T0303008

Our People

Our People

Discovering Lithuania's Hidden Holocaust

Rūta Vanagaitė and Efraim Zuroff

ROWMAN & LITTLEFIELD
Lanham • Boulder • New York • London

Published by Rowman & Littlefield
An imprint of The Rowman & Littlefield Publishing Group, Inc.
4501 Forbes Boulevard, Suite 200, Lanham, Maryland 20706
www.rowman.com

6 Tinworth Street, London SE11 5AL, United Kingdom

Distributed by NATIONAL BOOK NETWORK

British Library Cataloguing in Publication Information Available

Library of Congress Control Number: 2019952168
ISBN: 978-1-5381-3303-3 (cloth : alk. paper)
ISBN: 978-1-5381-3304-0 (electronic)

♾™ The paper used in this publication meets the minimum requirements of
American National Standard for Information Sciences—Permanence of Paper
for Printed Library Materials, ANSI/NISO Z39.48-1992.

Printed in the United States of America

Yitzchak Anolik
Born in Šiauliai, 1903
Murdered at Kaunas Ninth Fort, 1943
Lithuanian cycling champion, represented Lithuania at the 1924 Paris and 1928
Amsterdam Olympics.
Report from the 1924 Olympics in Paris in the magazine Sportas:
"Our cyclist Anolik also didn't go the distance because of seven flat tires.
At the starting line he had his tires pumped up so much that the British
and French cyclists were surprised by it. In actuality, stones on the route
quickly punctured the tires, and despite being in top physical shape
and despite his greatest desire, he could no longer ride, because along
the route no one was prepared to loan him tires or tubes, or even accept
money in exchange for them. Riders from other countries were taken
care of, and at each checkpoint were able to get food, inner tubes, and
anything they needed, because they were followed by a team automobile
which left them what they needed at the checkpoints."

Balys Norvaiša
Born in 1908
Lieutenant and commander of the Special Unit (*Ypatingas būrys*) from
November 1941, in charge of mass murder operations at many places in
Lithuania. Between 1941 and 1944 the Special Unit murdered approxi-
mately 100,000 people in Lithuania. Norvaiša's postwar fate is uncertain.
There are reports that he emigrated to the United States, although his rela-
tives claim that he was killed during the bombing of Dresden.

We, Alexander or Vytautas, by the grace of God, Grand Duke of Lithuania, grant rights and freedoms to all Jews living in our country. If any Jew, driven by great need, cries out for help in the night, and a Christian rushes not to his aid, then all neighbors, including Jews as well, must pay thirty shillings.

—1388

God, full of mercy, who dwells in the heights, provide a proper rest under the Divine Presence's wings, within the range of the holy and the pure, whose shining resembles the sky's, all the souls of the six million Jews, victims of the European Holocaust, who were murdered, slaughtered, burnt and exterminated for the sanctification of thy Name, by the German Nazi assassins and their helpers from the rest of the peoples. Therefore, the Master of Mercy will protect them forever, from behind the hiding of his wings, and will guard their souls within the package of life. The Everlasting is their heritage, the Garden of Eden shall be their resting place, and they shall rest peacefully upon their resting place, they will stand to be judged at the end of days, and let us say: Amen.

—"El Malei Rachamim," a Jewish
memorial prayer for the souls of the departed

Contents

viii   *Our People*

Preface

There are three good reasons why people write nonfiction books: to tell a good story, their own or that of someone else, to advocate a cause, or to expose an injustice. This book was motivated by all three reasons, which are even more valid today than when the original Lithuanian version appeared four years ago.

When we set out on our mission to visit sites of mass murder of Jews by Lithuanians during the Holocaust, we were not really sure what we would find, and whether we would be able to conduct a dialogue worthy of the subject. After all, no one had ever attempted to do so, let alone a descendant of the perpetrators together with a Nazi-hunter who was a descendant of the victims. Would we be able to travel together in the same station wagon from one killing site to another for what ultimately lasted forty days? Would be able to interact respectfully with each other with the shadow of the decimation of Lithuanian Jewry hanging over us? And most important of all, would this trip yield an experience that could create a basis for a book that would be read widely in Lithuania and reveal the true scope of Lithuanian complicity in the Shoah and the intentional cover-up of that unpleasant truth ever since the country regained its independence in 1990? While the research that Rūta did for many months in the Lithuanian Special Archives and studies by Lithuanian historians prior to the trip provided abundant information on Lithuanian complicity in the Shoah, it was fairly clear that, as convincing as this material was, it was the mission to visit murder sites that would make the book unique. And that feature would most probably determine whether or not we had a chance to succeed.

Whatever doubts we had about the logistics of the trip and the feasibil-
ity of the mission, they dissipated as time went on, and the impact of the
sites and the accounts of the eyewitnesses we interviewed, who had never
spoken to anyone about their experiences, strengthened our sense that we
had chosen an appropriate way to attempt to deal with the larger issue.
And as we continued, that sense became stronger and stronger, as did the
emotional burden of our encounter with the mass graves of the victims of
the Shoah, many of which were utterly neglected, while numerous others
were hard to find, and there were several which were not identified in
any way. And it was this neglect and indifference to the victims—men,
women and most of all children—whose bodies lay layer upon layer in
these pits, that also helped forge a mutual determination to do whatever
we could to inform Lithuanian society about the scope and nature of this
terrible tragedy.

Mūsiškiai; Kelionė su Priešu was launched on January 26, 2016, one day
before International Holocaust Remembrance day, at an Italian restaurant
in the heart of Vilnius that had been the headquarters of the Lithuanian
Special Unit (*Ypatingas būrys*), which had murdered tens of thousands
of Jews in Ponar—a fact studiously omitted from the speeches of local
officials at the state-sponsored memorial observances held annually at
that site. Joining us at the launch were national hero Tomas Šernas and
Ricardas Doveika, the two most popular priests in Lithuania, both of
whom had been interviewed for the book. A clip of seven mass murder
sites in the immediate vicinity of Vilnius added an important dimension
to our message.

Contrary to all expectations, the book became an immediate bestseller,
with the initial printing of 2,000 copies selling out in forty-eight hours.
Four additional larger printings sold out as well in several months, despite harsh criticism by government officials—some of whom who went
so far as to accuse us of endangering national security—and historians
who mocked the book as lacking scholarly authenticity. Large segments
of the public, however, ignored the criticism, and welcomed *Mūsiškiai* as
the first book of its kind to tell the truth about the scope of Lithuanian
complicity in the annihilation of Lithuanian Jewry in an interesting and
easily readable manner, accessible to all.

Since the book's success took the government by surprise, their revenge
only came a year and a half later. In late October 2017 our publisher,
Alma Littera, announced that they were severing relations with Rūta
and destroying all 27,000 copies of her six books (only one of which dealt
with the Holocaust), which were currently on sale in bookstores all over
Lithuania. Ultimately, they were not recycled into toilet paper, as originally publicized, but the damage was done, and Rūta was robbed of her
livelihood and harshly insulted and threatened on social networks. When

Vytautas Landsbergis, the father of Lithuanian independence, suggested that she should do her countrymen a favor and commit suicide, she realized that she could no longer reside safely in her homeland, and she moved to Jerusalem.

Recent events clearly show what an impact our book has had in Lithuania, as the subject of the Holocaust has become one of the most important topics of debate in local society. Thus, for example, the debates over whether anti-Semitic political leaders, such as Kazys Skirpa, or Holocaust perpetrators who were prominent in the anti-Soviet resistance after World War II, such as Jonas Noreika, should be national heroes have focused extensive public deliberation on the role of Lithuanians in Holocaust crimes. It is not yet clear what the results of these discussions and debates will be, but we can say that the efforts to hide these crimes have ultimately failed, and the first steps that might make possible an acceptance of an accurate historical narrative of the Shoah are being painfully taken. We hope and pray that this will indeed be the case, and if so, the many tears we shed as we traversed Lithuania will not have been in vain.

Rūta Vanagaitė & Efraim Zuroff
Jerusalem, September 2019

Introduction

Lithuania and the Holocaust

Efraim Zuroff

Among the numerous challenges faced by the new democracies of Eastern Europe created in the wake of the fall of the Soviet Union, one of the most daunting has been how to deal with their history during the Holocaust. These countries began this process, a particularly painful and difficult task under any circumstances, with two very significant handicaps. The first was the uniquely terrible nature of collaboration with the Nazis in Eastern Europe. Unlike the situation elsewhere on the Continent—where local collaborators assisted the Nazis in implementing the initial stages of the Final Solution (definition, Aryanization, concentration, and deportation), but did not participate in the mass murder of their Jewish countrymen—the Nazis' helpers in many of the post-Communist countries in Eastern Europe actively participated in the mass annihilation of local, and, in some cases, even foreign, Jews. Needless to say, this very important distinction made confronting the history of the Holocaust in these countries especially difficult.

A second disadvantage was the more than four-decades-long Soviet occupation or Communist domination, which profoundly affected local attitudes toward the destruction of European Jewry and the participation of the locals in these crimes. In this respect, three points are especially significant. The first is the highly politicized narrative of World War II and the Shoah, which was force-fed to the populations of the Soviet Union and Communist Eastern Europe. Ironically, in many instances, the treatment of the subject of local collaboration was close to the truth, but since that information was invariably formulated in harsh Soviet terminology—about "bourgeoisie Hitlerite fascists" who killed "peace-loving

1

Soviet citizens," and was exploited to advance Communist ideological goals—it was generally more commonly regarded as Bolshevik propaganda rather than historical truth.

The second point, connected to the first, was that throughout its existence, the Soviet Union purposely refused to acknowledge the unique tragedy of European Jewry, and the fact that the Nazis singled out the Jews for total annihilation. Such an admission would have run counter to the accepted Soviet narrative of the "Great Patriotic War," which portrayed World War II as an epic struggle between two ideological titans, Nazism and Communism. Thus, while the Western world had already fully accepted the narrative of Jewish exceptionalism in terms of Holocaust martyrdom, this concept was totally foreign to the peoples of post-Communist Eastern Europe. Another historical fact which was purposely repressed by the Soviets was the nationalistic element of local collaboration. Consequently, although patriotism was a key factor in the participation of many locals in the mass murder of the Jews, the Soviets, who were ideologically wed to the myth of the "brotherhood of Soviet peoples," highlighted the class origin of the killers and purposely ignored their nationality, which also damaged the credibility of their narrative.

A third point relates to the numerous postwar trials of local collaborators. On the one hand, the Soviets prosecuted a relatively large number of those who had perpetrated Holocaust crimes, but the charges against these defendants were not always for killing Jews. In many cases, the accusations were for political offenses, which had no legitimacy in the eyes of the locals. On the other hand, the large number of locals convicted created the false impression that the Soviets had completed the job (except in the case of those Nazi collaborators who had escaped abroad). This led to widespread resentment and resistance to efforts to convince the new democracies to prosecute unpunished Nazi war criminals, which made it much harder to convince the local authorities to do so.

Once independence was obtained, however, the question of how to deal with the Holocaust became very important in Eastern Europe, where relations with Israel and with world Jewry were considered to be crucial factors in achieving admission to the European Union and to NATO, which were the most important foreign-policy objectives of the new democracies. Thus, at a very early stage of their independence, these countries were already being forced to deal with six practical Holocaust-related issues, considered to be the basic requirements that Israel and the Jewish world expected would be implemented by the post-Communist countries of Eastern Europe, as part of the hoped-for reconciliation process. Ultimately, these issues also became the best indicators of the extent to which each country was making a serious effort to confront its Holocaust past. The issues in question were:

1. acknowledgment of guilt for Holocaust crimes and issuing an apology;
2. commemoration of the victims;
3. prosecution of heretofore-unprosecuted local perpetrators;
4. documentation (recording of an accurate historical narrative);
5. education (introducing Holocaust education and rewriting local textbooks); and
6. restitution.

On the surface, these demands appear to be understandable and not unreasonable. It was only natural to expect an admission of guilt and the requisite apology from countries where collaboration with the Nazis included active participation in the mass murder of Jews. By the same token, the demands for the publication of history books and textbooks which would accurately reflect the events of World War II and the Holocaust, as well as the introduction of Holocaust education into the school systems in countries where it was obvious that the materials on these subjects created by the previous regime would be universally rejected, should not have been considered excessive. Obviously, the calls for restitution and the prosecution of unpunished perpetrators would be more difficult to undertake, but they, too—especially the latter—should have been understood as a critical part of the reconciliation process. In that respect, it was clear from the beginning that absolute justice and restitution could never possibly be achieved, but if at least several of the more-prominent Holocaust perpetrators could have been punished for their crimes, this would have proven extremely beneficial. A genuine effort to return major communal property would also have been accepted, if accompanied by an honest and mostly successful attempt to deal with the other questions related to the Holocaust.

If there is anything that has been learned in this regard from the events of the past almost three decades, however, it is that when it comes to facing the Holocaust in post-Communist Eastern Europe, lip service is the dominant currency. In that respect, Lithuania is not only an excellent example, but is, in fact, the leader of efforts to elude an honest confrontation with Holocaust history, in the process robbing the Shoah of its justified status as a unique case of genocide. This process is known as *Holocaust distortion*, not to be confused with the far-better-known phenomenon of Holocaust denial. Yet it is those efforts—which have intensified over the past fifteen years, especially since the Baltics were accepted as full members in both the European Union and NATO—which currently pose a particularly dangerous threat to the future of Shoah memory and education and make this book of unique significance, way beyond Lithuania's borders.

No assessment of Lithuania's record in this regard can be presented without some historical background. Approximately 220,000 Jews lived in Lithuania under the Nazi occupation, of which only 3.6 percent—about 8,000—survived the war. These figures are the highest in Europe among Jewish communities of more than 5,000 Jews. (More than 99 percent of the Jews who lived under the Nazi occupation of Estonia were murdered, but only 1,000 Jews remained in that country when the Germans invaded in July 1941, 3,500 having managed to escape in time to the Soviet interior.) Almost all Jews murdered in Lithuania were killed individually, primarily by shooting, in close proximity to their homes, or at the major mass-murder site of Ponar (Paneriai) outside Vilna (Vilnius), in many cases by Lithuanian Nazi collaborators.

Only toward the very end of the war were approximately 30,000 Jews deported outside of Lithuania: 5,000, primarily the elderly and children, were deported to be murdered in the Auschwitz and Sobibor death camps in Poland; another 15,000 were sent to labor camps in Latvia and Estonia, where the overwhelming majority were killed; and 10,000 were deported from the ghettos of Kovno (Kaunas) and Shavel (Siauliai) to concentration camps in Poland and Germany, most of whom perished there.

Besides the unusually high percentage of Jews murdered, there are several other important aspects of the events in Lithuania which are noteworthy, and have had a powerful influence on the country's failure hitherto to openly and honestly deal with its Holocaust past. The first is the extremely large number of Lithuanians who actively participated in the murders, a factor which significantly facilitated the implementation of the Final Solution and greatly magnified its scope. Although there is no exact figure for the number of Lithuanians involved, our research indicates that at least 20,000 took part in the mass murder of Jews in a variety of functions, ranging from incitement to facilitating murder to actual shooting.

A second very important factor is the role played by Lithuania's prewar political leadership, many of whom fled the Soviet occupation of June 1940 to Berlin, where they organized the Lithuanian Activist Front (LAF), which enthusiastically supported the Third Reich and actively incited the local population to participate in the genocide of the Jews. Yet despite their tarnished past, some of these leaders have been glorified as heroes in democratic Lithuania. The same problem has arisen vis-à-vis some of the major figures of the postwar anti-Soviet resistance, who during World War II participated in the persecution and mass murder of Jews. One would assume that such crimes would have automatically disqualified them as heroes, but that has not been the case in Lithuania and elsewhere in post-Communist Eastern Europe.

A third factor of significance is that in many locations, especially throughout provincial Lithuania, the majority of the killers were Lithuanian volunteers, and in quite a few places, it was Lithuanians alone who carried out the murders, without any Germans or Austrians present. This was the case, for example, in Lazdijai, Telšiai, Eišiškės, Joniškis, Dubingiai, Babtai, Varėna, and Vandžiogala, whereas in Onuškis, Vilkaviškis, and Virbalis, the only Nazis present at the murder sites were photographing the crimes.

A fourth factor is that Lithuanians physically attacked Jews in more than forty different cities, towns, and villages, even before the Wehrmacht arrived, in many instances at the behest of LAF propaganda, which is yet another indication of the extent of independent Lithuanian initiative and zeal in harming their Jewish neighbors.

The fifth factor is that individuals from all strata of Lithuanian society, including the clergy, intelligentsia, and professionals, were among the local perpetrators of the crimes. And while it is true that many of the shooters were poorly educated or even illiterate, the role played by the Lithuanian elites—political, as noted above, as well as religious, cultural, and professional—was of great significance.

The sixth factor is the geographic scope of the tragedy, which encompassed every single one of the 220 Jewish communities spread out over all of Lithuania. The Jews comprised about 10 percent of the population of the territory considered Lithuanian under the Nazi occupation, and there were numerous Jewish communities in every district of the country, about 98 percent of which were obliterated, with local Nazi collaborators playing a role in every single one of these operations.

The seventh factor is that Lithuanians not only murdered Jews in their native country; at least several thousand men serving in auxiliary police units were also sent to help carry out the systematic annihilation of Jews in Belarus.

The eighth factor is that Lithuanian auxiliary police units were also involved in the murder of thousands of foreign Jews deported to Lithuania from Germany, Austria, and France. If we also consider that in quite a few cases the murders were preceded by the torture and humiliation of rabbis and prominent Jews (often carried out with extreme cruelty), and that extremist nationalism was a primary source of motivation for collaboration with the Nazis and active participation in the mass murder of Jews, it becomes abundantly clear why it has been so difficult for Lithuania to deal with Holocaust issues.

If we take the commemoration of the victims as an example—ostensibly the easiest of the tasks faced by the government vis-à-vis the Holocaust—the problems inherent in the approach of the Lithuanian authorities to such issues immediately becomes apparent. Several events are held in Lithuania every year to commemorate the tragedy of European and local Jewry, but when one carefully examines the programs and content of the speeches, the distortion of the historical narrative becomes obvious. Typically, the role of Lithuanians in the murders is not presented accurately; either their participation in the crimes is not mentioned at all, or it is greatly minimized and/or attributed solely to the criminal or marginal elements of Lithuanian society. Needless to say, there will never be any mention of the important role played in the murders by Lithuanian leaders, or of the cruelty exhibited by some of the murderers, or their patriotic motivation, or that the physical attacks on Jews began in dozens of places in Lithuania, even before the Nazis arrived.

An important example in this regard relates to the date chosen in Lithuania as a special memorial day for the victims of the Holocaust. The major dilemma faced by countries which sought to mark the tragedy on a specific day was whether to opt for January 27, the date of the liberation of Auschwitz-Birkenau, designated by the United Nations in 2005 as International Holocaust Remembrance Day, or a different date of particular significance to the history of the Holocaust in their country. The Lithuanian government chose September 23, the day on which the Vilna Ghetto was evacuated by the Nazis in 1943, an operation in which the local killers did not play a major role.

A far more appropriate date for a memorial day to commemorate the Holocaust in Lithuania would have been October 28, the day of the large-scale massacre of close to 10,000 Jews from the Kovno Ghetto at the nearby Ninth Fort, which was carried out almost exclusively by Lithuanians. Obviously the latter date would have focused necessary attention on the role played by local killers, but this was clearly something that the Lithuanian authorities wanted to avoid at all costs. (Another country which similarly chose a date for a Holocaust memorial day that had little connection to its own history was Estonia, which opted for January 27, despite the fact that not a single Estonian Jew was deported to, let alone murdered in, Auschwitz. The Estonians' choice could actually be regarded as a form of protest against the pressure they felt to designate a special day for a tragedy which they felt did not deserve special consideration by them.)

Another dimension of the Lithuanian campaign to create an alternative narrative of World War II and the Holocaust focuses on promoting the canard of equivalency between Nazi and Communist crimes, an approach often referred to as the *double genocide theory*. The rationale behind this effort was to undermine the hitherto-justified status of the Holocaust as a unique case of genocide and to categorize Communist crimes as genocide, as well, in order to help focus attention (and sympathy) on the suffering of Lithuanians during the Soviet occupations. Another reason why designating Communist crimes as genocide was so critical is because if that were indeed the case, which it clearly isn't, this would mean that Jews—in this case, Jewish Communists—were also guilty of committing the most heinous crime, thereby creating a false symmetry of criminality which would delegitimize, or at least significantly weaken, Jewish criticism of the role of local Nazi collaborators in the Holocaust. In fact, the Seimas (the Lithuanian parliament) passed a resolution redefining the term *genocide* to fit the crimes committed by the Soviets in Lithuania, and made it a criminal offense, punishable by a two-year jail sentence, to deny that Soviet (as well as Nazi) crimes were indeed considered genocide.

This aspect of the campaign was intensified in the wake of Lithuania's admission to the European Union and NATO in 2003–2004, and found expression in the document which can best be described as the manifesto of the Holocaust distortion movement in Eastern Europe, the Prague Declaration of June 3, 2008. Signed by thirty-three mostly Eastern and Central European politicians, and adopted by the Lithuanian Seimas, it calls for equality in the treatment of Nazi and Communist crimes, warning that "Europe will not be united unless it is able to reunite its history, recognize Communism and Nazism as a common legacy and bring about a thorough debate on all the totalitarian crimes of the past century." The practical manner in which such a unification of Europe should be implemented is formulated in several specific demands. One is the "adjustment and overhaul of European history textbooks so that children could learn and be warned about Communism and its crimes in the same way that they have been taught to assess the Nazi crimes." Another one calls for the "establishment of an Institute of European Memory and Conscience," which would function as a European research institute for the study of totalitarianism; support the local national research bodies that specialize in the totalitarian experience (all of which support the double genocide theory); and serve as a museum/memorial for all the victims of totalitarian regimes.

Luckily, to date these two demands have not been implemented, nor does it appear likely that they will be undertaken in the near future. The third demand, on the other hand, is the one on which the most progress has been made, and the step which poses the most immediate threat to the future of Holocaust memory and education. It seeks the "establishment of August 23rd, the day of the signing of the Hitler–Stalin Pact, known as the Molotov–Ribbentrop Pact, as a day of remembrance of the victims of both Nazi and Communist totalitarian regimes, in the same way Europe remembers the victims of the Holocaust on January 27." Within slightly more than a year after the publication of the Prague Declaration, three declarations or resolutions were passed by European forums supporting the designation of August 23 as a memorial day for the victims of Nazism and Communism, including two in the European Parliament (one of which passed by the huge margin of 533–44, with 33 abstentions) and one in the Parliamentary Assembly of the Organization for Security and Cooperation in Europe (OSCE). One does not have to be a prophet to realize that universal support for such a step will most likely ultimately lead to the elimination of the existing, separate International Holocaust Remembrance Day.

With the distortion of the Holocaust firmly entrenched and generously supported financially as government policy, it is hardly surprising that Lithuania has fundamentally failed in dealing with almost all of the practical Holocaust-related issues it faced upon obtaining independence from the Soviets. Thus, although ostensible efforts were made to solve all six of the pertinent issues, the problem was that the steps taken by the government were in reality not designed to honestly confront Lithuania's bloody Holocaust past, but rather to alleviate international pressure. A good example would be the question of an apology for the participation of Lithuanians in the crimes of the Shoah. Several such apologies were in fact made by Lithuanian leaders, all during visits to Israel, but when it came to dealing with practical Holocaust issues, the results clearly demonstrated that the apologies were, in fact, virtually meaningless.

An important example in this regard would be the impassioned speech made by President Algirdas Brazauskas in the Knesset on March 1, 1995, which included not only an apology, but also a promise that Lithuanian Nazi war criminals would be prosecuted "publically, consistently and conscientiously." Unfortunately, that has never been the case in Lithuania, neither before nor after his speech, and very little has been achieved vis-à-vis the prosecution and punishment of Holocaust crimes. Even though more than a dozen Lithuanian Nazi war criminals—who escaped after World War II to the United States—returned to post-independence Lithuania after they had been denaturalized and ordered deported for concealing their service in Nazi-sponsored death squads and local security police units, not a single one was ever punished for their crimes. Ultimately, under heavy pressure from the United States, Israel, and Jewish organizations, two senior security police commanders, Aleksandras Lileikis and Kazys Gimžauskas, were put on trial in Vilnius, but the Lithuanian prosecution waited until they were medically unfit to stand trial, thereby ensuring that they would not be punished. (In fact, they were not even obligated to appear in person at any of their trial sessions.)

In a third case, Saugumas (Lithuanian security police) operative Algimantas Dailidė was convicted and sentenced to five years' imprisonment, but the judges refused to implement his sentence, as he had to care for his ailing wife. Along the way, the Lithuanian parliament passed laws allowing the investigation and indictment of medically unfit genocide suspects, as well as a law allowing such trials to be conducted by video hookup, to ostensibly prove the seriousness of the judiciary effort. In practical terms, however, these laws merely demonstrated the Lithuanians' determination to alleviate external pressure on them to prosecute, while at the same time avoiding having to punish any local Nazi collaborators.

Even more shocking was a campaign launched by the authorities in 2006 to prosecute several Jewish anti-Nazi Soviet partisans on trumped-up charges of war crimes against innocent Lithuanian civilians. The campaign was accompanied by vicious incitement in the nationalist media against Yitzhak Arad, Fania Brantsovsky, Rachel Margolis, and Sara Ginaitė, with the term *murderer* freely bandied about in relation to these persons, who as young adults were only able to survive by joining the Soviet partisans.

Ironically, at the time these charges were made, Arad—a former director of the Yad Vashem World Holocaust Remembrance Center in Israel, and a noted Holocaust historian—was serving on the official international state historical commission to investigate the crimes of the Nazi occupation. Ultimately, the authorities dropped the four cases, since prosecutors were unable to find sufficient proof to mount a prosecution, but in the official announcement, they appealed to the public for incriminating information so that the case might be reopened. To this day, no apologies have been sent to any of the female suspects.

The same could be said about the rehabilitations granted upon independence (which came with a slew of financial benefits) to individuals who had been unfairly convicted and punished by Soviet courts. According to the law passed on May 2, 1990, individuals who had "participated in genocide" were ineligible for rehabilitation, but we discovered that in fact, at least several dozen men who had been involved in murdering Jews were indeed granted pardons and benefits. When we submitted the evidence to the government, they denied it, but ultimately were forced to establish a joint Israeli–Lithuanian commission of inquiry. The members of the commission reached an agreement with the government regarding the investigation process of the pertinent cases, but ultimately the Lithuanians did not keep a single promise they had made, thereby effectively neutralizing the commission. Under those circumstances, the local authorities were left to their own highly questionable devices to carry out their own investigation without any external supervision, so it is impossible to know whether their examination of the cases was done properly or not.

Any treatment of these issues would not be complete without referring to the Genocide and Resistance Research Centre of Lithuania. Established and funded by the Lithuanian government, its primary focus is on Communist crimes and the anti-Soviet resistance, but it is also the agency entrusted with all of the important official investigations related to Holocaust history. For example, it investigates cases related to efforts made to help save Jews, and decides whether individuals are worthy of the special recognition granted by the government to such persons. On the other hand, it also researches allegations of Holocaust crimes for the Lithuanian prosecution, and was commissioned by the government to compile a master list of all Lithuanians complicit in Shoah crimes in response to a list of 23,000 such persons published by Yosef Melamed, chairman of the Association of Lithuanian Jews in Israel. About three years ago, the Centre announced that it had compiled its list, consisting of 2,055 Lithuanians who had participated in the murder of Jews, a figure which is clearly far too small. At the same time, it has granted the status of Righteous Among the Nations to individuals who would never have been awarded this lofty designation according to the selection criteria established by Yad Vashem, the Israeli research and commemoration center which initiated the recognition of the Righteous.

Not surprisingly, the Centre's list of criminals, which initially appeared on its website, disappeared several days later, and has never been seen publicly since. Moreover, no action whatsoever has been taken by the government in connection with the list. Apparently, no attempt has been made, for example, to determine whether any of the people listed were alive and healthy enough to be prosecuted—yet more proof that when it comes to Holocaust-related issues, even historical research, not to mention legal action, continue to be negatively affected by government policy. Also reprehensible has been the Centre's role in attempting to whitewash the records of Lithuanian heroes who committed Holocaust crimes, and its role in overseeing the content of the government-sponsored genocide museum. An important example of the former problem was a statement issued by the Genocide and Resistance Research Centre in March 2019 supporting a decision made by the Vilnius district court to reject a suit filed by Grant Gochin to remove a plaque honoring Jonas Noreika, a leader of the Lithuanian post–World War II resistance to the Soviet occupation, who was an active participant in Holocaust crimes. In this case, the Centre not only claimed that Noreika was innocent of complicity in the Shoah, but virtually absolved Lithuanians of any responsibility for the annihilation of Lithuanian Jewry.

Another Lithuanian institution which starkly reflects the distortion of the history of the Holocaust and its aftermath is the Museum of Genocide Victims (only recently renamed, more accurately, the Museum of Occupations and Freedom Fights). Located in the heart of Vilnius, this museum is housed in a building that served as the base of the notorious *Ypatingas būrys* murder squad between 1942 and 1944, and during the entire Nazi occupation was the headquarters of the Gestapo and Saugumas (Lithuanian security police), and of the KGB during Soviet times.

Although it's touted as one of the city's most important tourist attractions, the museum's primary story has no connection to the genuine genocide that took place in Vilnius and throughout Lithuania. Rather, it focuses almost exclusively on the crimes committed by the Soviets (and especially by Jewish Communists), which, albeit quite terrible, cannot accurately be categorized as genocide (unless one accepts the altered definition of that term, approved by the Lithuanian parliament). Ironically, the only trials of Nazi war criminals held since Lithuania regained its independence—those of Lileikis, Gimžauskas, and Dailidė—were held in the same building, which also houses the KGB Special Archives, including the records of the postwar trials of Nazi collaborators conducted by the Soviets. On the other hand, the names of the most prominent anti-Soviet fighters are carved in stone on its exterior, among them that of Jonas Noreika, who played an active role in Holocaust crimes.

This summary would not be complete without mentioning Lithuania's International Commission for the Evaluation of the Crimes of the Nazi and Soviet Occupation Regimes in Lithuania, which has played a major role in promoting the canard of equivalency between Nazi and Soviet crimes (as clearly stated in its name), and the Prague Declaration. As one of its major functions, the commission is in charge of Holocaust education throughout Lithuania; for example, it chooses which teachers are sent to Israel for a seminar at Yad Vashem. Representatives of this commission urged the Seimas to adopt the Prague Declaration, which to this day remains on its website. The commission sponsors numerous events which reflect its support for the double genocide theory, and continues to actively advance that cause.

More recently, however, the subcommittee which deals with the Holocaust has begun to play a much more positive role in historical issues relating to the Shoah. For example, three years ago they issued a statement condemning the commemoration in the public sphere of individuals who "participated in any way in the persecution and/or murder of Jews and other victims during the Nazi occupation of Lithuania." Interestingly, the commission has not been convened since that statement was made. Of even greater significance was their unequivocal rejection of the statement issued by the Genocide and Resistance Research Centre supporting the exoneration of Nazi collaborator Jonas Noreika, which outrageously virtually absolved Lithuanians of any connection to Holocaust crimes.

One of the factors making the efforts to promote historical truth so difficult has been the staunch opposition of successive governments to cooperate. Regardless of the composition of the ruling coalitions, virtually all political parties have supported the double genocide theory and the false versions regarding limited local complicity in Holocaust crimes. This support has proven very important, as again and again individuals who initially supported our research and the writing of this book were influenced to switch sides in the debate, and in some cases were lured away by comfortable and lucrative employment in government jobs or government-financed institutions and organizations. Very few people were able to resist these temptations, which accounts for the hitherto dismal state of Holocaust-related issues the government has had to face since independence.

One person who stands out for his courage and bravery in this regard is Professor Dovid Katz, who for the past decade has devoted almost all of his time and energy to the fight for historical truth about the Holocaust in Lithuania. A native of Brooklyn, New York, and one of the world's leading experts on the Yiddish language, Professor Katz settled in Vilna after being invited to teach at Vilnius University, where (together with Mendy Cahan) he also founded the Vilnius Yiddish Institute. For eight years, he concentrated on his professional teaching and research, but when he learned of the government's attempts to prosecute Holocaust survivors who had fought as anti-Nazi partisans on charges of supposed "war crimes," he immediately began to campaign against these efforts, actively criticizing the cover-up of Holocaust crimes and the attempts to whitewash Lithuanians of any guilt for their role in the annihilation of Lithuanian Jewry. Professor Katz's efforts—and particularly, his excellent website, www.defendinghistory.com—did not go unnoticed by the authorities, and their response was swift and cruel. He was unfairly dismissed from his post at Vilnius University, a step which forced him to relocate for a good part of the year, making it much more difficult for him to continue his campaign against the authorities.

If the situation described above were taking place solely in Lithuania, then obviously the ongoing systematic efforts to rewrite the narrative of World War II and the Holocaust would not be considered as dangerous as they truly are. The sad truth is, however, that Lithuania is playing a leading role in promoting the canard of equivalency between Nazi and Communist crimes, and in hiding, or at least minimizing, the role of local collaborators in the implementation of the Final Solution. In that respect, Lithuania could be categorized as a laboratory for a wide range of initiatives to advance these goals and a locomotive to pull these efforts forward to the detriment of the historical record, as well as of Holocaust commemoration and education. This has clearly been the case as far as the other Baltic republics—Latvia and Estonia—are concerned, but also in the Ukraine, Hungary, Romania, Croatia, and Poland. And that is precisely why this book is so important, and why we hope that its message will not only reach the countries of post-Communist Eastern Europe, but a much wider audience as well.

We do not consider Lithuania a hopeless case, but without the whole historical truth about the Holocaust and Lithuanian complicity in Shoah crimes being delivered to the public, nothing will change. We hope that this book will mark the beginning of a turnabout and a different approach to Lithuania's past. Perhaps our collaboration—between a Jewish Nazi-hunter named for a victim of the Holocaust in Lithuania and a renowned Lithuanian writer who descends from perpetrators of Holocaust crimes—will help to pave the way toward a brighter tomorrow.

I

BEFORE THE JOURNEY

1

✝

My Connection to Lithuania

Efraim Zuroff

Ever since I was relatively young, Lithuania has always been a very special place for me. That was because it was the birthplace of my grandfather, *Zeide* (Grandpa) Shmuel Leib Zar (whose name in America somehow became Samuel L. Sar). He had a very strong influence on my life even before I was born. In fact, he was the person who gave me my name, the name of a victim of the Holocaust in Lithuania, a decision that mystics would no doubt claim greatly influenced my professional life. We'll never know if that is true or not, but it's a story that I sometimes tell when asked how I became a Nazi-hunter.

We still have the telegrams exchanged between my father and my grandfather right after my birth. "Esther gave birth to a boy," my father cabled his father-in-law, who had been sent to Europe by the Joint Distribution Committee to assist Holocaust survivors in European displaced persons camps. And my *Zeide* immediately responded: "Suggest name him Efraim." Apparently, by this time, which was early August of 1948, he had been able to confirm that his youngest brother (of six boys) had been murdered in the Holocaust; hence, his request, which my parents accepted, turning me from Moshe Daniel into Efraim Yaakov.

My grandfather not only chose my name, he also guided my educational path, influencing decisions as to which schools I would attend, closely monitoring my progress. I'll never forget a postcard he sent to me from a winter vacation in Miami. Responding to a letter I'd sent him in which I wrote that I had earned some money shoveling snow, he promised to match any sum I could make if instead I would sit and study. He was an enormous presence in my life, but in order to truly understand his role, I have to explain that he was one of the most important people at Yeshiva University, the flagship institution of modern Orthodox Jewry in the United States, and a prominent leader of religious Zionism in America. In addition, he traveled all over the world to help solve Jewish political and educational problems, and had visited Israel eight times. This was during an era when travel to the Middle East was primarily by boat, with each journey back and forth of four weeks' duration.

Perhaps even more important for our family was the fact that it was his idea that my parents start dating. You could say that he chose my father as a son-in-law from among the brightest young rabbinical students, and I have little doubt that this family connection also helped to launch my father's career as a very young high school principal, at the age of twenty-four. So in our family, my *Zeide* was really a genuine patriarch and role model.

This is no doubt part of the reason that I became so interested in his biography, but there was also something else. My grandfather was a very proud Litvak, someone who was utterly convinced that the Litvak tradition was the most correct, and that many Litvak Jews were unusually smart and talented—a conviction that he always shared with us. In that respect, he undoubtedly had a distinct Litvak superiority complex, which quite frankly I found convincing. The Litvak combination of sharp intellectual analysis and disdain for all sorts of *bubbe meises* (fairy or grandma tales) in approaching Judaism really appealed to me, and from a relatively young age, I identified with this approach. Given the fact that my father's parents lived relatively far away and that he had no knowledge of their history back in the Ukraine, my maternal grandfather's family of six boys, who had scattered all over the world, and his own personal journey and achievements, definitely occupied center stage in our family.

Ironically, the Holocaust dimension of our family history was never emphasized, and the fact that my namesake Efraim had been a brilliant Talmud scholar got far more play than his tragic fate, and that of his wife Beyla and two sons, Hirsh and Eliyahu. Indeed, it was only many years later that I would learn several details about what had happened to Efraim, and the fact that the entire family had been murdered in Vilna. By this time, I was already very involved in the issue of Lithuanian Nazi war criminals due to my work on several such cases for the US Justice Department's Office of Special Investigations. These facts only intensified the deep connection I already felt, for the reasons mentioned above.

This connection was further strengthened by my first visit to the *alte heim* (the old homeland), which took place under very uncomfortable circumstances, while Lithuania was still part of the Soviet Union. I had already been living in Israel for many years, having moved there in 1970 as a young graduate student, when in 1985 I was approached by the Israeli government to undertake a mission to the USSR to meet with "refuseniks"—Jews who had applied to emigrate to Israel, but whose applications had been rejected by the Soviets. The people we were supposed to meet were the Zionist activists, and especially Hebrew teachers, who were trying against all odds to teach Jews about their culture and history (and also, in some cases, about Judaism). The goal was to inspire a renaissance of Jewish identity, harshly repressed by the Soviets for decades, in hopes that all of the Jews would eventually assimilate.

The organizers sought out Jews living in Israel who had emigrated from Western countries and still retained their passports, so that they could travel to the Soviet Union under the guise of tourists. The idea was to meet with the activist leaders to encourage them in their struggle against the Soviet authorities, strengthen their Zionist and Jewish identities, and combat the very negative Soviet propaganda about Israel and life in the Jewish state. These "emissaries" were sent in pairs all over the Soviet Union, wherever there were Jewish communities. We usually did not have much say in our destinations, but I insisted that I wanted to go to Vilna, and luckily, I got my wish.

Thus, in the fall of 1985, I arrived for the first time in Vilna. I had no idea what to expect, but I was determined to at least try to get to Ponar, where, according to an account in a memorial book on the Jewish communities in the area of Shventzyan (Švenčionys)—among them, my grandfather's shtetl of Ligmiyan (today Linkmenys)—my great-uncle Efraim had been murdered. Unfortunately, there was no chance of getting to Linkmenys, as tourists could not travel freely around the country, but since Ponar was considered to be part of the Vilna area, I hoped that we could reach the mass murder site somehow. As things turned out, we were very lucky to get there, because the night before our planned visit, we had an encounter with the local KGB.

As was our custom in each of the cities we visited (Moscow, Riga, and, after Vilna, Leningrad), my partner Dr. Menachem Gottesman and I always went to visit the local synagogue. This was usually one of the only Jewish institutions, if not the single one, allowed to exist by the Soviets, who had outlawed Jewish schools and most communal organizations as part of their repression of Judaism and Zionism. These synagogues were the only places where one could openly meet local Jews, although there usually was at least one KGB spy in attendance at the services. When we attended the evening service that weekday in Vilna, we found a small group of Jews, almost all of them elderly, with one exception. After the services, that sole young person approached and offered to show us places of Jewish interest, an offer we gladly accepted.

We set off down Pylimo Street, enjoying the opportunity to speak to a local Jew, when we made a left turn on Basanavičius Street. Out of nowhere, we were accosted by two persons dressed as civilians who physically attacked our local guide and threw him to the ground. They then turned to us and told us to go immediately to our hotel, where "the authorities" wanted to speak to us the next morning. At this point, frankly, we were hardly surprised, having previously been "ambushed" by five police and KGB in the home of Hebrew teacher Chaim Goldberg in Riga, harshly warned the following morning that we faced expulsion if we failed to conduct ourselves "like tourists."

The next morning we informed the receptionist at the Lietuva Hotel that we were ready to meet with the authorities, and were told to wait in the lobby. The minutes ticked by without any progress, and I was beginning to be afraid that we would not make it to Ponar. So against my better judgment, I told the receptionist that we had a very busy schedule planned for the day and therefore could not wait any longer. "I am certain that if the authorities really want to speak to us, they will know where to find us," I said, and we set out for Ponar.

Given those circumstances (we were constantly checking to see if we were being followed), it was hard to concentrate on what I saw at Ponar. At that point, it seemed like a copy of the memorial we had seen at Rumbula, with the same Soviet caption—"To the victims of fascism"—but with one major difference: None of my relatives had been murdered at Rumbula. The fact that my great-uncle Efraim had been murdered at Ponar gave this visit special meaning. Nonetheless, our problems with the KGB remained at the forefront of our minds. As it turned out, we never heard from the KGB again, although this year I learned that I had a file in the Vilna KGB, and was able to receive a copy of the report filed by the local agents about our visit.

Fast-forward to the end of the Soviet Union. The exciting news about the impending breakup of the USSR and imminent Lithuanian independence lit a bright red light in my mind. The numerous difficulties under the Soviets in prosecuting local Nazi collaborators might now be eliminated under the new political conditions, and I wrote what would be the first of dozens of op-eds concerning the need for Lithuania to honestly confront its bloody Holocaust past. In that respect, "Justice from the Lithuanians," published in March 1990 in the *Jerusalem Post*, was the opening salvo on behalf of a cause to which I would devote a significant portion of my efforts over the coming quarter of a century.

My first encounter with independent Lithuania took place in June 1991 under far more auspicious circumstances. I had been invited to participate, along with many personages from Israel and survivors from Vilna, in the dedication of a brand-new monument at Ponar. No more Soviet captions which concealed the identity of the (Jewish) victims, as well as of the local (primarily Lithuanian) perpetrators. No more small memorials at a site where approximately one hundred thousand persons, among them seventy thousand Jews, had been murdered. Yet it was at the dedication ceremony which took place in the pouring rain that I began to fully grasp the extent of the difficulties that the Jewish world would face in attempting to reach a satisfactory *modus vivendi* with Lithuania and the other new post-Communist democracies in regard to a wide range of practical Holocaust-related issues. Ranging from acknowledgment of guilt to commemoration of the victims and prosecution of perpetrators, they also included documentation (history), education, and the particularly thorny problem of restitution.

The featured speaker at the event, Lithuanian prime minister Gediminas Vagnorius, basically tried to minimize both the time span of the tragedy and the highly significant role Lithuanian perpetrators played in the annihilation of the local Jewish community. "Let us not forget that this tragedy lasted for more than a wink of the eye, but at least three months," Vagnorius solemnly asserted, thereby reducing the time span of the Shoah from three years to three months.

Even worse, he tried to present local participation in the mass murder of Jews solely as the work of a group of criminals, despite the fact that in Lithuania, collaboration with the Nazis encompassed all strata of local society, from the clergy and intelligentsia to the hooligans and criminal elements. In this respect, according to Vagnorius, the assistance provided by those (relatively few) Lithuanians who helped to save Jews during the Holocaust, and the more-recent joint efforts of Jews and Lithuanians to restore the country's independence, proved that the activities of a group of criminals "cannot outweigh the good name of a nation, nor can it rob it of its conscience and decency."

Thus, at the highest level, from the very outset of the restoration of Lithuanian sovereignty, the historical record of the Holocaust was whitewashed by the creation of a false symmetry between the small number of Lithuanian Righteous Among the Nations and the many thousands who actively participated in the mass annihilation of practically the entire community. So if anyone hoped that the Lithuanians would honestly confront their bloody Holocaust past and make a serious effort to bring unprosecuted Nazi collaborators to trial, Vagnorius's speech, like the downpour during the dedication ceremony, should have washed away our illusions.

Besides the ceremony at Ponar, I was finally able to visit Ligmiyan (Linkmenys), the shtetl where my grandfather, long dead but never forgotten, and his five brothers had been born. This was where my great-grandfather Eliyahu had drowned at a relatively young age, leaving his widow, *Bubbe* (Grandma) Elka, to raise her six sons all alone. Needless to say, it was an emotional visit, even though—or especially because—there was not a single trace of the vibrant Jewish life which had existed there for decades, if not for centuries. The message I took from the visit was clear: The land of my forefathers was now open and accessible, but with very few reminders of our family's past.

These words are being written almost a quarter of a century later, twenty-five years in which Lithuania has enjoyed independence, and, for better or worse, for the first time ever had to take responsibility for its actions and how it deals with its Holocaust past. In effect, since 1991, this has been the essence of my ongoing relationship with the country in which my forefathers were born and grew up. For the past quarter-century, I have tried to honor the memory of the victims by helping to bring their killers to justice and by attempting to publicize the full historical truth about local complicity in Holocaust crimes, both in Lithuania and outside her borders. From the outset, it was clear that this would not be an easy task, and that my efforts would neither be welcomed nor even slightly appreciated. From my perspective, however, this mission was one which left little room for compromise or flexibility, and clearly was never seen as a popularity contest. There obviously would be a price to pay in public acceptance for any meaningful achievements.

Twenty-five years later, in retrospect, I do not regret the path I chose, but I frankly underestimated the difficulties I would face. To be honest, I never imagined that in many respects, Lithuania would be in a much worse situation today than a quarter of a century ago, with Holocaust distortion and the double genocide theory firmly entrenched in local historical consciousness, and brazenly exported as G-d's truth all over the world. I do not think that this battle is over, and I am fairly certain that the lies spread by the government officials and agencies will not ultimately prevail. That "victory," however, will only be achieved in the distant future, when Lithuanian historians and public figures will challenge the narrative fabricated by the first post-independence generation. In the meantime, I comfort myself that at least I did not betray the victims and violate their memory. If the price for that is the enmity of local public opinion and a totally false public image, so be it.

The journey that is the basis of this book is actually a farewell of sorts to Lithuania, and a symbolic passing of the torch of Holocaust memory to Lithuanians, in this case, Rūta Vanagaitė, a courageous seeker of the truth. It takes tremendous inner strength to respond to the knowledge that one's relatives were participants in Holocaust crimes, by seeking to educate one's own society of their scope and the nature of local complicity in the annihilation of Lithuania's Jewish residents. In that respect, *Our People* is an attempt to explain to contemporary Lithuanian society that the crimes committed against the Jews (local and foreign) were in reality a Lithuanian tragedy, one that will continue to cast its dark shadow over their beautiful country until the horrors are finally honestly confronted and internalized. Only when Lithuanians understand that, despite differences of religion, politics, traditions, and lifestyle, my people were actually also their people, will the true healing process have any chance of success. And that is my fervent hope and prayer.

2

✝

My Connection to the Holocaust

Rūta Vanagaitė

You see, Hitler back then hated Jews and took them away to Germany. Then it's like he pushed them into ditches and turned on the gas. That's why there are no more of them.

—My friend Dainiukas, age fourteen

I am a typical, average Lithuanian. I lived my whole life knowing as much about the Holocaust as the majority of our typical, average people do. Perhaps a bit more than Dainiukas, whose words I used to begin this chapter, but not radically more. I am a typical product of the lies of the Soviet regime and the silence of free Lithuania. *Homo sovieticus lituanus.*

Once upon a time, when I worked for a newspaper, I read the kind of news which is the least interesting to readers. The most boring headline in the world goes something like this: "Small Earthquake in Chile: Very Few Injuries." It has all the features of a boring news item: It happened far away, and to strangers, and there were few victims.

Isn't that how we view the murder of the Jews? It happened a long time ago, to strangers, and while there might have been many victims, what do we really know about them? Six million victims in the world, two hundred thousand in Lithuania—these are just statistics with lots of zeroes, and zeroes speak not to our hearts, nor to our minds. As Stalin once said: "The death of one person is a tragedy; the death of millions is a statistic."

I am a Lithuanian. I do not have Jewish blood. I am not just any Lithuanian—I'm an honored Lithuanian. This is because Jonas Vanagas (my father's father) was a political prisoner convicted of anti-Soviet activities, who froze to death within six months of being sent to Stalin's Gulag. His

whole family was deported to Krasnoyarsk. I was always very proud of
Grandfather Vanagas, who cut down a tree in Kavarskas in 1941 to block
the retreat of Red Army soldiers, and ripped Stalin's portrait off the wall
of the school. He was, of course, turned in by his Lithuanian neighbors
and arrested in 1944 when the Soviets returned.

At the Lithuanian Special Archives, I read the ninety-six-page secret
case file on my grandfather, as well as the testimony of the neighbor the
Soviets arrested with him, the interrogation papers, and the record of the
confrontation between the accused and the witness under the supervision
of the interrogators. For me, Jonas Vanagas's heroic deeds were some-
what eclipsed by information I discovered in the case file, showing that
during the German occupation, he had been a member of a commission
which compiled lists of Jews. He didn't take part directly in the mass murder of Jews, and he didn't covet their property, because he was already
sufficiently wealthy. Under interrogation, witnesses said that all ten Jews
from Kavarskas who were on the list were taken to Ukmergė in August of
1941. My grandfather's neighbor Balys, arrested and interrogated by the
Soviets along with my grandfather, transported those Jews to the execution site, and for this received compensation in the form of a Jewish house
and 4.5 hectares of land. That's what it says in the case file.

I am not just any Lithuanian. I'm a Lithuanian who suffered during the
Soviet years. In the bleak period of developed socialism, we were four
cousins, young girls, who wanted to dress up and listen to the Beatles, but
we didn't have any blue jeans, or records. What we did have was an aunt,
my father's sister, who lived in America and had an unbelievably kind
husband named Antanas. We used to write letters to them with lists of the
things we wanted. My aunt was very busy and worked as a dentist, but
throughout the Soviet era her husband sent us jeans and records and used
to write us warm letters, signing them "Antosėlė" instead of "Antanas."
Our parents told us the Soviets were looking for Uncle Antanas, so it was
better for him not to write his name or surname anywhere (after all, Soviet
security used to read letters from abroad). My aunt was happy with her
husband because he was a wonderful and honorable person, a colonel in
the army of independent Lithuania, and later, under the Germans, the
chief of police in Panevėžys.

As I write this book, all the jeans Antosėlė sent to us are long gone; he
is no longer with us, and my aunt is also gone, as are the Soviets. I now
know what the Lithuanian police did in Panevėžys and other cities during the German occupation, and why the Soviets were looking for Uncle
Antanas so intently. They didn't find him. "Antosėlė" passed away in
Florida, in a beautiful house near the ocean with a garden, a large mango
tree in the middle of it. They built a statue of him in a Lithuanian town.
His name, unfortunately, is among the list of five thousand Lithuanian

Holocaust perpetrators compiled by the Association of Lithuanian Jews in Israel.

So who am I—a descendant of Lithuanian heroes, or a member of a nation of despicable Jew-killers whose family bears the stain of crimes against humanity?

I also had a mother. She was born and grew up in Panevėžys, in a large and beautiful house with lodgers, where she was raised by her very strict mother, but also by one of the lodgers, a sweet woman named *Tante* Tzila (Aunt Tzila), who taught German at the Panevėžys Girls Seminary. My mother spoke German at home. Tzila was a German Jew. Did she flee to America to escape the Nazis? Perhaps. My mother was fourteen when the war began, when the Germans invaded Lithuania, and *Tante*, as my mother lovingly called her, quickly fled Lithuania. Where to? My mother never found a trace of her, despite trying to reach her at all of her former addresses.

Into which pit were you thrown, *Tante* Tzila—into which oven?

My mother didn't just lose *Tante* Tzila. A family of Jewish intellectuals lived next door to her on Respublika Street in Panevėžys. They had one child, Itzik, a year younger than my mother. They played together in my mother's yard throughout their childhood. Then came 1941 and the German occupation, and the neighbor family vanished one day. Mother said she heard shots fired far away in the forest, and later learned that Itzik's family, along with all the Jews of Panevėžys, had been shot on that day.

So who am I? Am I perhaps also a kind of victim, if my mother lost two people she loved in the Holocaust?

I am simply a Lithuanian whose grandparents and parents survived both the Soviet and the Nazi occupations. I accept all of the tragedies of my people without categorizing them as my own or not my own, as greater or lesser than other tragedies. I accept the guilt and losses of my relatives without recrimination and without trying to make what happened look better. I want to understand what happened, why it happened to them, and to all of my people. To my Lithuanians, and to my Jews in my Lithuania. And I want my children to understand—to know, and to remember.

At age fifty-seven I earned money from the Holocaust for the first time in my life. I didn't earn much—the equivalent of minimum wage for half a year. I accomplished a lot. The "Ponar Lullaby" Project received funding from the European Commission, which enabled us to hold ten wonderful events in Vilnius. The idea for the events was simple. We would bring forty people together and provide them with the conditions necessary to become Jews for a day: They would go to the synagogue and learn about Judaism (none of these Vilnius residents had ever been to the synagogue before); they would walk through the ghetto, visit the hiding places, hear Jewish music; they would learn a Jewish song and a Jewish dance, and eat what Jews might eat. And then, after a half-day of experiencing these things, having laughed, danced, and eaten together, they would get on a bus and travel to where the Jews were murdered. To Ponar.

But that wasn't the end of it. On the way to Ponar, we learned the song "*Shtiler, Shtiler*," also known as the "Ponar Lullaby," the music for which was composed by Alik Wolkowiski (who later changed his last name to Tamir), an eleven-year-old living in the Vilna Ghetto.

In 2012, I and forty others read, spoke, and sang Yiddish for the first time.

"Shtiler, Shtiler" (Ponar Lullaby)
Shtiler shtiler, lomir shvaygn kvorim vaksn do.
S'hobn zey farflantst di sonim: grinen zey tsum blo.
S'firn vegn tsu Ponar tsu, s'firt keyn veg tsurik.
Iz der tate vu farshvundn un mit im dos glik.

Shtiler, kind mayns, veyn nit oytser, s'helft nit keyn geveyn
Undzer umglik veln sonim zay vi nit farshteyn.
S'hobn breges oykh di yamen. S'hobn tfises oykhet tsamen,
Nor tsu undzer payn keyn bisl shayn

Quiet, Quiet
Quiet, quiet, let's be silent, graves are growing here
They were planted by the enemy, see their bloom appear.
All the roads lead to Ponar now. There are no roads back
And our father has vanished and with him our happiness.

Quiet, my child, don't cry, my treasure, tear no help commands,
Our misfortune was never understood by the enemies
Seas and oceans have their order
Prison also has its border
But to our pain there is no end.

We came to the Ponar woods bearing flowers and stones. For most of us, it was the first time we had been there. We stood and listened to the story of the mass murders. We sang, and then silently placed roses on the snow, which cleanly blanketed the largest of the six pits of death. There were rabbit tracks on the snow in the pit, left by a Ponar rabbit that had hopped across the crushed bones of thousands.

But that wasn't the end of it.

On the way from Ponar to Vilnius a daring experiment was performed. Should we return to Vilnius silently after what we had seen and experienced at Ponar? Or, on the contrary, should we come back inspired and united? After Ponar, after confronting the Holocaust, we opened a bottle of kosher wine from Israel on the bus and passed out homemade imberlach candies, and Mikhail, a musician with a Jewish ensemble, played "Tum Balalaika" for us. The feeling was so very unexpected: to drive through the Jerusalem of the North early on a Sunday evening, through a city devoid of Jews and of Lithuanians, singing with all our might, *Tumbala-tumbala tumbalalaika*, and toasting *l'chaim*—to life—with forty other voices. Forty Lithuanians who just that morning had known practically nothing about Jews, but now, toward evening, were excited, inspired, and sad, but also extremely happy . . .

After we arrived back in Vilnius, the participants found it impossible to part, and pressed our guide Simonas with questions, asking if their mother, brother, aunt, or friend could come next Sunday. Those who were part of the project told their families what they had heard and seen about Jews. More than one member of their families tilted their head in suspicion. *Well, they certainly made an impression on you . . . You're talking as if you were a cult member now . . . See how careful you must be with those Jews; if you give them an inch, they'll take a mile . . .*

A year has passed. The "Being a Jew" project has traveled to Kaunas and to other European cities where, unfortunately, everything became a bit more bureaucratic, "utilizing EU funds." But Kaunas affected me. The hour we spent in the suburb of Slobodka, now called Vilijampolė, affected me deeply.

The following took place in the area of one of the largest ghettos in Lithuania, where tens of thousands of Kaunas Jews lived and, over the course of several *aktionen*, including the "Children's Aktion," were almost all murdered.

Thirty teachers from Kaunas, led by a Jew, are standing in the middle of the Kaunas Ghetto, where there are buildings; sheds full of stacked firewood; storage spaces where thousands of Jews huddled during the war, brought here by the Nazis; where Jewish children played in the courtyards, after which everyone was taken to the square or to one of the Kaunas forts and shot. The buildings and storage sheds are new constructions, or renovated, and Kaunas residents who live there do not know where they are living and what happened before they came. How could they know? There are no signs; nothing is protected or commemorated, except for a stone near the entrance to the neighborhood. Also being renovated is the building where there was once a store, in whose window the head of a local rabbi was displayed. They cut the rabbi's head off as he was praying and placed it on the Talmud. That'll teach him.

An Audi sports car stops next to us. A man with a shaved head rolls down the window and shouts: "Well, what, Jews? What are you up to now? What are you looking for?" He receives a polite answer from our guide, almost an apology that we are here, and the man drives off down the small road in the ghetto, but several minutes later, he turns around and comes back toward us at full speed. The brakes screech and the car comes to a halt just before plowing into our group. I am afraid something bad will happen, and I go to the man in the car and try to defuse the situation. There is an unfinished bottle of beer on the car seat.

I say to the man: "Don't be angry; you know, we aren't Jews—this is a tour. This is where the ghetto was; did you know that?"

I see that this is news to him. He doesn't know what a ghetto is.

"Maybe you shouldn't drive," I tell the man with the shaved head, "because you've drunk a bit, and you might get caught by the police."

"I am a police officer," he shoots back.

Eventually he drives away without doing us any harm.

What wonderful people I meet, besides Simonas, for whom there is no place left in the Jewish community. The first time I met the other Simas, we talked about the project. After he'd heard about it, he said he had an idea. He took a photo out of a drawer: A hundred or more people had been photographed from above, forming the Star of David with their bodies on a city square. I got the shivers. This would be a wonderful idea for Vilnius, for the end of the project. Hundreds of Vilnius children standing and forming a living Star of David, photographed from above by a drone on the biggest square in the ghetto. Then they would board a train—I can get one; I know the head of Lithuanian Railways—and travel to Ponar. For the first time.

For the culmination of the "Being a Jew" project, we took seven hundred Vilnius schoolchildren to Ponar. We stood at the killing pits and asked what had happened there. About thirty hands went up. Of course, all the older students, those with twelve years of school, had already visited the most important museums in Lithuania, including the Horse Museum and the Chocolate Museum.

Everything happened as it had in that first photograph. On the train to Ponar, some of the children had begun to laugh rudely and make anti-Semitic jokes, but when they stood at the edge of the killing pit, they held each other's hands and listened as Simonas began to tell a story. It was about a beautiful Jewish girl with red hair. Someone who lived here had seen this girl through the window of a passing train. Returning to Ponar several hours later, he saw two soldiers playing soccer with that girl's head.

Seven hundred children went silent and listened without moving.

Ponar had been waiting for that silence—waiting for a long time.

3

Meeting the Enemy

And then the "Being a Jew" project came to an end. The most boring, but nonetheless necessary, part of the whole project was the conference on the theme of Holocaust education. Invitations, registration, conference materials, translating papers, boring characters at the podium, a yawning audience, and I still had to be the moderator . . . Sheesh . . . Well, maybe the Jewish lunch with live music during the break would provide some sort of fun for this hopeless event. Maybe we should provide kosher wine?

What could I do to make it less than absolutely boring? Whom should I invite to speak? There was much drinking of coffee with experts on the topic, my consultants. Besides historians from Lithuania, they suggested I invite two Lithuanians living abroad: scholar Saulius Sužiedėlis (whose name I was hearing for the first time) and world-renowned poet Tomas Venclova (wow—but would he really agree to speak?), and another person from the new Jewish museum in Warsaw. What I should not do is even consider inviting the ruiners of Lithuania's reputation, Dovid Katz and Efraim Zuroff from the Simon Wiesenthal Center in Jerusalem. They are uncontrollable. I had heard that Zuroff was very aggressive, and that he had recently made some Lithuanian schoolteachers, who had come to Jerusalem for a seminar, cry. Hmm. Not good.

But if they came, I asked my consultants, would there be fistfights?

No, they said, there wouldn't be. Perhaps you could talk to Zuroff so he wouldn't make women cry; he's a civilized person, after all. But if Katz and Zuroff come, we Lithuanian historians, we members of the academic community, will simply not participate in your conference. Because those two work for Putin. He finances them.

Well, I thought, this simply won't do. I don't want Putin's agents in Lithuania, nor do I want to be accused of the same myself if I invite them.

But I want to be sure, so I ask my consultants how they know about Putin's payments to these two Jews. One knows because someone at the US Embassy told him. Another is certain because Algirdas Paleckis is one of Zuroff's friends on Facebook. And from Paleckis to Putin, it is a short step indeed . . .

Now I'm starting to enjoy myself. After the consultations, I check Google and find out how both of these enemies of Lithuania have been ruining our reputation in the world for years and years, demanding that Holocaust murderers be brought to justice, and, even worse, requesting that neo-Nazi marches not be allowed in the center of Kaunas and Vilnius. Zuroff, it seems, is especially dangerous and out of control, because, according to the Internet, he's the most important Nazi-hunter in the world. Am I ready to face him?

After taking a deep breath, I wrote to these two Jews. How could I do without them? I planned to somehow isolate them from the academic community during the conference to avoid fisticuffs, but at least now it would be much more interesting. I wouldn't have to buy wine after all.

I received replies immediately. Both asked under what conditions they were being invited. The conditions were the same for all the speakers: We would cover the flight and hotel costs and pay each of them a five-hundred-euro honorarium.

Only later did I learn that both ruiners of Lithuania's reputation went into shock at this point. No one in independent Lithuania had ever invited them to such an event, never mind one to be held at Vilnius City Hall, with all expenses paid, and even a regular honorarium. I didn't know that at the time, and if I had, I wouldn't have offered to pay—but it was too late. Oh well . . .

Efraim Zuroff said he was going to be in Lithuania to monitor the neo-Nazi march on March 11, and that we could meet for coffee. He probably wouldn't try to beat me up or anything, but he'd surely blame me for all of Lithuania's sins. I would endure. I'm not a schoolteacher, after all.

When I entered the restaurant, I saw the Nazi-hunter in person for the first time, sitting at the bar, and immediately I understood why people are so afraid of Zuroff—and not just in Lithuania. We're accustomed to thinking of Jews as slight, often small people (how many Jews have we really seen?), but here before me was a giant. (I later read in one South African newspaper that he is of "mammoth stature.") An unexpected powerful presence seemed to ooze from his person. I didn't want to sit too close to him.

We sat down at a larger table. Zuroff's deep blue eyes evaluated me, the representative of the nation of Jew-killers, with unhidden distrust. His first question was straight and quite aggressive: "Why are you doing this project? For the money, which is paid by the European Union?"

"No," I responded to the ruiner of reputations. "I am doing it because I discovered that some of my relatives had most likely taken part in the Holocaust. And I feel that in remembering and honoring the Jews murdered, I will to some extent make amends for their crime."

Zuroff stared at me in surprise.

Then I told him about my aunt's husband, and about my grandfather.

"You are the first person in Lithuania I've ever heard admit their family's guilt," Zuroff said. "In twenty-five years of work in Lithuania, I have never met a single person who ever admitted that."

There was a long pause in the conversation. We drank bottled water. Now came my turn to strike: "Do you work for Putin? After all, it's to Putin's benefit for Lithuanians to be known throughout the world as Nazis. How much does he pay you?"

Zuroff spoke at length—about his work, his earlier anti-Soviet activities, and how the Russians sought to use him for their propaganda purposes. It turned out that Paleckis was one of Zuroff's five thousand friends on Facebook.

Zuroff said he'd like to speak at the conference, but unfortunately was already scheduled to give a series of lectures in the United States at that time. He suggested the names of several other people, and I sat there thinking how sad it was that we wouldn't have this mammoth presence at our conference. So I suggested a simple solution: We could film his speech while he was in Lithuania, and in that way be able to present it at the conference. It was a wonderful solution. We would have the mammoth presence, and there wouldn't be any fistfights.

So that's how my acquaintance with Lithuania's bogeyman, the person who makes Lithuanian schoolteachers weep, began. With a man who has resolutely hunted down Nazis around the world for more than a quarter of a century, hunting them down practically by himself, with minimal financing from the USA for his small office, but no support from the State of Israel. When Zuroff is in Vilnius, the Israeli ambassador to Lithuania practically cusses at him, because allegedly he ruins people's moods everywhere he goes.

We filmed Zuroff's speech in the foyer of a hotel near the train station, against a background of tourists speaking Russian loudly. After the recording, I said good-bye to the Nazi-hunter—not as one bids farewell to an enemy, but as one does to a person.

On the way home, I had an idea. It might be very interesting to travel with Zuroff someday, to visit several Jewish mass murder sites in

Lithuania to look for living eyewitnesses—to look for the truth about who had carried out the mass murder of Jews in Lithuania during World War II. Was it the Nazis themselves, the dregs of our society, or was it average Lithuanians? It might even make a good documentary film, which we could call *Journey with the Enemy*. The Jew and the Lithuanian, the Nazi-hunter and a member of the nation of Jew-killers, perhaps even the relative of Jew-killers. What would we discover? Whose version of the Holocaust in Lithuania would turn out to be correct: the official Lithuanian version that is being taught in our schools, or Zuroff's version? What if Efraim Zuroff was not a monster after all? And if he wasn't, then who was?

Before any planning took place, I had to do some homework. I had to prepare.

So I started searching for historical truth in the memoirs, in the archives, in the academic publications of Lithuanian historians.

II

PREPARATION
FOR THE JOURNEY

4

✝

Lithuania, 1941

Getting Rid of the Jews

Our sign is the right arm raised high.[1]

—from an LAF address to the nation

Hitler began the war on June 22, 1941. That same day the Lithuanian Activist Front, led by Kazys Škirpa, broadcast an address entitled "Let's Liberate Lithuania Forever from the Yoke of Jewry" on Kaunas radio, and its distribution began immediately throughout Lithuania.

Let's liberate Lithuania forever from the yoke of Jewry.

Lithuanian brothers and sisters, soon the hour we have been awaiting will come when the Lithuanian nation will get back its national freedom and restore the independence of the state of Lithuania.

Today we all rise to battle against one common two-faced enemy. That enemy is the Red Army, Russian Bolshevism . . . We are all convinced that the greatest and most hidden supporter of this enemy is the Jew. The Jew belongs to no nation, to no community. He has neither a homeland nor a country. He is eternally and exclusively a Jew . . . Russian Communism and its eternal servant, the Jew, are one and the same enemy. The ejection of Russian Communist occupation and the slavery of Jewry is the same thing and the most holy matter . . .

Vytautas the Great granted Jews the right of refuge in Lithuania, believing they would not transgress the obligations of being polite guests. This, however, was only seen as an initial opportunity for the bloodsucking tick of Israel to insinuate itself into the body of the Lithuanian people. Soon after the Jews began to spread ever more widely as hustlers and confidence men, usurers, percentage-gougers and builders of taverns . . .

---

1 Lithuanian Special Archives (LSA), K-1, ap. 58, case 12949/3, envelope 64-16.

> *The most evil Chekists, informants against Lithuanians and torturers of arrested Lithuanians were and are Jews . . . Put plainly, Jews are always and everywhere the most pig-headed torturers, exploiters and insatiable bloodsucking parasites of Lithuanian workers, farmers and urbanites.*
>
> *The Lithuanian Activist Front in the name of the entire Lithuanian nation most solemnly declares:*
>
> 1. *The ancient right of refuge provided to the Jews during the time of Vytautas the Great is completely and finally rescinded;*
> 2. *Every Jew of Lithuania without exception is hereby officially given notice to quit the land of Lithuania immediately and without hesitation for any reason;*
> 3. *All of the Jews who have distinguished themselves exceptionally through betrayal of the Lithuanian state or acts of persecution, torture or abuse of Lithuanian compatriots will be brought to account separately and punished accordingly. It is the duty of all good Lithuanians to take measures to arrest these sorts of Jews and, in grave cases, to mete out punishment; [and]*
> 4. *All real estate once or now controlled by Lithuanian Jews will pass into the hands of the Lithuanian nation.*
>
> *. . . In the newly reconstituted Lithuania no Jew will have civil rights or the means for making a living. In this manner the mistakes of the past and the evil deeds of the Jews will be corrected. In this manner strong foundations will be laid for the happy future and work of our Aryan nation.*
> —*Lithuanian Activist Front, June 22, 1941*[2]

After the war began on June 22, the Red Army fled Lithuania to the east, leaving behind storehouses full of weapons. The Lithuanian Activist Front began the uprising in Kaunas in order to show the Germans that Lithuania was not USSR territory, and to wash away the shame of 1940, when not a single shot was fired against the invading Soviet army.

In June of 1941, it was completely different. The Lithuanian heroes rose up against the occupier; the insurgents freed the prisoners jailed by the Soviets; they blew up bridges and battled against the withdrawing Red Army soldiers. According to the instructions issued by the LAF, all insurgents wore a white armband on their right arm with the letters TDA (*Tautinio darbo apsauga*, "National Labor Defense"). That white armband would have an extraordinary future . . .

One of the main symbolic acts of the uprising was the raising of the Lithuanian flag over the roof of the Church of the Resurrection. It was raised by uprising participant Lieutenant Bronius Norkus, soon to become one of the commanders of the National Labor Defense Battalion (TDA).

---

2 LSA, K-1, ap. 58, b. 12949 / vol. 1, envelope 64-18.

Propaganda cartoon sent to Lithuania by the Lithuanian Activist Front. (Lithuanian Special Archives)

SKETCHES FOR A PORTRAIT OF BRONIUS NORKUS

Kazys Bobelis, the son of the Kaunas commandant Jurgis Bobelis, recalls:

> *When the uprising began, maybe after three days or so, we young people were play-*
> *ing soccer at the corner of Kauko and Aguonų streets. All of a sudden we saw this*
> *guy shambling up. [He was wearing] the blue uniform of the Lithuanian Air Force.*
> *Without buttons, without epaulettes. With a lot of unkempt hair. Red eyes. In one*
> *hand half of a bottle, in the other a revolver. We were frightened. He came up to us.*
> *"Children, where are the Jews?" Jesus Christ! We hadn't seen any. There were none.*
> *Later it turned out this was Lieutenant Norkus, an officer in the Lithuanian Air*
> *Force. When the Bolsheviks came they put him in prison. After Kaunas was bombed*
> *he escaped the prison.*
>
> *He went straightaway to his wife and children in Žaliakalnis [a Kaunas neigh-*
> *borhood]. The neighbors said they had been deported on Saturday (June 21). I don't*
> *know the details, but that's when he began to drink vodka and shoot. He said he*
> *would shoot every Jew on sight. He became the commander of the battalion. He got a*
> *horse. He fell off, drunk, and the horse kicked him in the head and killed him.*[3]

---

3 From: Vidmantas Valiušaitis, *Kalbėkime patys, girdėkime kitus* (Let's Talk Ourselves and Listen to the Others), Vilnius: Petro Ofsetas, 2013, pp. 290–91.

Bronius Norkus was appointed a platoon commander and began service in the National Labor Defense Battalion in Kaunas. He didn't have to ask, "Children, where are the Jews?" after June 28, because men in his unit delivered them directly to him, at the pits.

Who were those insurgents? Against whom did they fight? No doubt against the withdrawing Red Army, but was it just against them? Whose orders did they carry out? The Lithuanian Special Archive contains a case file which relates how the workers at the Vilnius Psychiatric Hospital were invited at a hospital meeting held during the first days of the war to come to the police department and register as insurgents. By June 25, all of the men had received weapons, and their initial assignment was to arrest the Jews living on Vokiečių Street in Vilnius and march them all to Lukiškių Prison. The operation took several days, during which dozens of Jewish families were arrested, their property was seized, and their apartments were sealed. The Jews imprisoned at Lukiškių Prison were "turned over to the Special Unit" or "turned over to German security" (as recorded in the entries next to the names in the prison records preserved at the Central State Archive). Were these Jewish families Bolsheviks? Was the entire length of this street inhabited by Bolsheviks?

Many Lithuanian men took up arms believing they were serving their homeland, never imagining that their patriotism might be exploited to murder innocent people. The white armbands were supposed to remain white.

During the last days of June 1941, my grandfather, Jonas Vanagas, left his home in Kavarskas, joined the insurgents, and received a weapon. He too put on a white armband and joined the battle against the hated Soviets—or at least, that's what it says in the interrogation documents and witness statements found in his case file. This was right after the Soviets had confiscated his land and parceled it out to the poor. During the first days of the war, according to the NKVD and witnesses, my grandfather, along with other people, shot at the Red Army soldiers hiding in the Kavarskas schoolhouse. Then, with help from a neighbor, he dragged a log onto the main road through Kavarskas to prevent the Soviet tanks from retreating, so that the German army could catch up with them. For all this, when the Soviets returned, my patriotic grandfather was later convicted and punished under Article 58, for treason against the Motherland.

Lithuanians, especially military people, greeted Hitler's armies with hurrahs and flowers. Lithuanians escorted the Russian army out with gunfire. After the first wave of deportations to Siberia, people believed that any change at all meant salvation. For Lithuanians, Hitler's arrival meant liberation. For the Jews, the Nazi invasion meant death and destruction, so many of them tried to flee, but the Germans overtook the country so quickly that only about 6 percent managed to reach the USSR safely.

During the first days of the war, upon the initiative of the LAF, a Lithuanian Provisional Government (PG) was established, headed by Kazys Škirpa. Incredibly, the Germans, the LAF's friends and allies in Lithuania, immediately seized the Lithuanian prime minister in Berlin and placed him under house arrest. Every two or three days, a German official would visit his apartment to make sure that Škirpa was still at home. Škirpa claimed he could have tried to leave the house, but he just didn't want to annoy the friendly Germans. Juozas Ambrazevičius, a literature teacher and critic, who until then had been a schoolteacher, was appointed acting prime minister in Škirpa's stead.

Immediately during its first meeting, the PG sent an impassioned thank-you telegram to Hitler:

> *The liberating storm of war having passed through Lithuania, the representatives of the society of free Lithuania send You, the Führer of the German nation, our deepest and real gratitude for the liberation of the land of Lithuania from the all-destroying occupation of the Jews and the Bolsheviks and the liberation of the Lithuanian people, and express the hope that by Your genius the Lithuanian nation will be destined to take part in the victorious march led by You to destroy Judaism, Bolshevism and plutocracy, to defend the individual's personal freedom, to protect the culture of Western Europe and to implement the new European order.*[4]

Only a few days passed before the Germans issued orders to disarm the Lithuanian insurgents. On June 28, Kaunas commandant Jurgis Bobelis, who had been appointed by the PG, created a National Labor Defense Battalion (TDA) from the ranks of the volunteer insurgent-partisans. Gradually, about twenty such battalions were created in Lithuania. The belief was that they would form the nucleus of a new Lithuanian army. The Nazis immediately took command of two units of a TDA battalion, which were immediately put to work shooting Jews at the Seventh Fort in Kaunas. A third unit (led by Lieutenant Juozas Barzda) took part in one of the larger mass murder operations in which 2,514 Jews were killed. It is true that after the mass murder operations began, some of the soldiers of the battalion deserted (117 soldiers fled the battalion between July 5 and 11), but about 1,000 remained. They continued their national security activities at the Kaunas forts and elsewhere, murdering thousands of Lithuanian Jews.

The PG quickly restored the local administrative frameworks (i.e., municipal bodies and police departments), issuing laws that restored pri-

---

4 Kazys Škirpa, *Sukilimas Lietuvos suverenumui atstatyti* (The Uprising for Restoring Lithuanian Sovereignty), Washington, DC: Franciscan Fathers Press, 1973, p. 349.

vate ownership to property that had been nationalized by the Soviets—unless the original owners were Jews. Restrictions increased, Jews were concentrated at special locations, and steps were taken to facilitate mass extermination.

The PG was also busy corresponding with the Germans, informing them of their loyalty and asking for recognition, or at least a little attention. They received none at all. In his last speech, Lithuanian prime minister Juozas Ambrazevičius said: "The different agencies and ministries have done everything they could to satisfy the Germans' economic requirements, tolerating unfairness and so on. The Government had hoped that in exchange for loyalty and support the Germans would eventually grant Lithuania her dreamed-of independence. [. . .] To the different ministries with different desires and demands came German military officials from different services, and the effort was always made to satisfy their desires one-hundred percent."

The PG's loyalty to their liberators was impressive. As soon as they began work in the last days of June, they resolved to set up a concentration camp at the Seventh Fort in Kaunas and allocated funding for a battalion to guard the camp. Thus, the Seventh Fort began to operate as a prison for Jews in early July, with over two thousand prisoners who were guarded by the Lithuanian Auxiliary Police. No efforts were spared in the name of Lithuania.

In a conversation with Jewish representative and former Lithuanian military officer Yaakov Goldberg, PG finance minister Jonas Matulionis explained the situation in Lithuania this way:

> Lithuanians don't agree on the Jewish problem. Three views exist. According to the extreme view all Lithuanian Jews should be exterminated; the moderates demand concentration camps be established where Jews can atone for the crimes they have committed against Lithuanians through their blood and their sweat. The third view? I am a practicing Catholic. I and others like me are of the belief that a person's life may not be taken away from him. Only God may do that. I have never been predisposed against anyone, but under Soviet rule I and my friends became convinced there is no common path with the Jews and there never will be. In our view, Lithuanians must be separated from Jews, and the sooner the better. For that reason the ghetto is necessary. There you will be separated from us and you will not be able to hurt us. That is the Christian position.[5]

Robert van Voren, the author of an important book on the Holocaust in Lithuania, gives us an important insight into what happened in the summer of 1941:

---

5 *1941 sukilimo baltosios dėmės: Pokalbis su Sauliumi Sužiedėliu* (The White Spots of the Uprising of 1941: Talk with Saulius Sužiedėlis). From: *Shoah: Holocaust in Lithuania*, Part II, Vilnius: Vilna Gaon State Jewish Museum, 2004, p. 169.

A key factor that helps a potential killer overcome the barrier between not participating and participating is that of us–them thinking. In fact, it is in many respects a prerequisite, as killing "one of our own" is biologically, socially and morally unjustifiable, yet when the future victim has already become "one of the other," it opens the door to justification of the evil act. In the case of the Jews, physical death was preceded by social death, by excluding them from daily life. Parks, cinemas, theaters, cafes and restaurants, all public places became inaccessible. They were not allowed to walk on the sidewalks, were ostensibly marked as different with the obligatory yellow Star of David on their clothes and with the fat black stamp of "J" (Jude) in their identification cards. They were like trees in a forest that are marked before being cut—they were still there, but already selected for "production." It is only a matter of time until they were reduced to shadows in a society that continued to function without them.

Independent Lithuania remembers her heroes: The remains of Juozas Ambrazevičius were reburied in Kaunas in 2012, with full honors, and with the president of Lithuania in attendance. The central streets in Vilnius and Kaunas were renamed in honor of Kazys Škirpa.

The following assessment of Kazys Škirpa, prepared by the Genocide and Resistance Research Centre of Lithuania, was recently sent to the Lithuanian parliament:

K. Škirpa and the organization he led can be faulted that anti-Semitism was raised to the level of policy and platform in the actions of the Berlin LAF organization, and that the propagation of anti-Semitism among members of the anti-Soviet resistance and Lithuanian residents became one of the preconditions for the Holocaust to happen in the country. On the other hand, it has to be noted that the Berlin LAF organization proposed solving "the Jewish question" not through genocide, but by means of deportation out of Lithuania.

No reaction.

On August 5, 1941, the Nazis introduced what they called a civil administration in Lithuania under commissar general Theodor Adrian von Renteln, who had been sent by the Reich. The Germans proposed that the Provisional Government rename itself a council, but only three ministers agreed. They became subordinate to the Germans as general councilors, or advisers. Members of the PG resigned ostensibly because they wanted to stay true to their aspirations for Lithuanian independence, which had been thwarted by the Reich. Even so, historians perceive one thing that can't be glorified: As they were closing down their activity, the PG issued no public order or any other kind of instructions to police chiefs, military commanders, commanders of the Lithuanian battalions, or soldiers working within the administration that had been created, advising them to leave their posts. The Nazis made use of these structures.

Hitler's fiftieth-birthday celebration in Berlin in the center Kazys Škirpa. (Lithuanian Central State Archives)

After the members of the PG had resigned, everything remained as it had been in the lower echelons. The heads of the regional administration (the most important tool of the Nazis)—the mayors, the council members of the rural districts, the auxiliary police, and the courts—all remained in operation. Everyone managed to protect their salaries. My aunt's husband, Lieutenant Colonel Antanas Stapulionis, stayed in his post as the chief of the Panevėžys Security Police, and only at the end of August 1941 was he moved to the city administration, where he remained until 1944.

Under Nazi orders, the local municipalities were supposed to place restrictions on Jews, provide transportation for mass murder operations, find local residents to dig the pits and fill them in after the executions, and hold auctions of Jewish property (or otherwise dispose of those belongings).

On August 16, 1941, the chief of the Lithuanian Police Department, Vytautas Reivytis, sent a secret letter to the chiefs of all regional police departments:

After receipt of this circular, immediately arrest all men of Jewish ethnicity from the age of 15 up, and all women who distinguished themselves during the period

*of Bolshevik occupation by their Bolshevik activities or who are still known for
this sort of activity or imposture, at the locations indicated in the note. Collect the
arrested people next to major transportation arteries and immediately inform the
Police Department using special means of communications. In reporting, indicate
exactly how many Jews of this type have been arrested and collected, and at what
location.*

*You need to make sure to provide food and appropriate security, for which you
may make use of the auxiliary police, for the people arrested.*

*This circular must be fulfilled within 48 hours of its receipt. The Jews arrested are
to be guarded until it is possible to come and take them away to a camp.*[6]

Among the replies from police chiefs to Reivytis was this one, from the
chief of the Vilkija Police Department, dated August 18: *280 men and 120
women taken away out of Vilkija.*

And this one, from the chief of the Kėdainiai Police Department, dated
August 17: *913 Jews of the city and rural district of Kėdainiai concentrated in
the threshing shed and barn at the Kėdainiai Kulturtechnik School. Men sepa-
rated from women. They are being guarded pending the issuance of a separate
"directive."*

And from the chief of Šakiai Police Department, this reply: *I report that as of
today in the district assigned me there are no Jews. Local partisans and auxiliary
police took care of them.*

According to the historian Saulius Sužiedėlis, Vytautas Reivytis was
the greatest Lithuanian war criminal. In 1944 he and his wife and son left
Lithuania. They lived for a while in Scotland, and then resettled in the
state of Illinois in the United States, where he died in 1988.

During the years of 1941–1944, Zenonas Blynas, the general secretary
of the Lithuanian Nationalist Party, kept a record in his diary of all the
dealings he and his colleagues—councilors and national socialists—had
with the Nazis during the period of the civilian administration, right until
the end of the war. Here is a sampling:

August 13, 1941
*One person arrived from Joniškis. Supposedly it is difficult for the rural people
to get used to the massacres of Jews, in the villages [where] Jewish terror isn't as
especially rabid as there, and it is creating a discouraging and difficult atmosphere
in the countryside. He says it would be better to send them to work and shoot the
Communists instead. It is a bad thing we have shot too many, and that Lithuanians
have done the shooting. Especially if it is true that the Germans are filming those
shootings.*

---

6 Lithuanian Central State Archive, f. R-683, ap. 2, b. 2, 1.1.

August 14, 1941
I spoke with the head of the Rokiškis regional administration. This morning 9,000 Jews are supposed to be shot in Rokiškis. They dig a pit three meters deep, bring a group of 100 Jews in, lay them in the ditch and say whoever gets up will be shot, then several people with handheld tracer-bullet guns mow through the backs all in a row, then 20 or 30 centimeters of sand is sprinkled on top and the second column is laid down. Once they brought in 100 Jews. They were ordered to lead them out of the city. They left tied together. After a couple of kilometers they ordered them to leave the ropes and to undress to their underwear. The Jews understood their fate. It was a scene filled with tragedy. It affected the people doing the killing. He said another 2,000 people (the elderly, women, children) were left "for the second party." On humanitarian considerations, so that the children wouldn't have to be taken care of . . . now the younger, healthier men are being taken care of.

August 20, 1941
We cannot ask to be given an independent state right now. We have to be realistic. The Germans have promised us nothing specific, but if we are true to ourselves and unified, then we can serve as people and perhaps the battalions should be the ones to do that. For our loyal service we expect abundant realization of our aspirations, of our independent state.

August 24, 1941
One party colleague yesterday described the massacre in Rokiškis. It was done out in the open. The people were supposed to jump into a three-meter-deep pit, after half-undressing. People walking along the edge of the pit shot at them. Brains and blood splattered. The men doing the shooting were bloody. They were led out of the city tied together. At the pit they were told to half-undress. The women screamed and yelled. People from the surrounding area gathered. At first they were laughing and smiling but later became horrified, and the Aryan women also began to scream. A massacre. Shameful. The administration head is a Judas. I said, if the Germans are already doing this using our hand, then they should be doing it all calmly, without publicity, without scandal. Instead of doing all that, that freak did the opposite. I am going to remember him. Asshole.

September 18, 1941
One, two or three battalions are doing service. Everyone wears their own clothes. They don't have mattresses. They lie on the floor. They are given nothing. The morale of the volunteer soldiers is poor. Jews . . .

September 30, 1941
Today the soldiers of the battalion are walking around town completely drunk, saying they (they themselves are saying this) will travel to Riga. And what a life that will be there. But will it be finished with the Jews here by Friday? Perhaps the Lithuanians will ply this honorable trade of Jew murder-butchering there, too?

November 6, 1941

Commander Barzda has returned from the Minsk/Borisov/Slutsk region. The Lithu-anian battalion shot more than 46,000 Jews (from Byelorussia and transported from Poland). Hundreds of Germans filmed it. The soldiers are lice-ridden, and 30 percent have scabies. They are poorly equipped and freezing. They don't have clothes. Their shoes don't have linings.

There is talk that the Vilnius battalion is going to Lublin. The Vilnius people are saying that they are being sent to perform honorable duties. Well, those German guys sure the heck are honorable. The Ukrainians, Latvians, Estonians—none of them do [the] shooting. Only we alone have to shoot.

November 29, 1941

The Jews which the first battalion are now shooting are transported from Bohemia. They have visas for Brazil and the Argentine. They were told they were being transported to "quarantine." It's all legal; they just get lost along the way. The first battalion took care of them.

December 13, 1941

What's important to me is not the rescue of one or several Jews. I can't stand the fact that Lithuania is being turned into a cemetery-morgue, that we are being regularly forced to shoot Jews coming from Germany with visas, that we Lithuanians are doing the shooting, that we have become nothing more than paid executioners, that we are being filmed while the Germans are not filming themselves. I cannot stand this evil.

January 12, 1942

A certain drunk officer expressed his anger that Czechs refused to dig pits for them-selves, won't go into the pits, and instead they stand (while they are being shot), holding hands and singing the Czech national anthem. May these officers be damned forever.[7]

---

7 Zenonas Blynas, *Dienoraštis* (The Diary), LSA, f. 3377, ap. 55, pp. 105–228.

5

Lithuania Today

Minimizing the Crimes

Before leaving Lithuania, Efraim was talking about an important book. Twenty-one years ago, Litvaks—Lithuanian Jews—living in Israel, who had gone through the Lithuanian archives, came up with the so-called "Melamed List," named for Yosef Melamed, chairman of the association of Israeli Litvaks, and a former anti-Nazi partisan and Kaunas Ghetto survivor. The List, containing the names of alleged Lithuanian collaborators, was published in Israel in 1999, in a publication titled *Lithuania: Crime and Punishment.*

After Efraim left Lithuania, Rūta met with a historian who told her more. When the Melamed List was presented to the Lithuanian government, the authorities responded by sending it to the Genocide and Resistance Research Centre of Lithuania, requesting that it be researched. The Centre did so, and came to the conclusion that, of the 5,000 or so people named on the list, 1,050 had indeed participated in the mass murder of Jews from 1941 to 1944. During the investigation of case files and other historical sources, however, the Centre discovered more than a thousand other people who had also murdered Jews, whose names were *not* included on the Melamed List. According to the investigation, the total number of people found to have murdered Lithuanian Jews during the Holocaust was at least 2,055.

The Centre informed the Lithuanian government of the results of their study in 2012.

What did the Lithuanian government do?

Nothing. They did not respond. They didn't ask for further investigations. The results of the research were not released to anyone. The Centre has said that they cannot publish the List because they are not a court.

But there is no court. There are no prosecutions. There is no political will. Put more honestly, there is abundant political will to keep the List from being released.

Some detractors say that the list of hundreds of murderers of Jews contains a number of people who were arrested by the Soviets for "the mass murder of Soviet citizens" and other activities for the Nazis. Some of those on the list were convicted and punished. Some were shot, others sent to prison camps. After many years these people had been rehabilitated and returned to Lithuania with the halos of political prisoners, of martyr-heroes who deserved the greatest privileges and the right to participate in political life. Are we really going to rip the halos off the heads of these heroes, and those of their grandparents?

At the moment, there is another very important factor at play, and that is the current geopolitical situation. If the list of murderers were published, it would become apparent that Stalin hadn't just sent martyrs and heroes to the camps, but also hundreds of murderers. That would make Lithuanians Nazis, exactly what Putin is trying to prove.

So the Genocide Centre, without having received (or perhaps having received) a negative answer from the government, placed the list of 2,055 names in a safe and went on to the more-important matters for which it was established in the first place.

Rūta went to talk to the deputy councilor of the Lithuanian government about the list, to ask questions. "Why you are hiding it? Why is nobody investigating it any further? Why are Lithuanian historians not being asked to go on with their research?"

The answer?

"Whatever we Lithuanians do, it will not be enough. Jews will never forgive us, so what's the point of further research?"

6

✝

Mission Impossible?

In July 2015 Efraim Zuroff finally came to Lithuania. Was he really ready to start the journey with an enemy? Were both enemies ready for this?

Before we started planning the details of the trip, we had to sit and talk. We both had to clarify some of each other's attitudes and views. We had to find out if the journey was possible—if we, enemies at the start, would be able to conduct normal, civilized conversations.

Rūta: Many people I know warned me that you were a very aggressive and dangerous person, and that I should not get involved with you in any way. The first thing that the media and average people in my country say about you is that Zuroff hates Lithuania. Some even say that you would not be happy as long as we, Lithuanians, are living on this earth. Is that true?

Efraim: From the very beginning of my efforts in Lithuania, I always said that my activities were never motivated by hatred for the Baltics. On the contrary; I view them as something which in the long run would help Lithuania. Help it to deal with its past, make it a better place, and help the country to take its place among the liberal Western democracies of the world. What I tried to convince Lithuanians was that whatever positive steps they will take, they are not doing them for me or to please this or that Jewish organization. They will be doing this for their own benefit.

Rūta: Let's put it this way: Is there anything good you can say about my country?

Efraim: I would say two things: Lithuania is the most important country in the Baltics, certainly from a Jewish perspective. Two hundred and twenty thousand Jews lived in Lithuania under the Nazi occupation;

seventy thousand Jews were living in Latvia; and only one thousand Jews in Estonia. Lithuania is a country of a great natural beauty. My problem is that wherever I see a beautiful forest here, it reminds me of the unfortunate fact that there are hundreds of mass murder sites in such forests. Most of the sites where Jews were murdered are places of natural beauty, which is an absolute contrast to the terrible crimes committed there. And I must admit one thing: As hard as I tried not to make it personal, the fact is that as I get older, I think more and more about my great-uncle Efraim and his family who were murdered here, in your country, and most probably by your countrymen.

Rūta: You love your people. I love my people. Okay, your people were killed by my people, by Lithuanians. So I understand that you don't think of my people—both killers or bystanders—as people. We are enemies; that's inevitable. You represent the victims; in your eyes, I represent the killers. For me, both the killers and the bystanders were human. If I go on a journey with an enemy, I certainly will try to find out, to understand what happened to my people in those days. Why did they agree to shoot? They were not robots or monsters. What made them do what they did? And if this happened once, does it mean that it can happen again?

Efraim: I hate to say this, but yes, it can happen again. Because it already happened. If in 1930 somebody would have predicted that thousands of Lithuanians would go and shoot their neighbors, that person would have been sent to a mental hospital. But it happened. I am telling you from my long experience that the most horrifying thing that I learned in thirty-five years of hunting Nazis is that 99.99 percent of the people who carried out Holocaust crimes were normal people. They were not involved in criminal activity before the Shoah, nor after the Shoah. They lived normal lives with their families.

Rūta: One of the Nazis when questioned at his trial said the following. He was taught in police school the definition of a crime. Every crime consists of four elements: subject, object, intention, and action. In my case, said the accused, there was no intention, so there was no crime. Those young Lithuanians who joined the Lithuanian armed forces hoping to serve their country never intended to murder the Jews. They were brought to one place or another without knowing for what purpose, and then found themselves in a situation in which they were told to guard Jews or transport them to [camps]. . . . They had no intention of harming innocent people. Step by step, they were dragged into committing murder. Once in this situation, you need enormous strength in order to be able to refuse to do what you are told to do and what everybody else is doing. You are not in your daddy's garden; you are in the army, after all.

Efraim: First of all, as we all know, there was an option not to shoot. In other words, in the interviews of the people who were put on trial, some of them said the option of not shooting existed. How many people used that option? The sad truth is that these people did what their superiors expected them to do. In this case, it was mass murder.

Rūta: But you know how powerful inertia is. If you joined the army, you agreed to carry a weapon, you agreed to guard or transport people; there is practically no way back, no way to stop. You are carried down this road by the power of inertia and by being part of a large group of others.

Efraim: That's why international law recognizes individual criminal responsibility. No one is saying that these young army volunteers were the same as [Antanas] Impulevičius [an officer of the Lithuanian Army, and later, a Nazi collaborator who was the commander of a Lithuanian murder squad]. No one is saying that these people were part of the leadership. But these were the people who did it. They committed the crime, and the Holocaust would have never reached the scope that it did without those people doing what they did. They have to share the blame.

Rūta: I cannot help but pity those young guys . . .

Efraim: Listen, this is irrelevant; this is totally irrelevant. If the murders had been a one-time thing, that would be a powerful argument. But since the murders were murder after murder after murder in many cases—take the Impulevičius Battalion, or *Ypatingas būrys*—these people knew what they were doing and did it anyway.

Rūta: If the government of independent Lithuania told them to do so, if their superiors told them to do so, if all the other comrades did so, and if God agreed to it and allowed this to happen—so what can you do? Let's be realistic: The majority of these people were not well-educated; half of them were illiterate, and incapable of thinking in terms of moral criteria.

Efraim: You go to the people who lost their relatives in the Shoah and tell them, "I apologize, but you know what—my people were stupid." Does that sound convincing to you?

Rūta: No, it does not. But I also think about the responsibility of the Church. Or God, to make it simple. In some incredible and absurd way, the fact that the killers were almost all religious, attended church and believed in God, made them feel less responsible for their deeds. Why did God allow all this to happen? That is what some of them said in their testimonies.

Efraim: We are entitled to expect a certain level of understanding that what they were doing is the most horrific crime imaginable. Since when is stupidity a sufficient defense for mass murder? Here we are not talking about someone who under certain circumstances pulled a trigger once and ended up killing a single person. We are talking about murdering hundreds of men, women, children, the elderly, the ill. In a certain sense you have to be totally autistic to continue to carry out this task day after day after day. There were two different types of criminals in this regard. There were those people in the smaller towns who committed murder once or twice. But there were people from the special murder squads, like the 12th Battalion, Rollkommando Hamann, or *Ypatingas būrys*, who did it over a long period of time, with tens of thousands of victims.

Rūta: I am trying to understand even those people. Maybe it was difficult to shoot the first person, but once it was done, it became a sort of a job; killing was almost automatic. They did not see the faces of the victims, of the people they had to shoot, only their backs.

Efraim: You are looking for rationalizations. You want to free them from guilt. I do not want to make this personal, but if I think of the people who murdered my great-uncle Efraim, an innocent, wonderful, and brilliant person . . . How many wonderful people did we lose? Think what an important contribution these people could have made.

Rūta: I am thinking as a Lithuanian, of course. Some of these young, half-illiterate, confused guys perhaps killed someone who was very bright and could have become a top scientist or doctor and would have discovered a cure for cancer that later on would have saved, say, his sister's life. But he pulled the trigger . . .

Efraim: Brilliant statement. But this kind of thinking is the thinking of someone who has difficulty attributing blame.

Rūta: I cannot accept all the blame you are putting on my country. The book you sent me about the crimes of Lithuanians during the Holocaust made me sick. On every page, in almost every sentence, it says something awful about Lithuanians—that they robbed Jews, tortured them, raped Jewish women, and smashed the heads of Jewish kids—as if the whole population of Lithuania were monsters. Not all Lithuanians were like this; very few were. The book is soaked with hatred. I want to do this journey with you, so we can find out whether there were additional categories besides killers and righteous people. I want to see the full picture, not just black and white. I am from this country; they were my people.

Efraim: Listen, the majority of Lithuanians were bystanders—neither killers nor saviors. What you are trying to do is a partial attempt to rehabilitate the killers.

Rūta: No, no, certainly not.

Efraim: Are you sure about this?

Rūta: No, not entirely sure.

Efraim: Okay, at least you are honest. But you are taking all this a little too far. You want to soften the blow. Try to make it easier for Lithuanians to come to terms. But if you want to come to terms, it should not be a softer, sanitized version; you want to come to terms with the real hard facts. Look, this is something you owe to yourselves, not to me. I do not live here. I am going home. And my country did not do this.

Rūta: I know why you hate my country. Because my country rejected you. You came to us in 1991, right after we obtained our independence. You came to us to say that we were murderers. You came to spoil the wedding. You ruined the party. You should have addressed this issue delicately, step by step, and given us more time.

Efraim: How long did you think that the wedding would last?

Rūta: Hmm. Twenty years. Ten years. But now we have a hangover. It took us some ten years to understand that there was no real wedding, just a party. And there is one more thing you did wrong. You poured too much guilt over us. It was very hard for us to admit that we collaborated with the Nazis during their occupation. If this would have been the only accusation, we might have said, Okay, maybe; we will look into this. We will investigate. But on top of this, you accused us of starting to kill the Jews before the Germans arrived. That was too much. And then the third thing you did wrong was to try and kill our old people, like Lileikis and Gimžauskas, who looked almost like our grandparents.

Efraim: Because they killed my great-uncle and his family.

Rūta: But if you kill my grandfather, it does not bring your great-uncle back to life. These two people whom you wanted to put on trial were very frail, half-dead. Lileikis was living in the house next to mine in Teatro Street in Vilnius. He already looked like a corpse. Looking at him, we Lithuanians thought as Catholics that if he was really guilty, as you claimed, he would go to hell, and very soon. Let God take care of justice; it is too late for people to interfere.

Why did you concentrate your Nazi-hunting in Lithuania on just a few people? For example, you never looked for the man whom historian Saulius Sužiedėlis calls the biggest war criminal in Lithuania, Vytautas Reivytis. He issued the order to all the provincial towns to concentrate the Jews, so they could be killed throughout Lithuania. The national commander of the Lithuanian police moved to Scotland and died peacefully in Chicago in 1988.

Efraim: Look, when did we start to look for the war criminals? In 1991. If he died in 1988, that might explain why we did not look for him. Why didn't the Americans catch him? That is unbelievable. I am in shock. I did not know he was in the States. I did all I could. And I was alone here. But as I have said many, many times over the years, I realize how difficult it could be for Lithuania to admit its complicity. It took France fifty years to acknowledge its guilt. Germany had no choice. But for your sake and for your children's sake, the sooner you face this honestly, the sooner the healing process will start.

Rūta: If it took France fifty years, it will take Lithuania fifty years as well.

Efraim: No, it will take you ninety years. Because your crimes are greater, and your ability to deal with them is less. The French prepared the Jews to be sent somewhere and they sent them away to be murdered. Here the Jews were murdered by your people.

Rūta: My poor people . . .

Efraim: You can cry from today till doomsday, but it does not change the facts that have happened. This is the truth you have to face. You, not me. You know why everyone in Lithuania hates me? Because they know that I am right.

Rūta: So let me see if you are right or not. Let me face this truth. Let us face it together. Let's start the journey with an enemy. We'll split the gas. Hopefully, we will not fight all the time; otherwise, this journey could become a nightmare.

Efraim: Okay. Let it be a "No Violence Journey with the Enemy."

III

JOURNEY WITH THE ENEMY: THIRTEEN DESTINATIONS

7

✝

Kaunas / Kovno

At the end of the nineteenth century, 25,548 Jews were living in Kaunas (35.9 percent of the local population).

Before the Shoah—around 30,000.

JULY 2015

Efraim: We are standing in front of the Lietūkis Garage monument which says that several dozen Jews were killed here, but does not say by whom. Maybe it was a volcano, maybe a tsunami, maybe an earthquake. What we do know is that just a few days after German invasion, on June 27, 1941, several dozen Jews were beaten to death with crowbars by Lithuanians at the Lietūkis Garage. This was the very first public pogrom in Lithuania, organized by journalist Algis Klimaitis.

Rūta: We are with a professional Jewish guide from Kaunas, the one and only Chaim Bargman.

Chaim: My knowledge is based on the testimony of an eyewitness named Vaclovas Vodzinskas, whom I met at a seminar at Kaunas University. He was fifteen when this massacre took place. He saw a group of Jews who were brought here to the Lietūkis Garage from the Yellow Prison. This was a group of men only. That was at the time when Jews were being rounded up and brought to the Seventh Fort. They were guarded by only about four guards.

The Lietūkis garage pogrom. (Lithuanian Central State Archives)

This was the place where the horses of the Red Army were kept before the Germans invaded. The guards of the courtyard were ordered by the Nazis to clean this garage, which had been dirtied by the horses. They said that since the Jews were friends of the Russians, they should clean up all the shit. The guards brought the group into this yard. Vodzinskas put his bicycle aside and climbed up a tree and watched the event from there, together with other kids. The Jews were not given any shovels to clean the place. Meanwhile, a truck with four German soldiers came. The truck was also dirty, so the Jews were ordered to clean this truck as well. But the Jews' hands were so dirty that a water pipe was brought so they could wash their hands and clean the truck.

Efraim: What was the crowd doing here?

Chaim: The Jews were killed in a very cruel way. People on the streets who heard the screams came to see what was happening.

Rūta: A petty officer of the Lithuanian army who was one of the participants of the Lietūkis murder confessed several years after the massacre: "I am one of the executioners. When I got out of jail, I wanted to take revenge against the Jews. When the Jews began to resist, I lost my temper. Now you can condemn me. Today I do not understand myself how I could have done this."

Efraim: Is it true that the Jews were murdered in two ways—one, that they were beaten with metal crowbars; the other, that firehoses were shoved into the victims' mouths and the water was turned on to explode their stomachs?

Chaim: This is absolutely not true. The pipes were brought in so that the Jews could clean their hands. One of the Jews who had been ordered to clean the horseshit with his bare hands hit a Lithuanian soldier and began to run toward the Jewish cemetery. He was quick, but the bullet was quicker. There were four Lithuanians and four Germans. After that Jew tried to escape and was killed, the soldiers started to beat the Jews with iron bars.

Rūta: Efraim, you have been telling people all around the world for the past thirty years that the Jews were killed with firehoses which exploded their stomachs! It was not true. You lost!

Efraim: I have the testimony of a German photographer, who said that was what he saw. There was no reason for him to lie. This is the testimony of an objective observer.

Rūta: Big news! The chief Nazi-hunter trusts the testimony of a Nazi soldier more than any other testimony! Okay, I will be merciful. I read the testimony of a Lithuanian female doctor who said something about a water pipe being put into someone's mouth. Perhaps that supports your version.

Efraim: And did the crowd sing the Lithuanian national anthem after the massacre ended? That is what the German photographer said in his testimony.

Chaim: After all the Jews were killed and they were lying on the ground, two homeless men came by from the railway station. They had a harmonica. One of the killers saw them and asked them to play the "March of the Slobodka Jews" for them. The old people of Kaunas know this march very well, or at least the melody, not the words.

Rūta: The German photographer did not know what people were singing, he just asked someone there. That someone might have made a joke. So in his testimony he claimed that this was the Lithuanian national anthem.

Chaim: Yes, the legend goes like this. In reality, the "March of the Slobodka Jews" was played, and the legend goes around the world that it was the Lithuanian national anthem. The "March of the Slobodka Jews" was a song that the low-class people of Kaunas liked and sang, and it was a very anti-Semitic song.

Rūta: Efraim! For the past thirty years you have been spreading a lie about Lithuanians singing their national anthem after the Lietūkis massacre! Our enemy lost!

Efraim: I certainly was not knowingly lying. I had no reason to doubt the testimony of the German army photographer, but now I have to admit that Chaim cast some serious doubt on the story.

Rūta: Thank you, Chaim, on behalf of our people! After the garage we have to visit the mass murder site in the very center of Kaunas: the Seventh Fort. The place of the very first mass killing in Lithuania.

WHAT HAPPENED HERE IN 1941?

When the Germans entered Lithuania they immediately demanded that the Lithuanian insurgents should be disarmed. Kaunas military commandant Jurgis Bobelis issued an order to begin forming TDA battalions (an acronym for *Tautinio darbo apsauga*, or National Labor Defense). The insurgency lasted for less than a week. By July 4, the newly formed battalion included 724 petty officers and soldiers. Then the battalion, which was supposed to sooner or later become the army of an independent Lithuania, began to carry out the mission for which it was formed, by order of the Germans—the mass murder of Jews: 416 men and 47 women were shot at the pits at the Seventh Fort in Kaunas on July 4 (according to the Jäger Report).

The TDA carried out the shooting, and Lieutenant Bronius Norkus and Junior Lieutenant Jonas Obelevičius were in charge of the shooting. On

July 6, they began shooting victims with machine guns as well: 2,514 Jews were murdered, shot in the back. Lieutenants J. Barzda, A. Dagys, and B. Norkus led the shooting.

In the Lithuanian Special Archives, case no. 47337/3 contains twelve volumes about the crimes of Pranas Matiukas and another seven soldiers from the third platoon of the TDA battalion. During the period of independent Lithuania, Pranas Matiukas worked at a printing house and also studied to become a dental technician. As the Red Army withdrew from Kaunas, Matiukas ran into a soldier and threatened him with a pocketknife. The soldier turned over his rifle to Matiukas, who then went off to sign up for the TDA. At that point, Matiukas had two sons, ages seven and one. He admitted in court later on: "I kind of liked shooting people."

From the record of Pranas Matiukas's interrogation, December 3, 1961:

It was the summer of 1941. I don't remember the exact date; it might have been the month of July. In the afternoon our third platoon of the battalion, which was still deployed at that time on Laisvė Alėja [Kaunas promenade] near the so-called Sobor [St. Michael the Archangel Church at one end], commanded by the officers Barzda, Norkus and Dagys, went by foot to the Kaunas Seventh Fort which was in Žaliakalnis [a neighborhood of Kaunas]. There were soldiers from other platoons guarding the fort.

Inside the fort, in the deep ravine between the slopes, about 300 to 400 people were under guard, people of Jewish ethnicity. They were there under the open sky.

There were also about 100 to 150 women of Jewish ethnicity who were being guarded inside the underground fortifications of the fort itself.

The shooting took place in the following manner. A group of battalion soldiers, more or less 10 people, commanded by petty officers or officers, took about 10 people from that ravine where the condemned Jewish males were being guarded. They took them about 50 to 100 meters from there, where there was a large crater caused by an explosion. Then they stood them on the edge of the pit facing the pit and shot them from several paces. After the shooting, the corpses fell into the pit. The soldiers fired from the rifles which they had, while the officers—Dagys, Norkus, Barzda—shot from pistols.

Since evening was approaching, the shooting was halted. The next day, as soon as it was light, we again went to the fort and surrounded the ravine where the arrested men were held. There were two or three light Bruno-type machine guns set up on the slopes. Barzda and Norkus said we would have to shoot the condemned right there, from the slope above into the ravine. Then the command was issued to begin firing. The people under fire began to run around inside the ravine, but were not able to escape anywhere, and all of them were felled by bullets.

This disorderly shooting took about an hour and a half. During that time the bottom of the ravine was covered with corpses and blood. I can say that almost all of our third regiment did the shooting, except for a few people who for one reason or another had stayed in the barracks. I shot, too. I cannot say how many people I shot; that was impossible to determine.

The ravine was about 50 by 50 meters and the slopes around it were 10 to 15 meters high.[1]

Witness Jurgis Vosylius recalled:

Because there were so many residential homes near the fort, many local residents gathered to watch the shooting. As a guard I had to disperse them and not allow them to come closer, so I didn't see the shooting scene well.

Shooting of Jews from the Kaunas Ghetto in the Ninth Fort in Kaunas:

We were told not to drink too much the night before because at six or eight o'clock in the morning everyone would have be present in the barracks and go on an operation. Barzda or Dagys gave us this order.

The next day at eight o'clock in the morning the regiment was assembled and we all went to the ghetto. Our entire battalion participated in this operation.

Other soldiers transferred about 400 Jews—men, women and children—from the ghetto to us after which we, about eight to ten soldiers, took charge of guarding these Jews, and we began to march them towards the Ninth Fort, which was about two kilometers' distance from the city. We brought the Jews to the fort where there was a big depression. Here we handed them over to other soldiers to guard, and we ourselves returned to the ghetto to take other groups of people. After we delivered the second group to be killed, I didn't go back to the ghetto; I stayed at the fort.

In the back of the fort across from the Žemaičių road there were three long trenches dug, perhaps 100 meters long, 2 meters wide and the same number deep.

When I went to the ditches I found our third regiment soldiers, of whom there were about 30 people. From among the officers who were with them were Barzda, Norkus and Dagys. Besides them, there was a group of German soldiers and officers.

At the same time, about 30 of our regiment's soldiers, about 10 German soldiers using automatic weapons, and officers using pistols, shot the condemned. At that time I fired from my rifle and got off about 60 or 70 shots. I shot for about an hour and a half. I cannot say how many people I personally shot, because we all shot at the same time into a common mass of people who were in the depression. I remember that I personally participated in shooting about two groups of about 400 people each. Of course I fired with interruptions.

I cannot say in general who stood next to the ditch and shot because there was no order to it: one person shot and left, then another came up.

Of the condemned I knew Gravecas and Riveris.

I took gold items. At the Ninth Fort they passed out vodka, but in very small quantities. When we went to get more ammunition, Norkus and Barzda gave us a swig from a bottle of vodka. That day, as was said among the guards, about eight to ten thousand people were shot. After the shooting the soldiers selected the better things from the piles of the clothing of those murdered. I didn't take anything from the victims' things; during the shooting I took two watches from those being taken to the ditches, which they gave me freely. The second group we shot at the Ninth

---

1 LSA, K-1, ap. 58, b. 47337/3, t. 1., p. 208.

Pranas Matiukas at a mass murder site near Kaunas, 1962. (Lithuanian Special Archives)

Fort was Czechoslovakians. We were taken to the Ninth Fort, where the officers said that we would have to shoot about 2,000 people. The condemned were marched with shirtsleeves rolled up; the Czechs said they were being taken to be vaccinated against smallpox. In the ditches the Czechs tried to flee, but where can you run when you're surrounded?[2]

Matiukas's words in court in 1962:

According to my conscience I have committed a crime. But as a soldier I am innocent. I simply carried out an order. I don't know what my purpose was.

Testimony of suspect Jonas Raižys in the case:

After the shooting I saw Matiukas carrying a set of teeth. Matiukas himself showed the teeth on his palm. I asked why Matiukas needed teeth, and the soldier said he was a dental technician and his wife was a dentist. On Matiukas's palm I saw, it seems, four teeth, cleaned and polished.[3]

In total, Pranas Matiukas participated in the shooting of approximately eighteen thousand people.

---

2 Ibid., p. 142.
3 Ibid., p. 150.

On November 9, 1962, Matiukas and another seven TDA soldiers were executed by a firing squad. The dental technician's career was over.

The historian Afredas Rukšėnas examined the motivations of the murderers in the Kaunas self-defense battalions. He formulated four categories of people who joined the battalions:

Patriots: Those who joined the self-defense battalions out of a desire to defend the country from enemies, and who expected the battalions to become the nucleus of an independent Lithuanian army;

The unemployed: Former Lithuanian army officers and others who were out of work, who joined the battalions in order to receive a salary;

Those who suffered under Soviet rule: Lithuanian military officers who were mistreated by the Soviet regime, were retired under Soviet rule, interrogated by Soviet security, and who wanted to take revenge upon their oppressors; and

The insecure: Those who had served the Soviet regime and joined the battalions to avoid punishment, including those who were afraid of being deported to Germany as slave laborers.[4]

The following are statements made by the members of the third platoon regarding their motives for service, before the Supreme Court of Lithuania in 1962:

Aleksas Raižys:

I do not know why I joined the battalion. I cannot explain what I did. Maybe I joined the battalion because of poverty, I don't know. I don't know why I was shooting people.

Juozas Kopūstas:

When I joined the battalion my purpose was to get some goods. We did not get any salary. We were rewarded with the clothes of the victims. It was useful for me to be a member of this battalion. After the first shooting I did not realize I was doing something wrong.

Klemensas Skabickas:

I joined the battalion because of my poor health. The job wasn't difficult. I did not know the people I shot; they hadn't done anything to me. I am religious. When I was

---

4 Alfredas Rukšėnas, *Lietuvos gyventojų stojimo į Kauno savisaugos batalionus 1941 vasarą ir rudenį motyvai* (The Motives of the Lithuanian People Joining the Kaunas Self-Defense Battalions in Summer and Fall of 1941). From: *Genocidas ir rezistencija* (Genocide and Resistance), 2012, No. 2 (32), pp. 7–26.

shooting I didn't know what would come out of this. After the shootings I used to go to confess.[5]

After the mass murder operations in July by the third platoon, several soldiers deserted. One soldier, Captain B. Kirkila, shot himself in his apartment when he was on leave on July 12, 1941. Why? Couldn't he handle the stress? According to M. Biržiška, a Lithuanian historian living in the West, he was tortured to the point of madness by the Jews in the NKVD prison, having escaped there only to discover that his family had been deported to Kazakhstan, thanks to the efforts of Jewish Party members. He swore to take revenge on the Jews until he had killed a specific number of them. When he reached that number, Kirkila shot himself.

If this is true, Bronius Kirkila reached his quota very quickly, in just a few days. The number was huge—several thousand men, women, elderly, and children.

JULY 2015

The Seventh Fort is empty, or almost empty. No visitors. A children's summer camp is taking place. A young man, one of the camp counselors, takes us to the mass murder site, a pit overgrown with high grass. A memorial post marking the mass murder site stands there. When; who; how many died?

We ask the young man about what is taking place these days at the fort. There is a Cold War museum, as well as a chemistry laboratory. The children are engaged in various activities.

In June 1941, the Provisional Government of Lithuania decided to set up the first concentration camp in Lithuania at the Seventh Fort, allocating money for a battalion to stand guard over the Jews of Kaunas who were taken there.

On July 6, the first and third platoons of the TDA battalion found a way to save time while murdering people. According to the dental technician, Matiukas, on the night before, they had shot people in small groups, but the next day they shot everyone at once. All the Jews were pushed together into the pit and the shooting took only half an hour. They kept shooting until no one moved in the pit. How many people were only wounded and suffered until perhaps after another half-hour, one of the dental technician's many bullets ended their lives?

How is it possible that mass murder sites have been privatized?

---

5 LSA, K-1, ap. 58, b. 47337/3, t. 12, p. 154.

Kaunas VIIth fort mass murder site. (Rūta Vanagaitė)

During the Soviet period, the fort was a military site, so no one was allowed to visit, investigate, or honor the victims. For the first twenty years of Lithuanian independence, nothing was done to research the crimes or commemorate the victims. In 2009, the Kaunas Seventh Fort, with all of its five thousand buried Jews murdered by TDA soldiers, was privatized. The owner began cleaning up the seven-hectare territory, and in 2012, the following surprise occurred during the cleanup:

> Collecting the garbage we took many truckloads of junk away. In the pit we discov-
> ered a layer of lime, through which what looked like sticks were sticking up. They
> were the bones of the people shot.
>   After pumping the water out of the ditch and sticking a hand down there, I felt an
> endless number of bones; their depth might be several meters.[6]
>   —Vladimiras Orlovas, the owner

Orlovas went to the police, the Cultural Heritage Protection Department, and the Jewish community to report his discovery. No one did

---

6 Nerijus Povilaitis, *Nesutariam, kaip laidoti nužudytųjų žydų kaulus* (Disagreements over How the Bones of the Murdered Jews Should Be Buried). From: Lrytas.lt, October 3, 2014.

anything, so the owners packed the bones into three garbage bags and left them in a storage space somewhere.

When the media reported on this, the Kaunas city administration formed the "Commission for the Commemoration of the Burial and Human Remains Transfer Sites of Resistors and Other People Murdered during the Period of the Occupational Regimes of Lithuania." The commission met just twice over a period of two years.

It was only two years later, in 2014, that the bones were taken from the bags and returned to where they had been discovered, and this time most likely covered over with a thicker layer of soil.

So the city allowed the privatization of this mass murder site, complete with the corpses of all the people who were murdered by Lithuanians. Maybe we Lithuanians ought to be completely consistent about this. If mass graves can be privatized with all of their human remains, and a monument to the planner of this mass murder, Juozas Barzda, can be erected on state land in Plungė, then shouldn't that statue more properly be moved to the Seventh Fort, where that hero committed his crime? This is, after all, where Barzda commanded the first organized mass murders in Lithuania on July 6, 1941, an "exemplary mass murder operation," according to the Jäger Report.

The web page of the Kaunas Seventh Fort presents the site as "an oasis of nature and history." Midsummer's Eve celebrations and corporate gatherings are held here. The web page invites children to celebrate their birthdays at the site with such educational activities as blowing bubbles and even a "Treasure Hunt," which takes place throughout the seven-hectare area.

Kaunas residents and some visitors complained to cultural heritage protection specialists, who then approached the fort's owners, asking them not to hold celebrations, games, and similar events at the fort. The owners wrote back saying there was no problem here at all, since all of the events being held at the location are of an educational nature.

Seventy-five years ago, Pranas Matiukas, a murderer who loved gold, hunted treasure in the large pit filled with corpses. After the war, he worked as a dental technician in Joniškėlis. How many gold teeth pulled from the mouths of corpses were melted down and placed in the mouths of the residents of Joniškėlis? Maybe a few teeth are still left in the pit at the Kaunas fort, and it might be profitable for parents to pay the three euros for the "Treasure Hunt" there.

Efraim: Don't you think that on the way from this horrific place we should talk about anti-Semitism in today's Lithuania?

Rūta: Yes, we should. Many Lithuanian people of my generation have some anti-Semitic prejudices. I understand them. We are all from small

Monument to Juozas Barzda near Plungė. (Rūta Vanagaitė)

villages. Our grandparents were not educated people; they were very religious and full of prejudices. When our parents came to live in towns, there were no Jews left. No Litvaks, I mean. Lithuanians of my generation, or younger, have never met real Litvaks. The majority were killed, the rest emigrated, and what we encountered were mostly Soviet Jews who came here after the war and took empty flats in the cities, and took open positions in Lithuanian offices and factories. The official language back then was Russian, so they could get any job they wanted. They were Russian-speaking, not very well-educated, did not care about our culture, and were pro-Soviet.

These newcomers certainly were not in any way superior to us, so most of us had almost no chance to encounter real representatives of the Litvak tradition, representatives of the People of the Book. All we saw were just ordinary, unfriendly Soviets of Jewish origin. These Jews killed our interest in Jewish culture and reinforced our perception that Jews equal Soviets. We had very little possibility to meet the real Litvaks, to understand them, to get to know them. The Litvaks were killed; those who came here later were different. So how you can expect us to think differently about the Jews, and not be anti-Semitic? Our anti-Semitism came from our farmer grandparents and from our own experience with Soviet Jews.

Efraim: Unless you went to the university and encountered some smart teachers who taught you about philosophy, and history, and broadened your horizons.

Rūta: Don't forget that we went to Soviet universities and studied Marxist history and philosophy. Lucky me, I studied in Moscow, and met some incredible Jewish professors there. But what about those who lived and studied here, in Lithuania? So you see, it is very normal for us not to know anything about Litvak culture and about the Jewish religion because we never encountered it. And the less we know, the stronger are our old prejudices, and the longer they live in people's minds.

Efraim: That explains why some of people you talked to about this book were very hostile and expressed their anti-Semitic views.

Rūta: I know that this book will not be received with a positive attitude by people who were brought up in Soviet times. You Jews were swept away by the Holocaust and on top of this tragedy, the Soviet Jews came to our country.

Efraim: That is a very interesting argument.

Rūta: This is a very sad conversation that we are having right now. That is why the people who participated in the "Being a Jew" project were so overwhelmed by what they discovered, with the help of Simonas Gurevicius. I have met a lot of superintelligent Jews around the world, but hardly anyone here, among the people I live with.

Efraim: That explains a lot. But you are lucky; you met those people, and you met Simon, and you are open and you want to understand. But the people whom you were talking to, who are smart and educated, have something like a closed door in their minds as far as anything that has to do with Jews.

Rūta: I cannot kick this door open. Nobody can. The door will open when it opens, when the time comes to open it. In this sense, we are the lost generation.

Efraim: You might be right. It is a lost generation. The people I spoke to during the last twenty-five years were of that generation.

Rūta: They look at you and think that you are pro-Soviet and that you are making money off the Holocaust issue. You are part of the Holocaust industry.

Efraim: One second. What do I have to do?

Rūta: Give some of your money to Lithuania, to a charity here.

Efraim: Let's get serious. I am thinking about your friends, intelligent people with blocked minds. What does it say about Lithuanian society today?

Rūta: You know what it says: that we have more things to blame the Soviets for than we thought.

Efraim: Listen, you were anti-Semitic before the Soviets, then they made it worse.

Rūta: Yes, they made it worse.

8

✝

Linkmenys / Ligmiyan

At the end of the nineteenth century, there were 297 Jews (35.1 percent of the population) living in Ligmiyan.

Before the Shoah—less than 100.

Ligmiyan is the ancestral home of Efraim Zuroff's mother's family. His great-grandfather drowned in Lake Žiezdras, and even now Efraim is afraid of swimming in lakes. Twenty-three Jewish families lived in Linkmenys in 1941.

On the shores of Lake Žiezdras lies the village of Pažiezdris, only a kilometer and a half away from Linkmenys, from the Jewish homes. Adomas Lunius, the commander of the partisans who murdered the Jews of Linkmenys, was living there. The only school was in Linkmenys, so the killers and the victims must have attended the same school.

WHAT HAPPENED HERE IN 1941?

Witness Bileišis, Linkmenys resident, testifies:

I don't recall exactly when, but more or less at the end of July, 1941, Adomas Lunius gathered all the members of the unit in a building which had been a fire station earlier and which now served as partisan headquarters. There were about thirty or forty people at the meeting. I was there, too. Lunius addressed us, the "partisans" and "insurgents," and announced that it was necessary to place all the Jews in the schoolhouse in the village of Dvariškiai. Adomas Lunius then divided all the insurgents into groups of four or five people. Lunius gave orders to each group as to which specific Jewish family they should arrest and bring to the Dvariškiai village schoolhouse. I recall that together with two other "partisans" with whom I was not acquainted, I received an order to bring one Jewish family, whose surname I do not recall, to the gathering place. Carrying out this order, I went to the home of that family—and there were three or four people in the family—which was living in the house where Jurgis Šerėnas now resides.

When the others and I arrived to take away the Jewish family, we told them to come with us to the Dvariškiai village schoolhouse. At the moment that we delivered the Jewish family to the schoolhouse yard, we were met by Adomas Lunius, now sitting across from me, who told me and the other "partisans" and "insurgents" to take the Jews to a clearing outside Dvariškiai village near Ūsiai Lake. He said we would find a gathering place there. When we arrived with the Jews at the clearing near the lake, there were already Jews there who had been marched there by the other "partisans." I remember the Jews sat there on the ground in a single group while the "partisans" stood by and guarded them. We put the three Jews we had brought in the place where the other Jews were already sitting.

In total there were about fifty Soviet citizens of Jewish ethnicity collected in the clearing, perhaps more, perhaps fewer. When all the Jews had been collected in the clearing next to the lake, Adomas Lunius arrived, surveyed the gathering place and gave the command for all Jews to lie on the ground, facedown, which is what they did.

Then Lunius said that we were going to shoot the Jews and that the "partisans" must commence firing on his command, i.e., when he fires a shot from his pistol.

When the Jews lying on the ground heard they would be shot they began to yell and cry. Standing next to the shooting site, I clearly saw that Adomas Lunius shot from his pistol, although I did not see where he shot, whether into the air or at the Jews lying prone.

After he fired, this was at about eleven or twelve o'clock in the day, all the "partisans" (insurgents) who had weapons began to shoot the Jews lying on the ground. The shooting of the Soviet citizens of Jewish ethnicity lasted about fifteen minutes. After the shooting of the Jews, Adomas Lunius spoke to the insurgents who did not have weapons and announced that those who so desired could go home, which is what I did.

Several days later the possessions of the Jews were taken from the apartments of those Jews who had been shot and were collected at the Linkmenys Synagogue, and later, the "partisans," including me, received certain items. I got two towels, a tablecloth and something else, but I cannot remember what.[1]

Adomas Lunius, head of the white armbanders of Linkmenys, testifies:

I do not completely agree with some of the statements of the witnesses. . . . The insurgents asked my permission to shoot the Jews naked, to take away their watches, rings and other valuables, but I forbade doing this and gave the order to shoot the Jews in their clothes. . . . I do not affirm the statements by the witness that after I gave the

---

1 LSA, K-1, ap. 58, b. 46360/3, t. 2, pp. 213–15.

command "fire" he fled the shooting site. There were no cases at all of insurgents fleeing the shooting site.[2]

Witness Vladas Kliukas, who lived next to the shooting location, testifies:

I saw through my window how the members of the insurgent unit marched the Jews into the clearing next to Ūsiai Lake. I was curious [about] what the insurgents were going to do with the Jews. I went out into my garden and, hiding behind the trees, I went into a hay barn located on the farm of Mykolas Pilanis. After I entered the barn I climbed boards nailed to the wall like a ladder and began to watch through a large hole 30 cm across in the wall of the barn, through which the field next to Dvariškiai village was clearly visible. From my observation point I saw Soviet citizens of Jewish ethnicity sitting on the ground. One of the Jews began to beg the insurgents to allow them to pray before death. How the Jews prayed—whether sitting or lying—I do not recall because of the time which has passed since those events.

When the shooting was over, I left the barn and decided to go check on my horse, which was foraging about 300 or 400 meters away from the shooting location. When I went to check on the horse, after I had gone about 20 or 25 meters, one of the insurgents invited me over to the shooting site, and when I got there, Adomas Lunius showed me a shovel and told me to dig a pit.

Witness Alekna:

I recall that Lunius, sitting across from me, twice ordered me to guard the Jews' belongings in the Linkmenys Synagogue, which had been collected after the Jews who had lived in Linkmenys were shot. I remember Lunius told me, Go guard the Jews' things, because unit members might try to walk off with them. There was a room in the unit headquarters where the guns were kept, and I went and took a gun and went off to do guard duty. Lunius was in that room where the guns were and he also had the keys to the synagogue.

After about four or five days, Lunius told me to keep an eye on the other insurgents who were manning the post next to the synagogue, so that they wouldn't try to pull things out through the windows while they manned the post, which is what I did.

Several days after guarding the things in the synagogue, one of the insurgents told me I should come to the synagogue on a certain day and I would receive a portion of the Jews' things, which a commission headed by Lunius would distribute to the insurgents. I came that day to the door of the synagogue and one of the insurgents gave me some underwear, a simple necklace and some other small items. After I received these items I left.[3]

The unit of insurgents under Adomas Lunius's command killed about seventy people. Nine of them were children. Lunius received the order to carry out the murder at some headquarters, most likely from the local

---

2 Ibid., p. 230.
3 Ibid., pp. 210–12.

police. Not all of the insurgents in the unit murdered their neighbors—
only the ones who had served in the Lithuanian army—one such soldier
present in each group of insurgents. Only they had guns. That's what the
witnesses say in the interrogations in the case.

Lunius was only twenty-six at the time of the mass murder. He had a
wife and two children who lived right there, in Pažaizdris village. Adomas Lunius's first arrest was in 1950, at which time he was sentenced to
five years in prison under Article 117 of the Criminal Code. The KGB
didn't know then about his homicidal activities. After he came back from
prison, Lunius started a new family in a new location. His second arrest
came on December 25, 1959, Christmas Day.

When he was arrested, Adomas Lunius had on his person the following
personal items, which were placed in storage:

One leather belt
One wool scarf
105 rubles and 5 kopeks

They always take away those items with which the prisoners might
hang themselves.

While he was imprisoned during his interrogation, Adomas Lunius
complained of shoulder pain, so prison surgeon Dr. Ovsej began treatment on March 23, 1960. After taking X-rays of the shoulder area, the
doctor diagnosed stiffness in the shoulder joint. Treatment prescribed to
patient:

1. Heat treatment (paraffin, sunlamp)
2. Light physical therapy and massage

We don't know whether the massage worked. Several months later, in
September of 1960, Adomas Lunius was sentenced to death in Vilnius.
His daughter was five at the time.

JULY 2015

Seventy-five years after the mass murder of the Jews of Linkmenys,
Efraim Zuroff and I stand in the clearing where Adomas Lunius gave the
order in July of 1941 for the Jews to sit, and then to lie facedown. It's likely
that he did allow them to pray, after all. And he didn't undress them; he
shot them clothed. He acted humanely—didn't he?

The area glows red with raspberries, this year like no other. Perhaps
it was like this in July of 1941? Traveling throughout Lithuania for ten

Adomas Lunius at the exhumation site in Linkmenys, February 1962. (Lithuanian Special Archives)

days, we had seen gigantic raspberry patches at practically all of the mass murder sites. Zuroff had never seen forest raspberries in his life. This is where he saw them for the first time. And as I looked upon these raspberry bushes, the lines of a poem by Marina Tsvetayeva, which I had read long ago, came back to me:

> *Sorvi sebe stebel dikiy*
> *i yagodu emu vsled,—*
> *Kladbishchenskoy zemlyanki*
> *krupnee i slashche net.*

> Grab yourself the bramble,
> Pluck from it the berry,
> There is no strawberry sweeter of savor
> Than those from the cemetery.

Efraim Zuroff says Kaddish in Link-menys. (Rūta Vanagaitė)

Efraim Zuroff says Kaddish at the monument. I do not know what to do, so I move away a bit and wait for him. And then I hear a strange sound. Very strange indeed.

I hear the Nazi-hunter crying.

Right here, right next to the mass murder site and the monument, there is a farm. A man is cutting grass with a tractor; a woman is weeding the garden. I go over and ask about the mass murder which took place right under their windows—or, more precisely, the windows of their parents or grandparents, since these two people are too young to have seen anything.

The woman points to the old hay barn nearby. Her father was living there, on that day when Lunius's unit shot the Jews and the white armbanders locked all the children of Dvariškiai village in the barn for half the day, standing guard over them so they wouldn't escape and see anything. Mykolas Pilanis's shed on the hillock hasn't survived, but this barn is still here.

Who were the shooters? I ask.

Lithuanians—all Lithuanians, from Linkmenys, the woman replies. That's what her father told her. And my husband's parents, she relates, were also in that barn when they shot the Jews. And they knew those Jews. And those Lithuanians.

There is a farmhouse next to the barn, where an elderly woman of ninety named Janina lives. She recalls everything, her neighbor tells me. But she won't talk. Janina's husband was a partisan.

The woman takes us to Janina's house anyway, and we sit with her for an eternity.

I won't talk about it, she says.

Who did the shooting? I ask.

The Germans, she answers. Only Germans. Later she opens up and tells us more:

> I was young [not yet married]. When they took the Jews to be shot, I was at the home of the neighbor's girls on the other side of the road. They marched them right by us. We thought that they had taken them from their homes to a meeting, or so they said. We thought that while they were gone, their homes would be searched, and then they would bring them back home. We heard shots as we were sitting. When the shooting ended, I went home, and only later did I find out from my mother that they had shot all the Jews.

After the Russians came back, they killed Janina's husband, who had joined the Lithuanian partisans. Janina herself was deported to Siberia, apparently because of her husband.

Was young Janina's future husband, the partisan, in the clearing when they shot the Jews? I don't know. I want to ask the old woman her surname, but for what reason? So that I could check to see whether her surname also appears among the murderers mentioned in the archives? This very old woman living alone in her poor little house wasn't responsible.

As we are saying good-bye, I see a framed photograph of a handsome young man on the wall.

Who is he—was he your husband? I ask.

No. This is my son, she says. Her only child. Dead.

We're making our way to the car, ready to drive back. The neighbor who introduced us to Janina runs up to us and wants to give us some freshly dug potatoes and onions. She didn't want to say anything or even be with us in Janina's house. She recognizes me; she's seen me on television. As she gives us the potatoes she explains why she didn't want to participate or even talk to us: "Oh, then you'll write something or talk about me on television . . . I just don't want that."

9

Švenčionys / Shventzyan

At the end of the nineteenth century there were 3,172 Jews living in Shventzyan (52.6 percent of the population).

Before the Shoah there were 8,000 Jews.

WHAT HAPPENED HERE IN 1941?

On October 7 and 8, 1941, on Yom Kippur, the Jewish Day of Atonement, the holiest day on the Jewish calendar, 3,476 people were shot at the military base in Švenčionėliai. The Special Unit members came from Vilnius by truck. There were 30 of them, so the arithmetic is simple: Each member of the unit had to kill 115 people in just two days. In between the shootings they had a lunch break and came to the Švenčionėliai railway station canteen for a meal.

Witness Juozas Butkevičius:

When they began shooting people, I was working as a warehouse manager at the Švenčionėliai Union of Lithuanian Cooperatives. I supplied Švenčionėliai restaurants and cafeterias with food products. On the day they began shooting people, co-op manager Dudėnas told me we would need to feed some sort of military unit arriving from somewhere for several days. He didn't tell me what sort of unit they were or where they came from; he just said that we would have to give them lunch at the Švenčionėliai railway station buffet hall, and ordered me to set aside food products from the co-op warehouse for thirty people.

At about 1 o'clock, I went to the railway station buffet where the lunches were being prepared for them, since I wanted to see for myself what sort of people the mur-

derers were. They arrived in two uncovered trucks. They all wore military uniforms,
but I do not now recall of which army. There might have been about thirty of them.
After eating lunch at the buffet, they got back into the trucks and drove off toward the
military base, where you could hear them shooting again until the evening.

    I don't recall now on which day of the shooting cooperative manager Dudėnas told
me that there was an order (whose he didn't say) to prepare dinner for the murderers.

    When I learned from Dudėnas that the dinner was being held in a restaurant
located on Kaltanėnų Street, I suggested to him that he let the waitresses go, say-
ing that drunken murderers might try to harass the young girls. As I remember it,
Dudėnas did exactly that, assigning elderly women, selected from among the restau-
rant kitchen staff, to wait upon the murderers.

    I now recall that the order issued to Dudėnas to organize dinner for the murderers
might have come from the city burgermeister [mayor] Cicėnas.[1]

Witness Juodis-Černiauskas:

In the autumn of 1941—it might have been the end of September or early October,
I don't remember exactly—I saw a group of drunken men walking on Adutiškio
Street. They weren't walking in a row. There were perhaps about twenty or thirty
of these men, dressed in the uniforms of the former Lithuanian army, some of them
armed with military rifles, others with automatic weapons. A man in a German
officer's uniform was walking on the sidewalk. Some of them were very drunk and
shouting. One of them shouted that he was Stiopka Melagianskas, or Stiopka from
Melagėnai, I don't exactly recall now. He was shouting that he knew this city. He
and the others were shouting in Lithuanian.

    After they appeared, residents began to say that a group of "Jew-shooters," shoot-
ers of citizens of Jewish ethnicity, had arrived to relax and rest in Švenčionėliai.[2]

According to the records of the interrogations of Special Unit members, the following local men from the Švenčionys region arrived by truck from Vilnius on October 7 to shoot their neighbors, the Jews of Švenčionys and the surrounding communities: Hubertas Dieninis, Stasys Čeponis, Dioni-zas Golcas, Vladas Kliukas, and Vladas Butkūnas.

A monument to the victims of the Švenčionėliai military base was erected in Soviet times (1961), and the memorial was restored in 2001 with funding from the embassy of the United Kingdom.

JULY 2015

We visited the Švenčionys municipal museum, and spoke to the director. Our first question was about the Holocaust and educational activities.

---

1 LSA, K-1, ap. 58, b. 47746/3, pp. 115–16.
2 Ibid., p. 110.

Mass grave in Švenčion˙liai. (Rūta Vanagaitė)

Museum director:

Why is this issue always being emphasized? After all, there are other issues. We have to examine our own suffering, too, not just that of the Jews. For our residents, the issue is not very topical. And we have done so much already; no other Lithuanian region has done as much we have.

Later during the journey, we realized that the director was right. In other cities of similar size, or even larger cities, there are museums, but they do not mention the Holocaust or the history of the local Jewish community. Nothing at all.

The museum director showed us an educational publication which she distributes to visiting students free of charge, and I bought one. It's a pamphlet entitled "The Jews of the Švenčionys Region." We also saw an exhibit about the Holocaust which had eyeglasses, a wallet, and several other items—all that remains of the 3,476 people murdered at the Švenčionėliai military base. The events are described in the passive tense, over and over again: "The Jewish community of the Švenčionys region was destroyed on October 7 and 8, 1941, in the forest outside Švenčionėliai." "The executioners killed children without compunction." Who committed the murders? Who were these executioners?

The passive voice suddenly disappears when the discussion shifts to rescuers. They don't write "were saved"; they write: "Švenčionys city resident Elena Sakalauskienė rescued . . . ," and so forth.

(Several weeks later, Efraim and I returned to Švenčionys for the annual memorial ceremony for the local Jews murdered during the Holocaust. Those attending were mostly members of the Vilnius Jewish community, children and grandchildren of survivors. The local museum director gave a very emotional speech at the monument on the site of the former ghetto. Among her "pearls of compassion":

> *Jews were given the most central and most beautiful square in our town. Lithu-*
> *anians kept close relations with the Jews by visiting them and bringing them some*
> *food. There were two gates to eternity here through which Jews of Švenčionys left*
> *our town.*

The director was referring to the two gates of the Švenčionys ghetto. Through these gates Jews were marched to the murder site in Švenčioneliai military base, ten kilometers away. (This was their "journey to eternity.")

We drove all along the way that Jews were marched in 1941 and stopped at a small grocery store where we were supposed to turn toward the Švenčionėliai military area. Efraim saw an old woman on the street who could barely walk, although her face was bright and intelligent. I cautiously asked her where the killing site is, and whether she remembers what happened in 1941.

The old woman tells us a story:

> *I saw how they marched them . . . Oh, it is such a misfortune that we didn't save*
> *the young Jewish girls. Mother and I lived in Padumblė village. We got along well*
> *with Jews; they used to give us flour on credit . . . There were the two Bentski girls,*
> *one about fifteen and the other, seven years old. When they were marched by us, my*
> *mother and I cried because we couldn't save the little girl. How could we take them*
> *when they were guarded on all sides by armed men? And if we had taken her earlier,*
> *then our own people would [have] betrayed us to the Germans. The Germans would*
> *not have found out, if Lithuanians would not have said anything to them. It was a*
> *horrible thing. People became wild beasts. After they had shot them all, they said that*
> *blood bubbled out of the ground for two days.*

Who did the shooting?

"Everyone who wanted to shoot," she answered. "No one was able to stop them. How can you stop people who have gone mad? Only the priests could have done that."

We asked her name. The old woman told us, but asked that we not tell it to anyone. "I have to live," she said.

Of course we won't tell anyone. We said good-bye, and left her crying on the other side of the fence by the front door to her little house. She was crying for the Bentski girl whom she and her mother did not rescue seventy-five years earlier.

Efraim: The proximity of the homes of the residents of Linkmenys to the mass murder site is shocking. As if it is normal for people to come and live in a place like that. As if this murder was some kind of normal event.

Rūta: Listen, they did not come to live next to the mass murder site by choice! Their grandparents and parents had lived here for ages. It was their home, their land . . . They belonged here. Where were they supposed to go?

Efraim: These people do not want to talk about what happened here. Maybe they have some kind of connection to this horrible event, and they might say something they don't want to say or they might arouse memories they don't want to deal with. People, their neighbors, were wiped out, as if they never existed—all their things, even tablecloths, were stolen . . .

Going from Kaddish to Kaddish to Kaddish, Pabrade-Švenčioneliai to Polygon-Linkmenys. In such a small geographical area, mass murder after mass murder after mass murder. You want to yell and say to the world: How could this have happened?

Rūta: Were you surprised that people didn't want to speak?

Efraim: Yes and no. You would assume that since so many years have passed, you can open up. I have a sense that these people are hiding something. They refuse to talk out of fear or out of solidarity with other people, their neighbors. They were more scared of you than of me, who's an outsider, because you are on TV. They don't want Lithuanian TV to broadcast that they have been talking about the mass murders in Lithuania.

Rūta: These people are old. They live alone, and they are afraid.

Efraim: Let's talk about the element of fear. You say that because the people saw shootings, they think that it can happen again. And that this is one of their motivations not to talk.

Rūta: People are afraid to talk, and I fully understand them. Their grandparents, their parents, and they themselves have gone through so many upheavals and traumas, that for them it is safer *not* to talk. If you talk, anything can happen; if you don't talk, you are much safer. There is a Russian saying: Be more silent than water, be lower than the grass. Another thing: When they were very young they saw their neighbors being shot. Shot by other neighbors. So if anything changes, a new war or anything like that, the same thing might happen to them. They know that since murder was possible once, it can happen again. And one other thing: If you admit that you witnessed the crime, the person who committed it, or his relatives, might come after you and take revenge. People in Lithuania who have seen a crime most probably would not testify, because they would be afraid that the criminal or his friends would one day come out of prison and take revenge.

Efraim: The second argument is totally idiotic—you will excuse me—because almost all the murderers are dead. And even if they were not dead, how many ninety-year-olds do you think are going around murdering people? I want to address another thing. You said they saw the murders. You must remember something: The murder sites were in isolated places, specifically chosen so that there would not be any witnesses, except the shooters and those helping to dispose of the bodies. They saw people being taken out, not being shot.

Rūta: They heard the shooting. Afterwards, in every village, they were talking about what had happened and how the earth moved several days after the massacre, and bloody shirts were washed in the streams. They still talk about this among themselves.

Efraim: Maybe it is true for some people. It is possible that people start magnifying everything afterwards.

Rūta: Experiencing the Holocaust is horrifying for those who witnessed it as kids. Until now, nobody has talked about this in public, on TV or radio. Is it so surprising? If the police do not investigate the crime, you would not start your own investigation. If nobody ever spoke about the crime, this crime remains a secret. Who are you, an old lonely woman living in a village, to speak about this? Why you? Why now? For what reason? It will not bring the victims back to life.

Efraim: It is exactly the opposite of what should have happened. If the police do not solve the case and you have the information, you should be going to the police. She is ninety years old? Okay, why did she not do it before? I can understand why she would not go to the Soviets, but Lithuania has been independent already for twenty-five years, and there is our initiative, Operation Last Chance, which offered money for the information. Our ads were in all the newspapers in Lithuania. Why all you talk about is fear? You are living in a democratic country, a member of the European Union, for God's sake!

Rūta: Just remember—maybe some of their neighbors were killers, or were marching Jews to the pits, or took their property. The children of these people are living next door, or if not, they are living somewhere close by. If you start talking about what your neighbor did, your family will stop you. The whole village will think that you are a traitor. When I started talking about writing this book, and about my relatives and their role in the Holocaust, some of my relatives got very upset. I might be condemned by my family; I might become a black sheep! Do I want that?

Efraim: But listen—somebody has to pay the price for the crimes committed.

Rūta: Why me? If the government does not do it, if the police do not do it? Do you understand how much courage a person needs to speak out?

Efraim: You are right. It takes a lot of guts. And what you are doing is super important.

Rūta: I am not ninety years old. I don't live in a lonely house next to the forest. I am not talking about my neighbors from the same village. I am ready to become the black sheep in my family, because I believe in what I am doing. If not me, who? If not now, when? But you know what? If my grandfather would have shot the Jews personally, I would not be able to talk about this issue. It would be too painful for me. I know, I am sure, that no one in my family ever pulled a trigger.

Efraim: How can you be certain? You just don't know. Coming back to the issue of fear: You are trying to say that because people lived such a long time under the Soviet regime, they are scared of talking, scared of relating to the terrible tragedy that took place here. My question to you is, at what point does that stop being an excuse? If someone had a terrible childhood, at some point he or she has to take responsibility for their life and not blame their parents all the time.

Rūta: We are not talking about someone's childhood. We are talking about the entire life of an adult. That makes a big difference.

Efraim: Okay. So, in other words, in twenty-five years from now, they will start talking?

Rūta: By then they will be dead. Now they are already very old. And old age is not the right time to become a hero.

Efraim: So the only way for us to achieve what we want to achieve, to make an impact with this book, is to address the younger generation who did not live under the Soviets. But it also means that you are giving the older generation, including the government, a free pass.

Rūta: No; the government does not want the truth to come out because politicians want to be reelected—they want to be popular with their voters. But even for me, if I knew that my neighbor was killing people, it would be difficult to go to the police and give him up. In Lithuanian culture, to be a police informer, to inform on your neighbor, is a sin—a sin of betrayal. You would not testify about the crimes your neighbor's father or grandfather committed seventy years ago. Does it make any difference? It ruins your neighbor's life and your relations with the people living next to you. Nobody will pay attention to it anyway. A list of 2,055 Lithuanians, Jew-killers, was sent by the the Lithuanian Genocide Center to the Lithuanian government in 2012. Do you think anything was done? Not a single step was taken against any of them. So tell me who benefits if a ninety-year-old woman stands up and relates on TV that her neighbor's father, who is dead now, was a killer?

Efraim: What about the fact that the truth will finally come out?

Rūta: Who benefits from that truth?

Efraim: Lithuanian society will benefit from that truth.

Rūta: What is Lithuanian society? I am talking from the point of view of that woman.

Efraim: That is the society that she lives in, and hopes it will become a better society.

Rūta: But . . .

Efraim: I know what you are going to tell me—that she lives in her little world, in a poor little hut in Švenčionėliai. There is no society for her. It is all very sad.

10

Kavarskas / Kovarsk

At the end of the nineteenth century, 979 Jews were living in Kovarsk (63.3 percent of the local population).

Before the Shoah—around 400.

Kavarskas—where Rūta's grandfather, Jonas Vanagas, lived; where her father, Jonas Vanagas, was born. The house where they lived on the main Ukmergė street is still standing. There was supposed to be a well in the yard. Old Man Jonas Vanagas, as Rūta's family still call him, drew water by hand, sending a bucket down. One day, his ten-year-old son, Vytukas, Rūta's father's only brother, kneeled down next to the well. As the handle of the bucket hoist was turning, it hit Vytukas in the head. The child died ten days later, screaming in agony those entire ten days. Rūta's father's sister Valerija also died at the age of twenty-one, cut down by tuberculosis right before the war. The Soviets deported the rest of the family to Siberia because of Rūta's grandfather.

All of Rūta's relatives are buried in the Kavarskas cemetery. The graves are tended to; all have flowers growing around them, and are kept weeded. We are standing next to the Vanagas family grave.

"This is the first time in my life I've been in a Catholic cemetery," Zuroff says.

We don't stay long. Our journey is to other kinds of graveyards. Ones which are untended—where there are no names.

In this graveyard, there is also a monument for Rūta's grandfather, Jonas Vanagas, although he died somewhere in Karlag, a labor camp in Kazakhstan. His case file at the Lithuanian Special Archives is not large.

It is a single volume containing the ninety-six pages of the case against Jonas Vanagas and his neighbor, Balys Šimkė, father of six children, arrested by the Soviets on the same day, January 20, 1945. They are both part of a single case, and were convicted and later imprisoned together. When he returned from the gulag, Šimkė said Old Man Vanagas only survived half a year in the camp, and on January 16, 1946, he froze to death on his rough wooden bed. It seems they didn't make him work, because when he was sent to the camp his health certificate contained the entry *Physically healthy, but not fit for labor*.

Before the war Jonas Vanagas was rich. He had fifty hectares of land, six to eight horses, fourteen cows, sixteen to eighteen sheep, and a large house. Jonas Vanagas was angry. The Soviets confiscated twenty hectares from him and distributed it to the landless in Kavarskas. He was an elderly person, sixty years old, and had no business brandishing weapons around Kavarskas together with the young insurgents.

What did Rūta's grandfather actually do? Three witnesses all say the same thing. He was a person respected by the Germans, a member of a Nazi trial commission. At the very onset of the war, that commission had drawn up a list of ten Communist activists who were shot shortly thereafter. Who were they? Jews? The case file contains only one name of those murdered, Yakov Ovchinnikov, secretary of the local Communist Youth.

At his trial, Jonas Vanagas refused to admit any guilt. They sentenced him to fifteen years' imprisonment under Article 58 of the Criminal Code: treason against the Motherland. He was convicted based on the testimonies of Balys Šimkė and three witnesses. What was really going on there, Grandfather? Were those witnesses lying, all of them landless? Were they exacting revenge for something?

JULY 2015

We are here in Kavarskas. We don't know where the mass murder sites are, as their locations are simply not posted. On the central street of Kavarskas we see an elderly man named Romas. He is employed by the local council, in charge of all the buildings, and is well acquainted with the entire town. Romas has the time, and agrees to show us everything we are looking for.

We ask him where the synagogue was, the building where the Jews of Kovarsk and its environs, a total of about five hundred people, were incarcerated by the order of local police chief Mazeika in August 1941. The synagogue is still standing in the very center of Kavarskas. It has been privatized. In Soviet times, there was a farm products store here; now it is a storehouse and garage belonging to a Kavarskas businessman. Of course there is no sign or indication of what took place here before and during the war.

The mother of the Kavarskas businessman opens the door of the synagogue for us. We walk through the ruins and climb the stairs to the second floor. How could five hundred people survive here? How did they breathe for those two days until they were marched off to their deaths in Ukmergė? Were they thirsty, dying of hunger? Did they pray and still hope, imprisoned as they were in the stench?

We ask Romas about where the ten Jewish activists were murdered outside Kavarskas. One version of the story is that they were shot at the atheists' cemetery; another, that the shooting took place in the village of Pumpučiai on the Šventoji River. It was probably the latter. Romas rides with us to Pumpučiai village just next to Kavarskas. There are no signs or directions to the mass murder site. The small road ends, and we go down by foot for another kilometer or so. The path is difficult to find, the grass, high, and next to the river there is heavy brush. We can't even see the river.

"I should come here sometime to cut the grass," Romas says.

Amid the dense brush there is a small monument. Does anyone ever come here? Probably not. There was a couple from Israel last year, Romas

Monument for the victims in Kavarskas. (Rūta Vanagaitė)

says; he took them to the site as well. Efraim is standing there, silent. I see how he's gazing at a snail crawling across the monument. I remove it. Then he says Kaddish while Romas and I wait at a distance. We are silent.

Later all three of us climb up the hill and go to the home of some people living a couple of hundred meters away. At one farmhouse, at another, nobody knows; they don't remember. But if the Vebra family were still alive, they would know for sure . . . Yes, the Vebras are mentioned as witnesses in the case file on the mass murder of Kavarskas. But the Vebras are gone, gone are the murderers, and only the dense brush remains.

WHAT HAPPENED HERE IN 1941?

We learn a lot from the interrogation record of the case of witness Antanas Gudėnas, who was convicted in 1952. Antanas Gudėnas is named in Jonas Vanagas's case as being among the white armbanders. He was sentenced to twenty-five years and deported to a labor camp in Mordovia for his service in the unit and the crimes for which he was found guilty.

Antanas Gudėnas, the bell-ringer for the Kavarskas church, joined the white armbander unit on the fourth or fifth day of the war, and remained in the unit until October of 1941, when it was disbanded. By that time, all the Jews of Kavarskas had been murdered.

Antanas Gudėnas testifies:

> *In the month of July 1941, I don't remember the day, at about eight p.m., I, on what matter I don't recall now, left my home to go to the city. As soon as I had left the yard, I met three Kavarskas white armbanders, of whom I now recall only Jonas Misiūnas and Jonas Brigackas . . . All of them at that time were dressed in civilian clothing and each held a shovel in his hand. But one of them, I don't remember which, had two shovels.*
>
> *As soon as I met them, Jonas Misiūnas and Jonas Brigackas told me that I had been issued instructions to go with them to the banks of the Šventoji River and help them dig a pit. They did not tell me, nor did I ask, who had given them this order or for what purpose a pit should be dug. Initially, I wanted to refuse to dig the pit, but then Jonas Misiūnas and Jonas Brigackas told me that I must come with them because there were no other people, so taking a shovel from one of the white armbanders who had two shovels, and led by them, I went straight across the fields to the banks of the Šventoji River. When we had gone about one kilometer's distance outside Kavarskas and were in the territory of Pumpučiai village, Jonas Misiūnas and Jonas Brigackas stood on the banks of the Šventoji River by the bushes and said that this was the place where we must dig the pit.*
>
> *After Jonas Misiūnas and Jonas Brigackas indicated the place to dig the pit, all four of us began to dig at that spot. At that time, there were no other people there. When we began to dig the pit, the sun had set and it was getting dark in the field.*

As we were digging the pit, we saw a covered truck had stopped about 50 meters away on the Kavarskas-Ukmergė road which goes through the fields. After the truck stopped, we saw that there were people seated inside, surrounded on all sides by men standing inside the truck with rifles and automatic weapons. When I saw that, I understood that the armed people had brought arrested Soviet citizens to be shot.

After the truck stopped, one man whom I didn't know got out and went straight from the truck to us. When he came up to us he first looked over the pit we had dug, then ordered us to get out of the pit and go off to the side. After saying that, he returned to the truck. That man was dressed in civilian clothing at that time, but whether he had some sort of weapon or not, I do not recall.

After the man had gone away from us, we immediately got out of the pit and withdrew to about 20 meters away from it. That's how at that time we dug a single pit of about 2.5 meters long, 2 meters wide, and about 160 to 170 centimeters deep, next to the bushes on the banks of the Šventoji River.

The aforementioned man returned to the truck, and initially about eight to ten men armed with rifles and automatic weapons got out, then about ten to twelve prisoners were taken out—but how many there were, I don't exactly recall now.

After the prisoners got out, they were surrounded by the aforementioned armed men who then marched over to the pit we had dug. All of these armed people were dressed in civilian clothing and were of middle age. I was not acquainted with any-one among them. I likewise was not acquainted with any of the prisoners. One of the prisoners had a beard.

After the prisoners had been brought to the pit, the order was given for them to undress to their underwear and to put their clothes in a single pile. After they had taken their shoes off and undressed to their underwear, one of the armed men ordered them to go to the pit and to stand single file with their faces toward the pit. So the prisoners stood, undressed to their underwear, and barefoot, about 1 to 1.5 meters distant from the edge of the pit, facing the pit and with their backs to the Šventoji River. After the prisoners were standing there, behind them, about 4 meters away, all the armed men, who spoke Lithuanian among themselves, stood in a single line. There was nobody wearing any sort of military uniform among them, and there was also no one from the Kavarskas white armbanders among them.

After the armed men had formed a line with rifles and automatic weapons pointed toward the condemned, the command rang out: "Fire!" But who among them gave that command, I didn't notice. When they heard the command "Fire!," those ex-ecutioners standing in a line opened fire with rifles and automatic weapons on the Soviet citizens condemned to death standing across from them, and they fell on the ground from the shots.

During the shooting there wasn't any shouting among those condemned to death. The shooting lasted only a few minutes. When the shooting stopped, the execution-ers went closer to those corpses lying on the edge of the pit, but since one or two of the condemned were only gravely wounded, they finished them off with single rifle shots. In this manner, after the executioners ensured that all the prisoners were shot to death, they threw the corpses into the pit, and then took all the clothes and shoes of those people who had been shot and went back to the truck. They loaded all the things onto the truck, and then sat down in the truck and drove off on the same field road toward the Kavarskas-Ukmergė road.

> *When the executioners sitting in the truck had driven off, we four filled in the pit
> full of the corpses of those shot. After we buried the corpses we took the shovels and
> went to Kavarskas, and from there, without any other stops, we all dispersed and
> went to our own homes.*[1]

As Rūta read the case files, she discovered that the church bell-ringer
was not only a ditchdigger. He did much more. And it seems that it
wasn't a group of unknown outsiders who shot the victims that day. They
were shooting their neighbors, the residents of Kavarskas.

Efraim: We are coming from Kavarskas—Kovarsk, in Yiddish—and
there is a sign indicating that seven hundred meters from the road, there
is a mass murder site, but if you don't have a local guide, you would not
find the place in a million years. You can completely understand why
these murders were carried out there—out of sight, out of mind. If you
speak to the people who live nearby, no one knows anything. They know
that someone came from Israel a year ago, and a couple came two years
ago, but it seems that no one comes here, even on Holocaust Memorial
Day in Lithuania on September 23. This remote corner in the brush near
a river is one of the most shocking and painful places to visit. There is
no indication of the number of victims or the date of the murder. The
testimonies in the Soviet investigation files refer to the murder of ten to
twelve Jews, but the sources published in Israel speak about thirty to forty
people killed at this site.

We also visited the synagogue, or what is left of the synagogue, which
today is a private warehouse. It is not the Lithuanians' fault; years ago,
the Soviets turned the synagogue into a utility shop. We climbed the ladder to the second floor, to what was once the women's gallery. This is the
place where the Jews were held until they were taken to be murdered.
You can only imagine the horrifically anguished prayers that the Jews
must have prayed here to God to save them. Maybe they did not know
what would happen to them, but I am sure they had a sense of doom and
a sense of some potentially horrible fate.

This is just one little dot among many of other dots on the map of Lithuania. In a book called *Neighbors*, the Polish historian (of Jewish origin) Jan
Gross wrote about the murders in Jedwabne, where the local Jews were
murdered by Poles. Poland was traumatized, and for good reason. I say
to myself that right over the border, next door, there is a country full of
Jedwabnes, the whole country is one big Jedwabne, and they have not
yet been traumatized by these crimes. This is what we are trying to show,
Rūta. Despite the fact that we are coming from different sides of the fence
and completely different backgrounds, on a certain level our emotions are

---

1 LSA, K-1, ap. 58, b. 47397/3, t. 3, pp. 170–76.

the same, and so is our goal—that the truth finally become known, that it be taught and hopefully internalized.

Rūta: I am thinking about those ten to twelve, or maybe thirty to forty, Jewish men walking their last walk in the brush, down the hill, seven hundred meters through the thick grass, led by five gunmen, their Lithuanian neighbors. They must have sensed where they were being taken. I hate places like this—thick brush and high grass, full of ticks—the ugliest places in Lithuania. When I see such a place, I think that if someone murders me and throws my body into such a brush, I would never be found before my body rots. It is a very ugly last road to be taken. It is a very ugly grave. Before saying Kaddish you showed me the snail crawling on the monument to the murdered Jews. You did not say a word, but somehow I knew you wanted me to remove that snail. So I took it away. I removed our snail from the monument to your people.

Efraim: Yes, you did. Thank you. Now we are driving on Ukmergė Street, the main street of Kavarskas, which, according to the testimonies of Holocaust survivors published in Israel, was set on fire soon after the Nazi invasion, because this was a street where the Jews lived. Ironically, Rūta's grandparents, and her father, also lived on this street.

Rūta: I don't believe this. My father would have told me about it. He was born in 1921, so he was twenty years old then. He was studying in Kaunas, but during the summer he was back home to work on his parents' farm. My father told me about the prewar period, and said that there was no anti-Semitism in Kavarskas before the war broke out. He had Jewish neighbors, Jewish classmates. You keep repeating at every opportunity that Lithuanians were more than eager to hurt the Jews before the Nazis arrived. There might have been some cases here and there, but I refuse to believe that this was such a widespread phenomenon. I never ever heard from my relatives about such events or attitudes toward Jews among ordinary Lithuanians. I know what happened in Lithuania after the Nazis came, but—give me a break—that certainly was not the case beforehand.

Efraim: Let me read you the entry on the city of Ukmergė (Vilkomir in Yiddish and Hebrew) in Volume IV of *Yahadut Lita* (Lithuanian Jewry). In Ukmergė there were many Lithuanians, who, immediately after the war started, attacked Jewish homes, vandalized, tortured, and murdered.

Rūta: When you say "many," my heart sinks. What is *many*; how many? What you say makes the whole nation look like one big monster. All three million people waited for years for a golden opportunity to kill their Jewish neighbors, who had been living next to them for six hundred years?

Efraim: I did not say "all Lithuanians." I said "many." There were many. Ukmergė is a big city; eight thousand Jews were living there . . .

Rūta: How many is "many"?

Efraim: *Many* is a hundred, fifty, eighty, two hundred. What are you thinking? You are being oversensitive.

Rūta: Yes. I am sensitive when my people are attacked like this. It is normal. When you talk like this about my country, it makes me physically sick. I feel deeply hurt by the word *many*.

Efraim: Okay, you can start singing the Lithuanian national anthem now, if it makes you feel better. Like your people did when watching the murders at the Lietūkis Garage in Kaunas.

11

Ukmergė/Vilkomir

At the end of the nineteenth century, 7,287 Jews were living in Ukmergė (53.8 percent of the local population).

Before the Shoah—around 8,000.

JULY 2015

We drive along the road on which they marched Jews from the synagogue in the fall of 1941. My grandfather didn't march them. Fortunately, he was already sixty years old when those events took place, so no police chief would have been able to involve him in anything. Did Balys Šimkė, arrested and jailed with my grandfather, force-march the Jews? Interrogation records say that he did, and that Šimkė received a Jewish house and 4.5 hectares of land in exchange for transporting and guarding the Jews. Witnesses—and Šimkė himself—say that he only guarded Jews for a few days at the Kavarskas synagogue, and that he didn't get on the carts and didn't travel to Ukmergė. Nonetheless, he received payment for his efforts; after all, he had six children . . .

Five hundred Jews who lived in Kovarsk were brought from the Kavarskas synagogue to the Ukmergė prison. There were only thirty-seven cells there. During the month of July, the number of prisoners grew from 45 to 789. In the registers of the Ukmergė prison you can find figures for the number of people who were receiving food there during the first days of September 1941:

Vaitkuškis manor in Ukmergė where victims were held before being shot. (Rūta Vana-gaitė)

September 1: 667 adults, 8 children
September 5: 1,409 adults, 24 children
September 6: 11 adults, no children

We stopped at the ruins of the Vaitkuškis manor. Thousands of Jews were brought there. They were taken down the path in groups, and that is how they were shot. The manor is private, and fenced off. Of course, there is no sign at all. It seems that the manor is waiting for European Union funding and will be rebuilt. Then there will be a sign here, with the European Union logo.

Death has no logo, and so there is none here.

WHAT HAPPENED HERE IN 1941?

The third platoon of the TDA battalion formed the nucleus of the Rollkommando Hamann mobile death squad. Usually several members of the Gestapo and dozens of officers and soldiers from the battalion were "invited" to a specific operation in the Lithuanian countryside. "Hamann himself often didn't even come to the mass murders in the countryside; he just assigned the task to officers from the first battalion [to lieutenants A. Dagys, J. Barzda, and B. Norkus]."

According to Karl Jäger's report for December 1, 1941:

It was only possible to achieve the goal of cleansing Lithuania of Jews because of the Rollkommando consisting of select men under the command of Obersturmführer Hamann, who understood my goals implicitly and was able to ensure cooperation by the Lithuanian partisans and the appropriate structures.[1]

There were from thirty to forty Lithuanians in each operation of the Rollkommando Hamann. The local administration, police, and "partisans" made all the necessary preparations for the mass murders by isolating the Jews and bringing them to pits that had been dug previously. Hamann unit statistics:

Eight to ten Germans and about eighty Lithuanians altogether have participated in the murders carried out by the unit (mainly members of the third platoon of the TDA battalion). Hamann himself most often would not go to the sites. *"The Germans usually stayed in Kaunas to carry out other functions, and usually just two or three Germans traveled to the shootings in the countryside. They often came in a passenger car, while the main forces came in one or two trucks, or sometimes on a Lietūkis bus. Local police and activists often collaborated with the Hamann group in the countryside."*[2]

Ukmergė Jews were murdered in Pivonija Forest. Witness Adomas Daniūnas, hospital disinfector, provided the following account:

In October or September of 1941, I don't remember exactly when, I and other members of the Kavarskas nationalist unit participated in the mass shooting of people of Jewish ethnicity in Pivonija Forest.

At about ten o'clock in the morning, Karolis Čiukšys came to my home and told me to go with him to Ukmergė. He said that I was under orders of the police chief to come to Ukmergė to do guard duty. But he did not say what I was supposed to guard.

After dressing, I left my apartment, which was on the premises of the school, with Karolis Čiukšys. On the road, outside the school, I saw carts in which members of the Kavarskas nationalist unit sat. I don't recall now how many carts there were, and I also don't recall to whom they belonged or who the drivers were. About twelve of us, all men, drove away from Kavarskas. We were all armed with military rifles. Čiukšys, who was the leader of the group, gave me a gun at that time. I received a Russian carbine. The carbine lay on the bottom of the cart where I was placed. There was ammunition in the cartridge, i.e., the carbine was loaded with rounds of bullets.

After leaving Kavarskas, at about 10:30 a.m., we went straight toward the Vaitkuškis manor. The manor estate was about four to five kilometers outside of Ukmergė. The ruins of the manor still stand and are now very close to the road from

1 Jäger Report from December 1, 1941. From: *The Persecution and Mass Murder of Lithuanian Jews during Summer and Fall of 1941: Sources and Analysis*, Vilnius: Margi raštai, 2006, p. 230.
2 Arūnas Bubnys, *Vokiečių okupuota Lietuva: 1941–1944* (Lithuania under the German Occupation: 1941–1944), Vilnius: LGRTTC, 1998, p. 203.

Ukmergė to Vilnius. *After arriving at the manor, we stood in the courtyard and everyone got out of the carts. We arrived at about one or two o'clock in the afternoon. Once we arrived, we found that about one hundred armed men were already gathered there. Of them, a portion was uniformed Germans and police officers. We were all dressed in civilian clothing. Besides us, more than half of the rest of the armed men who were at the Vaitkuškis estate were also dressed in civilian clothing. The Germans were dressed in pale-green uniforms. The police were wearing the uniforms of the former bourgeois Lithuanian police.*

More than an hour after we had arrived at the manor, a group of men armed with rifles, whom I did not recognize, brought a group of citizens of Jewish ethnicity, including men, women, and elderly people, out of the threshing barn. The group included about fifty people. Čiukšys ordered all the members of the Kavarskas nationalist unit to take charge of this group of Jews, who were in the manor courtyard, from those who had taken them out of the building, and to march them along a small road going toward the forest. At first we didn't grasp why we were supposed to march them into the forest. They told us they were being sent to do some sort of work somewhere.

We marched them along the narrow road through the field toward the forest and into a clearing about 40 to 50 meters away from the edge of the forest. I don't remember now how big the clearing was. There were several large ditches in the clearing that were more or less identical. They might have been about 20 meters long, 2.5 meters wide, and about 2 meters deep. The ends of the ditches sloped down. We found a group of people next to the ditches. Among them were about twenty uniformed Germans and police. They surrounded the forest clearing on all sides. There were also about ten or fifteen armed men in civilian clothing.

After we had marched them into the clearing, Karolis Čiukšys ordered the Jews to undress to their underwear. After they had undressed, Čiukšys told them to go into the ditch. Some went, but others did not want to. Then Čiukšys and the armed men whom I do not know, who were dressed in civilian clothing, began to beat them with wooden sticks and force them into the ditch. They broke the sticks off bushes growing in the forest.

We all stood at the edge of the ditch. On the other side of the ditch stood five or six Germans with automatic weapons. When all the citizens of Jewish ethnicity had been herded into the ditch, they ordered them to lie down next to one another. They lay down together in whatever position they found themselves. When all the citizens of Jewish ethnicity had lain down in the ditch, they ordered all of us to form a single line at the edge of the pit. All of us members of the Kavarskas nationalist unit who were there lined up at the edge of the pit without exception. When we had formed a line, someone ordered us to load our weapons, which we did. Then someone commanded in Lithuanian: "Fire into the ditch!"

After the command "Fire!," we all shot into the ditch. I shot just once, but I didn't see where it went. After that shot my hands began to tremble and a German standing on the other side of the ditch who saw that sent me away from the ditch. One of them, speaking in Lithuanian, ordered me to put down the weapon and pick up a shovel. The shovels were near the ditch. Our group shot only the first group of citizens of Jewish ethnicity. After shooting them, we filled the ditch with our shovels, grabbed our weapons, and returned to the manor, and didn't shoot anymore that day.

Question: Why, during the earlier questioning, didn't you tell us about the mass shootings of Soviet citizens in Pivonija Forest?

Earlier, I didn't want to admit that I had participated in the mass shooting of Soviet citizens in Pivonija Forest, because I was ashamed.[3]

P.S. Karolis Čiukšys was not convicted by the Soviets. Did he have something to offer in exchange for his freedom?

JULY 2015

Efraim: Pivonija Forest: 10,239 people were murdered here. That's the information I have. All of them were brought from Ukmergė, Kavarskas, and the surrounding villages and towns. The most horrible thing is that it's impossible to find this site. We are standing next to huge graves, marked by one, two, three, four . . . fourteen pits. Oh my God—we are standing on top of one of the graves. We are standing on the remains of thousands of people!

Rūta: It's impossible for the rational mind to understand what is under us—heaps of bodies, bones, and skulls, strewn every which way, mountains of them, layer upon layer, meters and meters. In my notes from the Special Archives there is a record of one exhumation which I know almost by heart. You want to hear it? It will be hard for you to listen.

Efraim: It's okay. I want to hear it.

Rūta: It's about the findings of the exhumation in Lazdijai, but I think that they discovered the same things everywhere: The human remains in the graves were buried in two to three and sometimes four layers. The corpses were curled up, their extremities folded next to their stomachs or chests, and, in the majority of cases, their hands are next to their faces, eyes, or around the corpses of children.

Efraim: It's absolutely horrifying . . .

Rūta: You know, there is this famous Polish psychiatrist named Antoni Kępiński who survived Auschwitz. He wrote that after they returned to the normal world, the survivors of the concentration camps could not attend any sort of funerals. They couldn't help but laugh at so much ado being made over a single dead person. I'm ashamed to say it, but sometimes I think about how I will visit the graves of my relatives after this trip. Every grave is identified and so nicely tended. I will pick up the flowers, clean the headstones, and light candles as I am used to doing, but now I will also think about other graves—about tens of thousands of people who are not my relatives, people without names, stuck under the ground, with broken skulls, jawbones torn off, teeth pulled out, hugging their

---

3 LSA, K-1, ap. 58, b. 47397/3, t. 3, pp. 277–82.

children who were buried alive. And there are 227 such sites in Lithuania. How can it be that the Lithuanian earth isn't still moving?

Efraim: Everyone in Lithuania should be thinking the way you are now.

Rūta: That's what will happen someday. Look, there are already positive signs. Here the metal rails around the grave and the metal chains haven't been stolen, as they were in Kavarskas.

We are driving toward the center of Ukmergė. I am thinking about the children and adolescents murdered in Pivonija Forest. I remember the lines of a poem by Justinas Marcinkevičius, which we recited at school—one of my favorites:

> *And how many Einsteins and Galileos*
> *Aged sixteen, sleep in the ground . . .*

The poet was writing about the Lithuanian partisans fighting the Soviets after the war, not about murdered Jews. It was probably just a coincidence that he mentioned Einstein, a Jew. It's only a coincidence that sixteen-year-old Jews, future Einsteins, were murdered in 1941 by Lithuanians no older than they were. Not Galileos.

We go to the city center of Ukmergė and enter the local museum, where we ask about the Holocaust, and about Pivonija Forest. One of the workers points us toward an exhibition panel about the Holocaust, prepared thanks to funding from the International Holocaust Remembrance Alliance. There are a few photos and the traditional requisite text, the same sort as the one at the museum in Švenčionys and in the pamphlets. The Jews were arrested, transported, and murdered. Who arrested them? Who murdered them? What's the difference? After all, it happened long ago. And in the final analysis, is this really part of Ukmergė's history?

Efraim: On the third floor there is an entire section devoted to the history of the Jewish community of Ukmergė that was created with the support of the International Holocaust Remembrance Alliance (IHRA). It describes the Holocaust as follows: On August 18–19 and September 5, 1941, more than 6,354 people were murdered in Pivonija Forest near Ukmergė, which was one of the favorite places of the town's residents. But there is no mention of who did it. The most outrageous detail in this museum is the fact that this special corner was created by IHRA, so, in fact, IHRA is spending money to hide the crimes of the Lithuanians, a phenomenon which is so typical here. We are talking about a city in which more than eight thousand Jews were murdered.

Rūta: I think that the best Holocaust education is not putting up one or two abstract sentences in a museum, but to put a plaque on every building which was used for guarding people, during the Holocaust. On a private garage in Kavarskas where the Jews were held, as well as at Vaitkuškis manor (which is currently private property), there should be signs about what happened there during the Holocaust. In ten years, nobody will know anything. Even now, nobody knows.

The city of Ukmergė, like all the other Lithuanian cities, wants to have a heroic history. It has a monument recently built for one of the postwar heroes. So we are trying to find the square which the city of Ukmergė recently renamed in honor of an anti-Soviet partisan named Juozas Krikštaponis. None of the locals seem to know where the square is, or the statue, or who Krikštaponis was. They only know that there is a statue to which the archbishop of Lithuania, Monsignor Svarinskas, used to come to pay his respects. And that's the one.

Next to Vytauto Street near the public library there is a huge monument with a cast bas-relief of the hero. Krikštaponis is famous for being the nephew of Lithuanian president Antanas Smetona, but more infamous for having served the Nazis loyally in the Impulevičius battalion before becoming a partisan. He participated in every massacre, especially in Belarus, where he was one of the commanders of the mass murder operations. Lithuanian historians calculate that the Impulevičius battalion murdered about twenty-seven thousand Jews in Belarus. In 2014 the Genocide and Resistance Research Centre of Lithuania admitted that Juozas Krikštaponis was a war criminal, but yet the monument is still there. Monsignor Svarinskas is dead, so he no longer comes. Some other Lithuanian patriots now come.

We wonder if Lithuanian municipalities—before they decide for whom to erect statues, put up memorial plaques, and rename streets—ever bother to ask historians what these heroes did before their heroic anti-Soviet deeds. How many people did they murder?

We stand next to the monument to the executioner and Rūta is ashamed to look Efraim in the eye. Efraim is looking right at the bas-relief, at the handsome face of the executioner carved in stone, and is cursing: *"Shit. Shit. Shit."*

On the way to Vilnius we visit two more shameful sites. One is on the way to Želva, at the Antakalnis II site, where the prison warden, J. Kuzmickas, turned Jews over to the murderers of Pivonija, and personally, with his helpers, hanged about one hundred Jews in a barn. Why did they go to the trouble of hanging them, when it would have been much simpler to shoot them, as they did the other ten thousand victims in Pivonija Forest? The mass murder site is not marked. There are no signs or

Monument to Juozas Krikštaponis in the center of Ukmergė. (Rūta Vanagaitė)

directions. At the site where these Ukmergė Jews were hanged, there was
a slaughterhouse or a meat-processing plant built some time ago. Now
this huge factory produces something else.

In the postwar period, Kuzmickas was put on trial. He wrote an appeal, addressing the Supreme Court with these words: "Please take into
consideration my low level of education and give me a lighter sentence."

Driving on, we would discover yet another mass murder site not worthy of a monument, near the village of Šešuoliai. No one knows the identity of the Jews who were murdered here, nor how many of them were murdered, and when it happened. We see a marker on the road and climb through heavy brush up a hill. Once we are on top of it, we see a huge pit filled with tree trunks, branches, and garbage. Here it is—the death pit, and the final resting place of the murdered Jews of Šešuoliai, shot as entire families.

Rūta: I think about the negligence in tending to the mass graves all around Lithuania. If nobody takes care of the graves, the message that all the people around the area get is that this is not important. The death of those people is unimportant, so their memory is also unimportant, as are their lives. A Jew? Who? When? Ah, that happened such a long time ago! Butrimonys—three hundred kids are buried here. So what?

Efraim: It sends a horrible message: These people don't count.

Rūta: If the pigs around here are dying from pigs' plague, and that is what it said on the warning sign right before the entrance to Butrimonys, the Jews apparently died from some kind of Jews' plague, right? Is there a very big difference?

Efraim: Apparently not.

Rūta: There is some difference. There were more pigs than Jews. Is this humor too dark? The Holocaust was a plague suffered by the Jews. If you want to slap me, say so.

Efraim: No violence in this Shoah-mobile.

Rūta. Let's listen to a song that schoolchildren sang at this past year's Yom HaShoah event, which was held on April 17 at the Town Hall square [in Vilnius]. It was pouring rain; two hundred kids were singing one of the psalms, and another five hundred formed a human Magen David, holding hands, waving their hands to the music . . .

Efraim: . . . .

[long pause]

Efraim: I just broke down. I just broke down. And it's obvious why. The events here affect me a hundred times more than a visit to Auschwitz. Apparently it's because it is personal. I always felt that the only way to be able to do what I do, as a Nazi-hunter, was to make sure that the work never became personal. And, in fact, for many years, I think I succeeded in doing so. But now I feel that my defense wall is crumbling, because this journey feels very personal.

I will never give up, but this is the first time I have a Lithuanian partner. The reason my efforts here were only very partially successful, and I am the first to admit it, is because I was basically alone. I was a foreigner, and it was too early. I came here at the very beginning, already in 1991, very shortly after independence, and as you say, I came to spoil the wedding and I even didn't realize that I *was* spoiling the wedding.

Rūta: Look, it was not your wedding.

Efraim: No, it was not my wedding.

Rūta: Nor were you invited.

Efraim: You're right. I was not invited. And, as a result, the efforts did not yield the results we hoped for. Now there is a real last chance, in a sense. We come with a different team. The team includes a person named Rūta whom Lithuanians trust, at least they did until now. She has credibility after her books on elderly care and on the challenges facing women at age fifty were extremely successful. If you would see how people on the street who read her books come up to her and hug her, you would know that she is tremendously popular here and this credibility should give them pause to listen, to read, to try to understand, and to think about the content of this book. That is the best we can hope for. Because the story is so dramatic and powerful, we hope that the people who will read it will be moved by it and changed by it, and will begin to look at their country in a different light.

Rūta: I just got an idea. I will have these kids learn to sing five or six psalms, and go to the most neglected and forgotten places in Lithuania where Jews were killed, and honor their memory with this performance. What drives me crazy is not the fact that Jews were murdered, but that they are totally forgotten, and that their memory has been erased. They are buried in the wild brush. I did not know this before our journey. We Lithuanians respect death; we honor the memory of our deceased. You saw it in our cemetery in Kavarskas, where my relatives are buried. What happened to us? Why do we not respect the death of the Lithuanian Jews murdered in the Holocaust? Because these victims are not our people? Because our people killed them, and we do not want to remember? Just think: Two hundred kids will go to the most neglected places, and we will make people shiver with shame.

It is no longer an issue for me that Lithuanians killed the Jews, or how many, etc. I have discovered two other important things: First of all, that after nearly eighty years, people are still afraid to talk about this; and the other thing is the total indifference. Human bodies, bones, and skulls are covered not by grass, but by a thick, wild brush, and everybody is okay with it. Lithuanians are obsessed with death; they never allow flowers to dry up on graves, we pay the staff of the cemetery to water and weed the flowers, and we travel many hundreds of kilometers on All Saints' Day to visit every grave of our relatives. We even light candles on the graves that nobody visits. A neglected grave is a thing your relatives and your neighbors would talk about, and you would be severely criticized. So all this should be our second nature—respect, remembrance, and honoring the memories of the deceased.

The women we spoke to in Kavarskas live one or two hundred meters from a mass grave. They should come to the grave at least once a year, in the spring, and plant a flower. Or they should ask their husbands every now and then to cut the grass next to the monument—because this is a grave. What is wrong with us?

That's why I came up with an idea that two hundred kids should come to sing psalms in the wild brush for twelve murdered Jews. People would see this on TV, and this would affect them—wouldn't it? Fear and indifference are two things that I have already discovered during this trip.

12

Šeduva / Shadeve

At the end of the nineteenth century, 2,513 Jews were living in Šeduva (56.2 percent of the local population).

Before the Shoah — 800.

AUGUST 2015

Efraim: We are on our way to Šeduva. This is the town where my grandmother Bertha (Beyla Zar) grew up. Apparently her family was fairly succesful. The reason I know this is very simple: There was a branch of the Telz [Telšiai] Yeshiva in Šeduva, and the boys who studied there did not have a dormitory or a dining room. They therefore were sent to different local families, and used to eat their meals with the same family each day of the week. One of the families that volunteered to host some of yeshiva boys was the Gifter family. That is where my grandparents met. My grandfather was a student of this branch of the Telz Yeshiva, and he and Beyla Gifter fell in love. Later on, before World War I, all the kids of this family went to America and settled in different places. Jews were more than half of the population of Šeduva. Today it goes without saying that there is not a single Jew here.

Oh, here is a guy who might be able to help us find the Jewish cemetery. Let's just stop and ask him.

Today, in the city center, there are several temporary commercial huts where the synagogue used to be. In Soviet times, the synagogue building was still standing, Romas recalls, and they used to hold livestock shows there. Later it was torn down.

Romas, who has worked for the town administration for thirty years in land improvement, knows the entire area perfectly. We drive to the Jewish cemetery, and then to the airport, where Jews were held in the hangars before being taken to be shot. Romas is the first person we meet on our trip who tells us both his name and surname.

Romas tells his story:

> *My father was a farmer who raised cattle. His best customers were Jews who paid him in gold. We went to school together with Jewish children, we played together, and there was enough room under the sun for everyone. When the Germans came, our people thought they would be here forever, and they began to cozy up to them, trying to please them. Others murdered for property. Primarily they looked for those who had more wealth. It all happened here; people talk about how they used to ride Jews like horses, and cut their fingers off—that's how they took the rings off. There were also those who offered to hide a certain Jew who then brought some valuables over, but the Lithuanians ultimately turned him in. That's how so many chairs from Jewish homes appeared in my father's brother's house. Many white armbanders were from Vaidatonys village; they were sons of farmers. I remember how the priest during his sermon told the mothers of those young men: "How do you allow your sons to commit murder? After all, you already have everything, and everything is enough."*

Efraim: There is one question I want to ask you: Is the word *žydšaudys* (Jew-shooter) just a name, or does it have some kind of negative connotation?

Rūta: *Žydšaudys* only refers to the people who pulled the trigger. But I think we need to invent additional words to cover the other categories of those who participated in the process: like *žydgaudys* (Jew-catcher), similar to *šungaudys* (dog-catcher) and *žydvedys* (transporter of Jews), and maybe even *žydvagis* (thief of Jewish belongings).

Efraim: What about the people who were behind this entire process, like the Lithuanian Activist Front or the Provisional Government?

Rūta: Those are the people who made a mockery of the words of the Lithuanian national anthem. We used to sing: *Vardan tos Lietuvos / Vienybė težydi* (For the sake of Lithuania / let there be our unity). I think that after they came to power in 1941, the words should have been changed to *Vardan tos Lietuvos / Vienybė be žydų"* (For the sake of Lithuania / our unity without Jews).

Efraim: It is a sad joke. But that is what they were trying to achieve—Lithuania without Jews. It can be said that they more or less succeeded.

Rūta: They did not succeed. They did not get any unity.

Efraim: They succeeded in getting rid of the Jews, but they did not achieve any unity among Lithuanians.

Rūta: What is wrong with this town which no longer has any Jews? Look at how many houses we have got.

Efraim: I am used to this kind of dark humor. At Yad Vashem and the Simon Wiesenthal Center, the staff allow themselves to occasionally make this kind of jokes. So you do not shock me, Rūta. I want to ask Romas, our guide, how many people now live in Šeduva? Only three hundred people? So they murdered more than twice as many Jews during the Holocaust—eight hundred—as there are people in Šeduva today!

Romas suggested that we drive to Radviliškis where his elder sister Jūra lives; she remembers these events very well.

Romas's sister Jūra picks up the story. Jūra is a Lithuanian language teacher. She was born in 1929, and was twelve years old in 1941.

WHAT HAPPENED HERE IN 1941?

Jūra tells us:

It was truly horrible. We knew the people. There was one Jewish girl whom I liked very much. She was perhaps eighteen years old and worked in a shop owned by her father. Now there is a store there, called Aibė [a Lithuanian chain of small convenience stores]. There was no conflict at school; the classrooms were right next to each other. When the mass murders began, young men wearing white armbands drove the Jews from their homes, didn't allow them to walk on the sidewalks, and I saw how they marched them along the street. There were children as well. I don't know where they took them. It was said that they were first taking them to the synagogue where the market is now. They constantly marched them. They began in the month of July and marched them very often.

At that time there were no Germans here. There was not a single one of them in the town. People said all sorts of things. Many of those who knew Jewish people were sympathetic. When our parents came back from the village they always used to park their carriages in a yard belonging to Jews. And when the Jews celebrated their Easter, they used to give my parents matzah.

I also heard that priest's sermon in which he spoke to the mothers of the murderers. He yelled: "How can you allow your children to commit murder? Blood will exact blood!" They used to come home with piles of clothing, and the mothers would wash those clothes in the creek. None of us saw the mass murders, we just heard talk. After all, none of the murders were carried out inside the town. Those who lived by the forest related how they brought the Jews, and they heard the shooting. By the time they started shooting, there no doubt were also Germans there. The first time we saw Germans was when they took away our beloved young filly. Everyone knew that a certain Senulis had murdered many people . . . Grinius was a math teacher. Then the Russians came back and deported him to Siberia. A son survived, and there are grandchildren. There are others who murdered as well, and were deported and later returned from Siberia.

The people in Šeduva talked about the Jew-shooters. In Šeduva they all died shortly after the war. They simply drank themselves to an early death. They kept visualizing the mass murders again and again, and were driven to drink. Perhaps they had some sort of conscience after all. And they had the means to drink. Not that they worked anywhere. They all got drunk. People said they had set themselves on fire from within. That's the sort of people they were, really simple. Very simple. I don't know whether the farmers' sons shot the Jews; perhaps they just transported them. There were unemployed alcoholics who just wanted to get something for themselves. People did not respect them and called them "Jew-shooters." A "Jew-shooter" was the lowest sort of person. We were frightened to say anything against such people. We were very afraid. It was war, after all. It was a horrible time. I don't remember whether anyone tried to rescue or hide Jews, because everyone knew: If you were caught rescuing them, you would be shot.

Efraim: Both Romas and his sister told us one important thing that I had never thought about. When the Germans arrived in 1941, many Lithuanians thought they would remain for a very long time. Thus, most young Lithuanians probably thought that they should cooperate with the Germans in order to survive—or, to be more precise, to succeed and build their future. That was among the factors which explain why they started collaborating with the Nazis.

There is no question that those Lithuanians who were ready to carry out the murders wanted to find favor in the eyes of the Germans. This is another aspect of the motivation of the killers. I would look at all this in a different way and say that one of the main motives of the Lithuanians was to convince the Germans to restore Lithuanian independence. On the one hand, the Lithuanians wanted their independence back. On the other hand, they knew that the Germans hated the Jews, and therefore assumed that it obviously would please the Germans if the Lithuanians would get rid of the Jews for them. All this is speculation regarding the reasons why people were doing what they did. There are all sorts of reasons, but the bottom line is what they did. This is the hardest part to swallow.

This trip from mass grave to mass grave is absolutely horrifying. Once you get over the horror, you are struck with a feeling that takes over—one of sheer anger. Anger that such a thing took place, and that there is nothing we can do to bring these Jews back to life. This is the price that the Jewish people paid for all those reasons, all those "motivations" we are talking about. Someone who sees it from the point of view of the victims is far less open to understanding the "motivation" of the killers. You Lithuanians, whose people were involved in the mass murders, naturally look for the motivation to try in some way to lessen the anger, the pain, and the disgust some of you might feel after you found out that your relatives were part of this, even if they did not pull the trigger.

Rūta: Listen, I want our readers to look at those people, the killers, and not think of all of them as outcasts of our society. I have to look at them as people myself. That brings us to another important issue.

Efraim: Which is . . .

Rūta: Which is the diary of a killer. The dreams in the prison of the *Ypatingas būrys* member thirty years after the mass murders. When I e-mailed it to you, you said you could not read it because it made you sick. I was thinking, how was it possible that someone who has been dealing with Holocaust murderers for thirty-five years cannot read the dreams of a killer without feeling sick? Now I know the answer. All the testimonies you read were written by the survivors. You never thought that the killers were people too. They had their fears, nightmares, and dreams, loved their children and were afraid of death. That human dimension made you feel sick.

Efraim: No. That's not true. Of course they were people. My problem is this: The minute I start thinking of them as people and this whole "try to understand" starts, this weakens the resolve to bring them to justice. The issue of justice faces so many obstacles as it is, that this is a luxury I cannot allow myself, and that is one of the differences between me and you.

Rūta: If I paint some kind of portraits of these monsters, or non-monsters, it means in a certain sense that I am justifying them, doesn't it? If you read someone's dreams, listen to someone, that person becomes human to you.

Efraim: Here is the bottom line: The most horrific thing about the Holocaust is that these crimes were committed by normal people. Before the Shoah they were law-abiding citizens, and after the Shoah they were law-abiding citizens, but during the period of the Third Reich, they committed the most horrific crimes imaginable.

Rūta: I think that these people were normal all the way, all their lives. Just ordinary regular people, doing what the law, the authorities, expected them to do. Before the Third Reich, during the Third Reich, and after the Third Reich, they were the same. Normal. They haven't changed. The norms changed for a couple of years, and they obeyed these norms.

Efraim: Maybe . . . You have a good point here, an important point—sad and horrific. Very interesting, very important. You got me.

Rūta: You know what is so good about our conversations? You have been dealing with this issue for thirty-five years, and I am a newcomer, who knew almost nothing about the Holocaust until a year ago. I posed stupid questions. But sometimes my stupid questions or naive insights made you look at things differently.

Efraim: Yes, they shed light on some things that I never fully analyzed. The Third Reich created a reality in which moral deeds were only possible for people who were unusual and unique. Too many went with the flow. The flow to Auschwitz. The flow to mass murder sites in Lithuanian forests.

13

Telšiai / Telz

At the end of the nineteenth century, there were 3,088 Jews living in Telšiai (49.8 percent of the local population).

Before the Shoah—around 3,000.

WHAT HAPPENED HERE IN 1941?

Efraim: I will read you the testimonies of what happened to the Jews in Telz and Rainiai Forest:

Rabbi Bloch asked the Lithuanian commander of the camp, Platakis, to allow the Jews to pray the evening prayer. Rabbi Bloch then asked the Jews to promise that if they would survive, they would observe Shabbat, Kashrut, and the laws of family purity, and all the Jews said "Amen." As Shabbat began, the Jews emptied their pockets, since it was forbidden to carry anything on Shabbat. In the evening, the women and children were sent home and the men stayed in the camp. They understood that the men's fate had already been decided. Rabbi Bloch received permission from Platakis for the Jews to cover their heads, and prayers were said, including the prayer of vidui, which Jews are supposed to recite before they die.

On the next day, toward evening, the women and children were taken from their homes and brought to Rainiai Forest. They found their men there. All the Jews were kept under the skies for several days, until they were put into wooden barracks—men, women, and children together.[1]

---

1 Telz (Telšiai), *Sefer Yahadut Lita*, Volume IV, Tel-Aviv: Hotza'at Igud Yotzei Lita B'Yisrael, 5744, 1984, p. 291.

Rūta: The Rainiai tragedy—our tragedy—happened nearby on June 25. Now I will stop the car and want you to listen to our testimonies. What happened to seventy-two of my people here, in Rainiai Forest, seventy-five years ago? The documents tell the story:

After the war broke out, the NKVD and NKGB considered shooting prisoners as a form of evacuation. In the documents this is called "evacuation" under category I. Of the 162 prisoners in Telšiai Prison, 76 were prisoners who had been interrogated by the NKGB. . . . Red Army soldiers took those prisoners from their cells to the guard headquarters. Then they put them in trucks lying one on top of the other. As dawn broke on June 25, the trucks drove off in the direction of Luokė and into Rainiai Forest.

What happened then isn't well known. This was perhaps the only mass murder operation carried out in Lithuania in which none of the victims survived. Only the perpetrators of the mass execution have testified. Domas Rocius said: "Red Army soldiers did the shooting. From among us, those who were there were: NKGB department head Raslanas, authorized representative of operations Galkin and the prison guard Pocevičius. Among the 26 NKVD employees who participated in the arrest, interrogation and murder of the Telšiai prisoners, I find Jewish surnames as well: Nachman Dushansky, Telšiai representative of operations, and Daniel Shvartsman."

Pranas Sabaliauskas:

I was born and grew up near Rainiai Forest. . . . I know about the murders from the stories of Antanina Rocienė, who participated in the massacre with her husband. Two Chekists (Soviet security personnel) came to the executive committee and ordered them to go to the prison, taking along shoelaces, nails, hammers, and knives. When they got to the prison they brought the prisoners in and ordered them tortured. The Chekists demonstrated the method of torture: cutting through the lips and breaking arms behind backs. When they hammered nails into their heads, the prisoners began to really shout. To stop them from shouting, they cut off their genitalia and stuffed them in their mouths, and took them out to a waiting automobile.

They finished them off by torturing them in the forest, where the pots of boiling cabbage were set up. They stuck their hands into the boiling cabbage and laid them in pits while they were still alive. From the top of the pit some crawled out of the forest into the rye fields, and three more corpses were found there. There were three automobiles idling their engines to cover up the people's screams. I myself saw what happened in the forest.

Jewish men dug up the corpses. It was said that when the corpses were floating, they ordered the Jews to drink that water, and whoever didn't, was immediately taken away and shot.[2]

Efraim: My turn.

2 *Rainių tragedija: 1941 m. birželio 24–25 dd.*, Vilnius: LGGRTC, 2000, pp. 6–7.

A few days later, the Lithuanians discovered the corpses of the murdered prisoners. Bishop Staugaitis and the Lithuanian leadership decided to turn the funeral of the Soviet victims into a victory celebration. Every day Jews were brought to the murder site in Rainiai Forest, and were forced to dig up the corpses, wash them, lick them, and lay next to them in the caskets. Many could not do this. For several days, the Jews were tortured like this. On July 13, Staugaitis decided that the corpses of the Soviet victims would be buried in a religious ceremony and interred in a Catholic cemetery. This day would symbolize the victory over the Soviet regime. The Jews were concentrated in one place near the cemetery, and every Lithuanian participating in the funeral was allowed to spit in their faces or slap them.

On July 15, before the murder of the Jews of Telz, Revisionist Zionist leader Yitzchak Bloch turned to the Lithuanians and said: "Your country will be covered with your blood! But our revenge will grow out of our graves! Our blood will water the trees, your blood will wash the sidewalks."[3]

Rūta: Later studies of the Rainiai tragedy found that both then—at the beginning of the war—and later, the events of Rainiai were, and remained, a political issue. The specific method of torturing the victims was considered evidence of "Jewish" participation, and also, because [Nachman] Dushansky participated in the torture, and his preferred method of torture was supposedly damage to the genitals. The main organizer of the Rainiai massacre, Pyotr Raslan, fled to Russia, and Dushansky did the same, to Israel. All of Lithuania now knows that the perpetrators behind the Rainiai massacre were Jewish NKVD workers. Why is Israel protecting Dushansky as Russia is protecting Raslan? You want us to punish Nazi criminals but refuse to surrender the Soviet criminal Dushansky.

Efraim: I am well acquainted with the Dushansky case, and I even met him in Jerusalem several years after he came to Israel. As I understand, there were basically two major accusations against Dushansky: One was that he was among the Soviet officers who murdered and tortured about seventy Lithuanian inmates from the Telsiai prison in Rainiai Forest right before the Nazi invasion of June 1941. The second charge was that he played an active role in the punitive measures taken against thousands of Lithuanians in the aftermath of World War II.

As far as I know, Dushansky has always denied the first accusation, claiming that he was already out of Lithuania when the murders took place at Rainiai. When Lithuania requested judicial assistance from Israel in this case, the International Department of the Israeli Justice Ministry sought my advice and that of Lithuanian Holocaust survivors Professor Dov Levin and Adv. Yosef Melamed, then chairman of the Association of Lithuanian Jews in Israel. I remember that Irit Kahan, who headed that department of the ministry, convened a meeting in her office in Jerusa-

3 Telz (Telšiai), *Sefer Yahadut Lita*, Volume IV, Tel-Aviv: Hotza'at Igud Yotzei Lita B'Yisrael, 5744, 1984, p. 291.

lem to discuss the Lithuanian request. The consensus at the meeting was that the motivation for seeking to investigate Dushansky, with a view to seeking his extradition to Lithuania to stand trial, was anti-Semitic, and that he had purposely been singled out because he was Jewish. The proof presented was that twenty-four Lithuanian KGB officers of equivalent or higher rank, who were in Rainiai at the time of the murders, had never been questioned, let alone investigated.

Israel indeed refused Lithuania's request for judicial assistance in the Dushansky case, on the basis of a law which stipulated that if the ministry believed that the basis for the request stemmed from anti-Semitic motivations, Israel did not have to agree, and could refuse to provide any help in the case.

Rūta: Let's leave Dushansky in peace—or in turmoil, if he is really guilty. Because Dushansky is dead, as are many of the other criminals. Neither you nor I know whether he is guilty or innocent. We just know that the events in Rainiai served to inflame anti-Semitism in Lithuania, even up to the present time.

Efraim: And we now know, since we have just seen it, that the seventy-two Lithuanian victims of the Rainiai massacre are honored in the form of a huge chapel built alongside a road which has an oak grove planted on the other side. For the seven hundred Jewish victims of the Rainiai massacres, there is nothing at all. Not even a sign to the site of their murder. Next to an overgrown fence, next to a new factory, there is a small old Soviet marker.

Rūta: Our wonderful artist, Antanas Kmieliauskas, whose testimony about the murders in Butrimonys is in this book, decorated the chapel. There is a chapel for seventy murdered Lithuanians, but not even a sign for seven hundred murdered Jews. Does that mean that the life of one Lithuanian is worth more than the lives of ten Jews? Lithuanian martyrs deserve a chapel and an oak grove. They are worthy of a dozen books written about the massacre, because, after all, it was our people who died at Rainiai. Your people died at 227 or more Lithuanian locations, so Rainiai is not a unique place. And there is no oak grove, because the oak is not an appropriate tree to commemorate Jews, since under the oak trees our people shot yours.

Building of the Telšiai yeshiva. (Rūta Vanagaitė)

Fence around the mass murder site in Rainiai. (Rūta Vanagaitė)

14

Plungė / Plungyan

At the end of the nineteenth century, there were 2,502 Jews living in Plungė (55.6 percent of the local population).

Before the Shoah—around 2,000.

AUGUST 2015

Efraim: We are on our way to Plungyan, to meet Eugenijus Bunka, son of the last Jew of Plungyan, Yakov Bunka. Yakov was studying in the *mechina*, a program for younger boys at the Telz Yeshiva, and ironically, later on in Soviet times, he worked in the very same building, which had been converted into a factory producing souvenirs. Next door to the yeshiva was the synagogue, which is now a store which sells windows and doors. All three buildings—the yeshiva, the synagogue, and a dormitory and canteen for the students—all stood next to each other on the same street. On the building of the yeshiva there is a small sign which says that after the Soviets occupied Lithuania, "The Telz Yeshiva moved to Cleveland."

My only previous visit to Telz was in 1991; there were three Jewish women still living there, all of whom were married to Lithuanian men. Today there is not a single Jew in a town that used to have one of the most important Jewish communities in Lithuania.

In Plungė we are visiting a seventy-six-year-old woman named Vanda, who gave us a wonderful homemade blackberry drink.

Vanda tell us a story:

Who destroyed the Jews here? In Alsėdžiai it was Baltiejus, the blacksmith. There were 134 Jews here. Everyone got along well until the war started. When the Germans came, Baltiejus changed his skin immediately. The Germans didn't shoot here. They just had a command post. After the war Baltiejus went away, leaving his wife and three children here. They arrested him in Poland, and when they brought him back, his whole arm was all twisted up. See, there is justice. He shot twenty-nine women.

We hid three Jews, and a servant woman turned us in. The Jewish women were from Alsėdžiai. The servant woman worked around the farm and noticed we were making porridge and that Mama carried it off somewhere. The three Jewish women we hid were the seamstress Sara Braudienė, her daughter, who was about twenty years old, and Brikmanaitė, a total stranger, who was about forty. They came to us naked, of their own volition, and were with us for three years, but sometimes they moved around. They were with us once for a year and a half. They raised me since I was two years old.

On Sundays my father used to drive the servant woman to church, but one Sunday she decided to come back. When she arrived at our house, the three Jewish women were in the room, carrying me and my brother in their arms. No matter how much my father begged her, it was to no avail . . . She was friends with a policeman who shot Jews, and she was young and stupid. My father took the Jewish women away immediately. The police conducted a search and arrested my father, and held him for three months. Later they came back to our home again. We were always looking out the window, and if anyone was coming up the road we went to hide the Jews in the basement right away.

Baltiejus and other white armbanders would come to visit my father, who would sit down with them at a table in the kitchen and put down a bottle. They all sat there and drank, while the Jewish women were hiding with me in the basement, holding a hand over my mouth so I wouldn't make a sound. They drank, they left, and several hours later we came back upstairs. Baltiejus ran into my father in town and said, I know that you, Mr. Kareiva, are hiding Jews. My father said, Let's go have a drink and talk about it. As they were drinking beer, Baltiejus kept screaming: "I'm going to catch you." Our neighbor was sitting next to them and heard everything, so he either jumped on his horse or somehow got word to his wife to go warn us. They shot all the Jews in Alsėdžiai on Christmas, but the ones we hid all survived. My father, Pranas Kareiva, was recognized as a Righteous Gentile and received a medal. But other people, including priests, also saved Jews.

Rūta: It seems that here, in the region of Samogitia, people trusted—and still trust—each other more than in other parts of Lithuania. Are they different people? Or perhaps they have incredible solidarity. Thus, when people who were born in Samogitia meet, they normally speak to each other in Samogitian, even if they meet forty years later in Vilnius. They have a very strong identity, a very strong sense of local pride. It seems important that many were living not in small towns, but in isolated single houses quite far from one another, which made it easier to hide a Jew.

Efraim: Do you know how many Lithuanians participated in mass murders? Between twenty-five thousand and forty thousand.

Eugenijus: I can say that around Plungė alone there were about seven hundred who participated. When the Germans came, these people thought they had come for good. Other people who tried to save Jews also thought that the Germans had come to stay. They knew that hiding Jews would probably become a lifetime commitment. They would have to live with people hiding in their cellars until they die. Their children would also have to share this burden . . . It is not courage. It is something more.

Efraim: That is something I've never heard. No one ever said these things to me. But then again, my subject was not the righteous, but the killers.

Rūta: But you have to listen. Even if you are our enemy, you have to listen and hear everything that we have to say.

Efraim: I am listening. I am listening. Eugenijus, what, if anything, do you think those people who saved Jews have in common? Were they farmers? Devout Christians? What made them different from their neighbors? Have all these people been honored in Israel? If not, we should get them honored.

Eugenijus: It is not important for them. They had good relationships with the Jews before the war. They knew them. Maybe they were working in a Jewish home, taking care of a household or of children. One woman was asked by her Jewish neighbor to hide his gold and valuables and send them to him once he arrived in Palestine. She refused. "If me and my children ever are in need," she said to him, "I will have to sell your gold, and therefore I would not be able to send it to you." Where is this gold now? I think the killers found it.

Rūta: Who were the killers? Were they less educated? Less Christian? More stupid? Unemployed?

Eugenijus: Some of them were teachers, some doctors, civil servants . . .

Efraim: I have been saying this for twenty-five years: Collaboration with the Nazis encompassed all strata of Lithuanian society. And the Lithuanian government has been trying to say for twenty-five years that they were just a bunch of hooligans.

Eugenijus: Jewish property was important to them. The other thing was, there was something not right with their minds. There were about thirty murderers in the town. One murderer, when asked in court why he murdered the Jews, said: "The Jews are scam artists; I used to sell them geese and they always haggled over the price." One Jewish man from Užventis, named Tsik, was arrested along with other Jews and put under guard. He asked to be able to leave, and since the person guarding them was a friend of his, he told Tsik: "Get out of here." Tsik ran to a farmer's house on the hill and the farmer hid him, and he kept him hidden for the entire duration of the war. The most horrible thing was that they marched the Jews through that farm when they were taking them to be shot, and Tsik watched it all through a crack in the wall. Later he married the farmer's daughter.

15

Plateliai / Plotel

At the end of the nineteenth century, there were 171 Jews living in Plateliai (28 percent of the local population).

Before the Shoah—around 100.

AUGUST 2015

A meadow. A steep hill called Bokštakalnis, right next to Plateliai. Stairs lead up to the monument. The strong young Jewish men of Plateliai were shot here. There is a farm nearby where a man and a woman are tying sheaves. We go over to them. They speak the Samogitian dialect, and while it is hard to understand them, I do understand. The Samogitians are strange people; they don't talk much, but for that very reason, every word is significant. Is it perhaps because they talk so little that they betray so little?

I ask them: Did you witness the shooting of the Jews?

I saw everything. I was eight. I remember everything. There were ten of them. They came down from the hill. A car pulled up and some woman, a beautiful German, got out and gave the command. They shot all of them and drove off, but left one drunk person to stand guard. He dozed off, sitting near the road and that pit. Later Norvilas came to do the burying. Norvilas was such a handy person that he pulled out the teeth. I didn't see that; my parents just told me.

Then one person rose from the grave, bloody, but not even wounded. The poor fellow could have run to the hills and gotten away, but no, he ran to the guard. That snake still had a bullet left. And he shot him. He was so drunk, he didn't care whom he was shooting. He pulled the body by the legs and threw him back into the pit.

Were you friends with these Jews?

How could it be otherwise? We knew all of them. My father was a [black]smith, so he used to make wheels for the Jews. They shot strong young men here by the hill. They put five or six of them next to the pit. They shot them with rifles. None of them cried out. It was as if they were already dead. Then they came with lime and sprinkled it [over the bodies]. Those who hadn't shot did the burying.

Did you tell your parents what you saw?

How could I do otherwise? But they didn't allow me to go over there. They said, "Where do you think you are going? They'll shoot you." My father was so sorry for the Jews; how could he not be? We got along best [with them], we got along famously . . . When they were still alive I used to go to the shop and bring back armloads of buns for five cents. They baked cakes, slaughtered lambs. And there was a smokehouse, and a slaughterhouse. We knew all of them, but when they were shooting I didn't know whom, because it was so far away . . .

Two weeks later the women of Plateliai were shot.

WHAT HAPPENED HERE IN 1941?

About one hundred people remained imprisoned in the synagogue. At the end of August, Jakys (chief of the Kretinga security police) sent an order to the commander of the insurgents, the teacher Barkauskas, to liquidate them. A meeting was called at which the place, date, and time were set, and there were deliberations on how to gather the women who were working with farmers, without causing a lot of noise, and where to find enough carts to carry the children and the elderly. Among those at the meeting were Barkauskas, Žvinys, and Zubavičius, who before the war had worked as a secretary of a municipal board of directors. After everything was discussed, twelve people were called in, police and insurgents. Six volunteers appeared among them.

When the Jewish women had been brought to the pit near Lake Plateliai and clearly understood what awaited them, nerve-shattering screaming and wailing ensued. They undressed and the grown-ups were shot in an orderly fashion, one at a time. They behaved differently with the children. They shot them a ways off from the pit and then threw them into the pit. In total there were about twenty children ages one to ten. Police officer Grišmanauskas's wife Berta Grišmanauskienė shot them all. The shooting lasted about an hour. The participants divided up the clothing. The next day Barkauskas sent Jakys a report on how the order was carried out.[1]

---

1 Rūta Puišytė, *Masinės žudynės Lietuvos provincijoje* (Mass Murder in the Lithuanian Provinces). From: *Žydų muziejus: Almanachas*, Vilnius, 2001, pp. 182–83.

Before the shooting. (Lithuanian Central State Archives)

Efraim: There is one thing that bothers me, and it is only natural on such a trip with an enemy, and that is that you, Rūta, reject the facts that I read in Volume 4 of *Yahadut Lita*, which is very critical about people in Plungyan. I do not know why you find it so hard to believe that people were cruel to the Jews. I do not see any reason to reject this testimony. It does not mean that all the people in this town were like that; it means that there were some people who treated Jews in a very cruel way. We will see how to deal with this issue as we continue our journey. Maybe in Samogitia there was greater solidarity among the citizens themselves, which meant that they were less afraid of their neighbors informing on people who were hiding Jews. This could be a very critical factor. We have to think about this.

Rūta: Why should I trust the testimonies published in Israel? People tend to magnify what they experienced. The horror becomes multiplied twice or three times as time passes. The whole idea of this journey is not to read to each other what other people have written, but to go together to see the places with our own eyes. To speak to people who have witnessed the Holocaust.

Efraim: We remain divided on this issue.

Rūta. We spoke in Plateliai with a man who had witnessed the murders at Bokštakalnis. I asked him why he thought the killers were doing what they did—perhaps to please the Germans? For money? Were they drunk? And he said a very interesting thing: They did it for power—to exercise power over other people. The same thing other people were saying. Young, primitive, power-hungry people enjoyed humiliating other people because they could do it legally, without harming themselves or putting themselves at any risk. They did it legally. And they did it with a group of other guys, which created a comradeship and made them feel not only strong, but also part of a strong group.

Efraim: Finally they felt stronger than the Jews.

Rūta: It did not all start with shooting. Shooting might not have been possible for them in the beginning. They started by humiliating Jews, transporting them, guarding them, etc.

Efraim: It means that these people felt a certain weakness—and therefore, anger—that their new independent state had been "taken over" by the Jews.

On the course of our journey one thing became much stronger in my mind. The issue of the alienation between Jews and Lithuanians. I think about the sense of superiority the Jews may have felt, especially in the smaller provincial communities, which could easily have led to hostility between these two groups. Lithuanians, especially illiterate Lithuanians, must have felt this hostility. These are the people who played an important role in the murders.

Rūta: That is something I never thought about. How might the Jews have conveyed this sense of superiority?

Efraim: First of all, they kept to themselves. That's how they preserved their way of life. Listen, I have no doubt that many Jews have a sense of superiority because they are taught that they are the chosen people. I sense that there was a very strong barrier between the more primitive elements of Lithuanian society and Jewish society. Many of those who killed Jews came from among those people.

Rūta: According to the research of historian Rimantas Zagreckas, half of the people who pulled the trigger had virtually no education at all. One-fourth of them had only a few grades of elementary school.

Efraim: I want to take off my hat—or in this case, my *kippah*—to the man who did this research. This is very important research in trying to understand what happened here. But all the research that has been done, or will be done, in Lithuania does not solve the problem, because almost 99 percent of the research that has been done by serious historians in Lithuania has received absolutely no coverage in the local media. It has not affected the speeches by politicians, and/or is not being taught in the Lithuanian educational system.

Rūta: But you must agree that the Holocaust research done by our historians is a step forward.

Efraim: Yes, I agree, it is a step forward.

Rūta: All we have to do is to make their findings better known, and more accessible to the general public. Many aspects of the history of the Holocaust in Lithuania have been researched accurately by local historians, but almost none of this research has been either read or discussed seriously by the wider public.

Efraim: There is an enormous gap in Lithuania between local academic research and public perceptions of the Holocaust.

Rūta: Who has to fill this gap?

Efraim: Ironically, the person who has to do this is you! I am counting on you to break the glass ceiling and get past the distortion, minimization, double genocide theory, and all that. There is a classic example in that regard, a book called *Neighbors*, by Polish historian Jan Gross, which was published about five years ago, about the murder by local Poles of the Jews of the town of Jedwabne, their own neighbors. This book was a shocking wake-up call for Polish society. Poles classically saw themselves as victims, the same way Lithuanians do. And of course, all the nationalists in Poland raised a scandal: What? *We* are the murderers? You are ruining our martyrdom. The same thing might happen here, with this book.

Rūta: But it could have happened with the books and articles of our historians, the ones I read and quoted from in this book.

Efraim: No way; nobody wanted this to happen. These guys are lucky that nobody outside academic circles ever read what they wrote, or talked about it. They have secure jobs, secure academic careers, and all this would have been ruined by a scandal, by the people who are trying so hard to hide the truth. The less people who read what Lithuanian historians write, the better their chances to continue writing the truth.

Rūta: When I told some of my relatives that I had started writing this book, which would also deal with some of our family members' possible role in the Holocaust, one of them told me that I was doing this for some rotten euros. Every time I was in the Special Archives and read the interrogation files, I thought that I should let this relative of mine read what I read. Lithuanians do not know about the cruel crimes committed by our people, and do not want to know. Let them read the confessions of the Lithuanian killers; I do not have any reason *not* to believe the testimonies.

Efraim: Your relatives might say that these people confessed because they were tortured.

Rūta: I read the testimonies of some ten to fifteen witnesses, and every detail of a particular event they described is the same. Were the witnesses tortured as well? Were they told by the Soviet interrogators what to say? Lithuanians trust every testimony in the KGB files of any person who fought against the Soviet regime. Based on these testimonies, we make him our hero. But if a person has confessed that he murdered Jews, we start talking about KGB torture and refuse to believe them.

Efraim: People who don't want to believe something will find every reason in the world not to believe it.

16

Tauragė / Tavrig

At the end of the nineteenth century, there were 3,634 Jews living in Tauragė (54.6 percent of the local population).

Before the Shoah—around 3,000.

WHAT HAPPENED HERE IN 1941?

I, Antanas Šėgžda, state my desire to voluntarily join the police force. The reason for my joining the police is to acquire more rights, thanks to which my life will always improve, because I will have more opportunities to get everything I need.

Antanas Šėgžda began studying at the Tauragė teachers' seminary in 1939. On June 15, 1941, summer vacation began for the seminary students. Antanas was nineteen.

On June 25 or 26 two friends stopped by and suggested I join the volunteers unit. They said if I entered the unit, life would be easier for me. While on the police force I wore civilian clothing and was armed with a rifle, and on my left arm I wore a white armband made of material upon which I wrote in my own hand Ordnungsdienst, which translated means "Order Service."

At the end of August 1941 I took part in shooting Jews three times. There were fifty of us police officers. During the first operation I personally shot ten Jews. Regular police officers transported them from the town into the forest. They transported them early in the morning so the residents of the town wouldn't see. We took their money and valuables from them and put their clothes in a pile, and then we took the clothing to a storage facility and distributed it to people who had suffered from the war, including my mother. She brought me a new blue woolen coat from the storage space.

Also, I found large sums of money on the Jews brought to be shot. That is, when they brought a party of Jews to the pit dug for the shooting, I proposed that they give me their money, because they were about to die anyway. They gave me different sums of money, which I used to buy a fedora for 50 rubles. I bought a violin in Kaunas for 700 rubles, and spent the rest of the money on food. I took about 4,000 rubles from murdered Jews over the entire period. Over the course of my service I shot about fifty Jews.

I served in the security unit for about three months—that is, from June 26 to the end of August, and on September 15, I went back to school.[1]

After the war Antanas Šėgžda had a job as a member of the choir at the Šiauliai City theater. In 1948 he was arrested and sentenced to imprisonment for twenty-five years.

AUGUST 2015

We visit the Tauragė Regional History Museum. A friendly museum worker greets us. We ask if there is any information about the Jewish community who lived here—about the four thousand Jews of Tauragė who were murdered?

No, we don't have anything about the four thousand Jews who were murdered, but we are very proud of other parts of our exhibition, he says, like the collection of pennies from the United States. The young man tells us that visitors are amazed by this unique exhibit of one-cent coins. The next panel is dedicated to the writer Honoré de Balzac, who passed through Tauragė and decided to stop here for a while.

The tourist information center directs us where to look for the mass murder sites. We search, driving down dirt roads, braking next to trash containers by the side of the road, which from afar look like the small black obelisks scattered throughout Lithuania to mark the places at which you need to turn to find the mass murder sites.

Rūta: After driving to so many mass murder sites, I now know in which sort of forest to look for them. I now recognize the "right kind" of forest for mass murder. It must be large, dense, and near a town or the road. The site has to be in a clearing where it is easier to dig a pit, and there also has to be enough space for both the people to be shot and the shooters themselves. This is the right kind of forest, for example. And there's the sign, that they murdered Jews here.

---

1 LSA, K-1, ap. 58, b. 43767/3, pp. 5–6.

Efraim: Several thousand people murdered. Why? What have you achieved by killing them?

Rūta: Lithuania is such a beautiful country, and you recognize that. We can think of it as a beautiful young woman whose blossoming body is covered with wounds hidden from view. Two hundred wounds—two hundred mass murder sites. We might think the maiden is healthy and the wounds have healed long ago, but they aren't going to heal just because we are thinking they will. We have to do something about these wounds. The historian Alfonsas Eidintas said: "The wounds must be opened to allow the pus to drain out." Lithuania doesn't have any other neglected festering wounds besides this.

On our way we pass an old Jewish cemetery of Jurbarkas, next to whose fence is the local mass murder site. The two thousand Jews of Jurbarkas, the entire Jewish community, were murdered here on July 3, 1941.

Rūta: These murderers had mercy; they murdered people right next to their cemetery instead of in a swamp or bushes somewhere. The grandparents and parents heard the screams of their children and grandchildren. The children who were shot next to the graves of their parents and/ or grandparents probably had time to think what I would be thinking, if I were killed 30 meters away from my father's grave: "Father, help me . . ." What did the people think before dying? What prayers did they say, what psalms did they sing, or did they meet the bullets in silence?

Efraim: There are many different stories about the Jews' last moments. I heard about four different songs that Jews sang before being murdered. There is a very well-known song about the Jewish belief in the coming of the Messiah. "I will wait for his arrival every day until he comes, and even if he tarries, I will [continue to] wait for him." Another song is *"Hatikva,"* originally the anthem of the Zionist movement [and today the anthem of the State of Israel], which expresses the longing of the Jewish people to return to their homeland and establish an independent state, which did not exist at that time, and therefore could not do anything to save them. The third was "The Internationale," sung by the Socialists, and the fourth was the Czech national anthem. Many Jews from Czechoslovakia were Czech patriots, and they sang that song before they were murdered in the gas chambers in Auschwitz.

Rūta: When I was writing my book about care for the elderly in Lithuania, I read a lot about death. It seems that death is quite merciful. Before you die, your consciousness gets blurred. You are not thinking, seeing, or feeling clearly anymore. You become either unconscious, or semiconscious. This must be some kind of a defense mechanism. I just hope that those people who were waiting to be shot were not seeing or thinking too clearly, and that they became semiconscious. Perhaps sensing that death was imminent, they became mentally paralyzed. Many of the killers mentioned in their confessions that the Jews they were about to kill were silent, almost "as if paralyzed," or "already half dead."

There must be a big difference between death in a concentration camp and death at a mass murder site in a forest. In a concentration camp people saw death all around; they knew what was waiting for them, which perhaps in a way prepared them to die. But here it was totally unexpected. They did not know until they were brought to a pit or to the edge of a pit. They were told they were being taken to work, to a meeting, to be vaccinated, out of their houses so that the houses could be searched . . .

Efraim: Yes, in many cases they did not know what fate awaited them and were told all sorts of lies by the killers, to lull them into a false sense of security. There obviously was no need to fight and probably be killed in the process, if they were being sent "to work," or "to Palestine," or G-d knows where. As long as they were alive (or thought that that would be the case), that was preferable to risking death by fighting or fleeing.

I am also thinking about the whole issue of resistance. Why was there so little resistance, so few attempts to fight against the badly outnumbered killers guarding the Jews? One of the things that came to mind was the Jewish tradition of martyrdom. Throughout the centuries, we Jews have glorified our martyrs, those who died rather than betray their faith. And there were many such cases—during the Crusades, for example, or the Inquisition—of thousands of Jews who preferred to die *al Kiddush Hashem* (glorifying G-d's name), rather than convert to Christianity. That was perhaps one factor; another was the Jews' lack of power, having constantly been a powerless minority everywhere they lived, for centuries. In the Holocaust, all these factors came together, and there was very little physical resistance.

Rūta: Almost all the killers said that the Jews behaved like sheep, so easy to handle . . . Four hundred Jews were taken from the Kaunas Ghetto to the Ninth Fort by eight Lithuanians. Then another four hundred, another four hundred—a two-kilometer walk. No escape attempts. Incredible. Ten thousand people were slaughtered in the pits of the Ninth Fort in Kaunas, and only one eleven-year-old boy escaped.

On the Klaipeda-Vilnius highway, we pass Raseiniai.

WHAT HAPPENED HERE IN 1941?

Among the testimonies of outstanding Lithuanian writers and artists who witnessed the Holocaust, but have never been interviewed about their ex-

periences, is that of Marcelijus Martinaitis (1936–2013), one of the most renowned poets and essayists in Lithuania. His works have been translated
into fourteen languages. Martinaitis, a winner of the Lithuanian National
Prize, was one of the leaders of the "Sajudis" movement during the years
1989–1991, before the restoration of Lithuanian independence. Marcelijus
Martinaitis was just five years old in the summer of 1941.

*I saw the mass murder of Jews twice. Those images are lodged very deeply in my
memory.*

*. . . My father and I returned from the market in Raseiniai. There was a Jewish
ghetto in the pasture, and the Jews were being marched in columns on what was
called Jurbarkas Road. We were riding in a cart and overtook them as they were
taken to be shot. It was very strange that so many people were being marched, but
there were only four people with automatic weapons guarding them. As a child, I
wondered, Why don't they run away?*

*The next time, as we were returning from Raseiniai, they stopped us at the turnoff
onto a dirt road. A group had been brought there. They ordered them to undress. And
the women were naked. For some reason they shot them without lining them up. The
men shot the victims in the pit while walking along the side of the pit.*

*It was August, the beginning of August. Beautiful warm days. There were a lot
of shootings, several times every day. Screaming was heard, heard awfully far away,
from over the hill. And we knew that the shooting would soon begin. People heard
the shooting in the fields and stopped what they were doing. Women kneeled down
and prayed when they heard the shouting. Then automatic weapon fire was heard.
Then silence, silence, silence.*

*When they used to shoot, they used to sprinkle a little earth over [the victims],
then the next group, and the next. There were survivors. At night they used to come
to our village, having crawled out of the pits, crawling and digging themselves out
from the ground. I don't know what happened to them, because they [the adults] hid
everything from the children very carefully, [since] children would tell everything.
Those people remained; they weren't turned in. I saw one bloody man shambling
toward our house, and then later he disappeared. Maybe he spent the night at my
parents', maybe someone took him in, I don't know.*

*And there was another atrocious thing. I didn't see it, but there were stories that
they didn't shoot the children, they beat them to death. They smashed them against
a tree trunk, split their skulls and then threw them into the pit. Because it's very
difficult to shoot a child; there's not a lot to aim at.*

*Who did the shooting? The scene I saw was like this: There were Germans, but
they were somehow removed, farther away. Locals did the shooting. There were two
from our village, Uleckas and Savickas. There was another man from the neighboring
village. Neighbors who lived a few hundred meters away used to come to our house
after the shooting. They were a bit drunk. They wore uniforms with a skull on the
sleeve. They were very proud of that symbol and kept showing it off. They wanted
to drink, so they used to bring clothes and items [from the Jewish victims] and offered them to my parents, but they didn't take them. Nobody in the entire village
took them. After the war, Uleckas went into the forest but he wandered around by*

himself, because the partisans wouldn't accept him. Later he was shot. Savickas hid;
they found him on a farm in the winter, and he ran away barefoot in the snow. They
shot him, and his bloody footprints remained in the field.

After the war, cows were sent to pasture at the place where the Jews were shot.
Later they began to build the Kaunas-Klaipėda highway. They were building the road
and didn't know there were graves there. They dug, and skulls and bones began to
turn up. Later they paved asphalt over the graves.[2]

—September 28, 1998

---

2 Credit to: Jeff and Toby Herr Collection at the United States Holocaust Memorial Museum in Washington, DC.

17

Butrimonys / Butrimants

At the end of the nineteenth century 1,919 Jews were living in Butrimonys (80.1 percent of the local population).

Before the Shoah—around 800.

WHAT HAPPENED HERE IN 1941?

Butrimonys was one of the oldest Jewish communities in Lithuania. The local Jewish community had a brick synagogue, a school where Hebrew was taught, and charity and welfare associations. Fifty-two (of fifty-four) shops, breweries, bakeries, and other small enterprises belonged to Jews.

And then it all started:

> The chief of the Butrimonys rural district police department reported to the regional policy chief that the "Jewish question is very urgent because there are over 2,000 Jews living in the town who need to be taken care of in the near future."[1]

On September 8, the Butrimonys police chief, L. Kaspariūnas-Kasperskis, ordered that all Jews who were still alive should be taken to the town's primary school that night. The mass murder of the Jews of Butrimonys was planned for the next morning.

---

1 Arūnas Bubnys, *Holokaustas Alytaus apskrityje 1941 m.* (Holocaust in the Alytus County in 1941). From: *Genocidas ir rezistencija* (Genocide and Resistance), 2012, No. 1 (32), pp. 37–38.

It seems they were waiting for the third platoon of the TDA battalion, under the command of Bronius Norkus, to complete the mass murder of the Jews of Alytus, so they would be free to come to Butrimonys. The largest massacre in Alytus was carried out on September 9, 1941. According to the Jäger Report, Norkus's men murdered 1,279 Jews that day: 287 men, 640 women, and 352 children. The killers had no chance to rest afterwards, and got right on the bus. No time for a party; that would have to wait until later that day, in Butrimonys.

> *On September 9, 1941, a bus arrived from Alytus with about twenty mobile-unit [Rollkommando] soldiers on it. In the afternoon the local police and white arm-banders began to march the Jews from the school in columns. Jews wearing better clothes were ordered to undress down to their underwear. The columns of Jews were marched to Klydžionys village, about two kilometers from Butrimonys. The shooting ended in the evening. Then the murderers returned to Butrimonys and celebrated the end of their "work" at the town cafeteria.[2]*

When L. Kaspariūnas-Kasperskis, renowned for his brutality, was transferred to become chief of the Birštonas police department, "he left Butrimonys with fourteen or fifteen large carts full of looted property. Local residents saw this and said: 'There goes Kasperskis, King of the Jews.'"[3]

TESTIMONY OF A WITNESS:
ANTANAS KMIELIAUSKAS, PAINTER AND WINNER
OF THE LITHUANIAN NATIONAL PRIZE (BORN IN 1932)

Since 1994 Antanas Kmieliauskas has held the position of professor at the Vilnius Academy of Arts and is considered to be one of the most outstanding contemporary Lithuanian artists. He has been working simultaneously in the fields of sculpture, painting, fresco, and graphic art.

Antanas Kmieliauskas was nine in the summer of 1941:

> *In Butrimonys where we lived, the majority of the residents were Jews. Building next to building, shops everywhere. These stores were full of a bit of everything, and after church, people would go to those shops.*
>
> *Later they began to register Jews and pinned yellow stars to their lapels. That wasn't so bad, but it was somehow very unpleasant when they did it on their backs, too, as if they were some sort of target to shoot at.*

---

2 Ibid., p. 39.
3 Ibid., p. 40.

On the day of the shooting, I heard from my parents that all the Jews had been brought to the square and were ordered to take their clothes off. Everyone was horrified by this. We children understood something terrible was about to happen. And later in the evening they beat them, and the moaning could be heard. We wanted to go and look, but they didn't allow us to see. The pits in the forest had already been dug; everyone knew they would shoot the Jews, and were waiting for it to happen.

The next day, we children went off toward Klydžionys Forest in the late afternoon. The sky to the west of Butrimonys was so red, but perhaps I just remember it that way because of the terror. We went, hid behind a house, and watched. They brought them, almost completely naked; they were naked, without clothes. Maybe just with underpants. There were maybe ten of them. They stood right at the edge of the pit. There were shots, and everyone fell down. They shot them in the back, and the hands of those people were behind their backs. There were about ten people who shot and they were all wearing green uniforms.

They brought the people in groups from town. They neither spoke to them nor made them wait at the pit. They brought women mostly, and older people, because they had already taken the younger people to Alytus to shoot them. Maybe they were afraid of resistance. They brought them, shot them, and then brought others.

After those shootings I had nightmares. About pits. Perhaps all the children had nightmares. Whoever saw those shootings was changed for the rest of their lives. There is no justice at all, not even a fingernail's worth of dirt.

My parents later said that the Jews' clothes had been put on the second floor of a certain house, tied with cord into bundles which were lowered from the second floor through the window. There were people who took them. That's the sort of ugly affair it was.

Those who participated in the shooting of the Jews later tried to convince people that the Jews had exploited them. Later those same people participated when the Soviets deported people to Siberia. Mostly they were people who had been unsuccessful in life, whom it was easy to convince that they were living impoverished lives because the Jews were exploiting them. They thought they would take something from the Jews after they were shot. Later these same people said they were exploited by the rich, by Lithuanians. And they deported those exploiters to Siberia. Both the Germans and the Russians used the same methods. There was a man who used to sell grain to a Jew in Kaunas. The Jew allowed him to make a living, but the man said he was supposedly a servant of the Jew, and that the Jew had exploited him.

There are people capable of shooting anyone, even a child. If in the future some Chinese or someone comes and says that the artists need to be shot because they don't work, and only exploit others, then enough people would come forward willingly to do the shooting. All that is needed for that is for some kind of government, or an organizer, to tell them to do so. There is this type of person, of lower intellect and low education, and it's not difficult to convince them.[4]

—April 19, 1998

---

4 Credit to: Jeff and Toby Herr Collection at the United States Holocaust Memorial Museum in Washington, DC.

AUGUST 2015

Before going to Butrimonys, Rūta visited Antanas Kmieliauskas, now eighty-three. He added some new details to his original testimony, given in 1998:

> *When the shooting was over, we, the children who had been watching it from behind the house nearby, came out and approached the pits. More people from the village came to see their murdered neighbors. Some people in the pit were still alive. One person was badly wounded; blood was blocking his nose, so he could not breathe. This man moved his head to get some air. The killers did not want to waste the bullets on the victim, so one of them went to the forest to get a stone.*

Rūta asked the artist to draw the scene from nearly eighty years ago, and Antanas Kmieliauskas obliged, creating a sketch of the murder he witnessed in 1941, before the Jews fell into the pit.

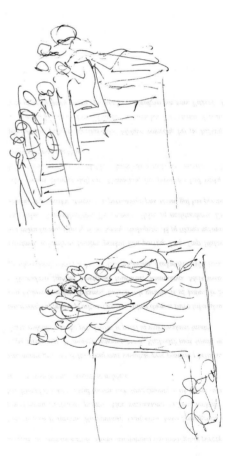

Antanas Kmieliauskas's drawing of the mass murder in Butrimonys. (Antanas Kmieliauskas)

Butrimonys is a small town. Empty. We look for some older person, as we have done in all the towns we've previously visited. We see an old man with a broken-off walking stick, completely hunched over and very frail. He agrees to show us the mass murder site in the Klydžionys Forest in exchange for a pack of cigarettes. Right beside the road is the place where the artist Antanas Kmieliauskas saw the mass murder being committed when he was nine years old, which he sketched for us. They murdered old men here, because the young and strong Jewish men of Butrimonys had already been shot in Alytus.

But where is the second mass murder site, the one where our guide told us three hundred children had been shot? We trek through fields and meadows without directions or understanding where we are being led, or how much further we must go. The elderly man goes in front, supported by his stick as his lungs croak and wheeze. The sound is bloodcurdling. The man really has a problem with his lungs. Finally the old man stops and says, "I cannot go with you any further; I am not healthy enough. You go in that direction, you will find the place where the children were murdered."

He leaves us in the middle of a field. It is a hot 35 degrees Celsius (95 degrees Fahrenheit) today.

We go on, but where should we go? Toward which field? To the left, where the horse is running away from us, or to the right? Efraim stops. Rūta goes on. She wants to find the gravesite of the children.

She did not find it. Oh, well. Somehow we are both very sad for the old man with his wheezing and croaking lungs out in that heat. We go back.

The old man is sorry he couldn't find it, and says, almost as a sort of excuse, that his wife died long ago and his son was killed in Italy. As we say good-bye, he points out the house of the last Jews of Butrimonys. Rivka Bogomolna and her sister saved themselves, and continued living in their own house.

Efraim: Rivka Bogomolna was one of the few Butrimonys survivors, and she and her sister continued to live there after the war for a very long time, in order to preserve the memory of the Jews of Butrimonys. This was very rare, because those Jews who had survived the Holocaust in the provincial towns and villages almost never stayed in the place where they were born and lived before the Shoah. Two hundred and twenty Jewish communities had been destroyed. The Lithuanian provincial towns were left with almost no Jews. Jews were concentrated in Vilna, Kovno, with some in Shavl and Ponevezh.

I first met Rivka Bogomolna in 1991. She was the first person to alert the world that starting in 1990 rehabilitations had been granted by the Lithuanian government to people who had murdered Jews, even though the rehabilitation law specifically forbade granting pardons to anyone who had "participated in genocide."

Rūta: Who were these people, the murderers of Butrimonys?

Efraim: Their names were Juozas Krasinskas and Kazys Grinevičius. Rivka gave me this information in 1991. Afterwards, Professor Shmuel Kukliansky gave me documents on twelve other cases of people who had been granted rehabilitation. The *New York Times* published a front-page story on the issue, the day after Lithuania was admitted to the United Nations. Tens of thousands of people were rehabilitated starting in 1990, and either their records were not properly checked, or their wartime activities were purposely ignored. The people who were granted rehabilitation got their property back, and received 5,000 rubles in compensation from the local municipalities. Only around two hundred rehabilitations were subsequently canceled in the wake of the protests and extensive media coverage of the scandal. That was, at least, a partial victory.

Rūta: One of the members of the *Ypatingas būrys* was granted rehabilitation . . .

Efraim: According to the law, anyone who had "participated in genocide" was ineligible for rehabilitaton.

Rūta: There were a total of twenty-six thousand applications for rehabilitation, of which seven hundred were rejected. I am afraid they didn't investigate very carefully. I have seen the application form. It only has a few questions: Where were you born? What was your sentence, and how long did you spend in prison or the gulag? That's it. If you applied for rehabilitation you were supposed to get an aswer from the General Prosecutor's office in three weeks. The commission that handled the applications was made up of just three people. What happens if the case file consisted of twelve volumes, or even only seven volumes, each two hundred to three hundred pages? Do you think that these people could investigate properly? You have to understand that rehabiltations were granted in the 1990s, so it's too late to review everything and start investigating all over again. If we would do so, we have to admit not only that we made a huge mistake back then, but also that there were more war criminals than we are ready to admit . . .

Efraim: Yes, they would have to admit that they made a terrible mistake.

18

Panevėžys / Ponevezh

At the end of the nineteenth century, 6,627 Jews were living in Panevėžys (51.1 percent of the local population).

Before the Shoah—around 10,000.

WHAT HAPPENED HERE IN 1941?

Efraim: The Ponevezh Yeshiva was one of the most important yeshivot in prewar Lithuania. Among the students was my great-uncle, Efraim Zar. This yeshiva was closed in 1940 by the Russians. Then Rabbi Kahaneman moved to Israel and opened a yeshiva with the same name, one of the most important yeshivot throughout the world.

Rūta: What made this yeshiva so important?

Efraim: Two things. First of all, the advanced level of Talmud studies, and second, it had some of the best rabbis in the world, who naturally attracted the most talented students. Some of them became rabbis, others became educated Jews by learning Torah. Now I will read you what your people did to my people here in Ponevezh during the Shoah.

Rūta: I am listening.

Efraim: There were ten thousand Jews in Ponevezh, the third-largest community in Lithuania, after Vilna and Kovno. Let me read about what happened to the Jews in Ponevezh:

One day the notorious [Lieutenant] Izonas led a group of Jews to work at the railroad station. Their task was to move barrels of gasoline, each one of which weighed

200 kilos, from one place to another, and each barrel had to be carried by two men. The job was very hard, especially for the weaker men, who were unable to carry out the task, and were therefore beaten and tortured continuously. That, however, did not satisfy the lust of the Lithuanians for murder and torture.

When the task was completed, Izonas announced that the men "would take a hot bath, after which they could rest in the crisp and cold air."

Izonas and his men then led the Jews to the cement factory. There were large pits there full of unextinguished lime, and the Jews were ordered to pour water into the pits, whereupon the lime began to boil. The Jews were arranged around the pits, and then were forced to jump into the pits and swim in the boiling water. Whoever wouldn't jump was pushed by the policemen. Whoever tried to climb out of the pits was beaten with rifle butts.

Among the unfortunate men was a bearded elderly Jew who tried to keep his head above the water. The murderers suspected that he was doing so in order to save his beard. They hit him in the head with their rifle butts, and he dived deeper into the pit. By the time the other Jews were able to get him out of the lime, his eyes were burnt and he was blind. Badly injured, the Jews were taken out of the pits, with some being sent straight to Pajuostė Forest to be murdered, and some being taken to prison.[1]

Rūta: This is way too much. Nobody can swim in boiling water . . .

Efraim: Do you think that this testimony is a lie? One of the Jews tried to keep his head above the water, so the killers decided he wanted to save his beard. They started beating him with a gun until the man's head sank. Other Jews took him out of the water. The eyes of this man were burned out, totally white. Then the killers took all these Jews to Pajuostė Forest and murdered them.

Rūta: Look, there are limits to what I can take from you. Yes, these Jews were swimming in the boiling lime and thinking how to save their beards. After the swimming they got out and only then were taken to the forest. I respect the victims of the Holocaust, but there are limits to every fantasy.

Efraim: Regarding torture of the Jews in Lithuania, there were no limits.

Rūta: Let me tell you about my family member, Lieutenant Colonel Antanas Stapulionis. He was the husband of one of the most wonderful people in my family, my aunt Gene, and was the commander of the insurgency against the Soviets in Panevėžys in June 1941. After the Germans arrived, the insurgents joined the local police force or the white-banders. Stapulionis, who had been the Lithuanian Army commandant for the Panevėžys district, was appointed the head of the local security police. After all the municipal employees returned to work, except the mayor, Stapulionis appointed a temporary replacement, who remained at his post until the end of the Nazi occupation.

Stapulionis was responsible for maintaining order in the city, but it is not clear exactly what role, if any, he played in implementing the orders

---

1 "Ponevitch (Panėvežys)," *Yahadut Lita*, Volume IV, Tel-Aviv: Hotza'at Igud Yotzei LitaB' Yisrael 5744, 1984, p. 330.

of the German *Ortskommandant* regarding the city's Jewish population. Starting July 11, all the Jews of Panevėžys were forced to live in a poor section of the city, from which all the Lithuanian residents had been removed. The homes of the Jews who were forced to move to the ghetto were vandalized by local poor Lithuanians, despite the efforts of Antanas Stapulionis's office to stop the robbery. Out of the 4,423 Jews who entered the ghetto, only 3,207 had a roof over their heads; the remaining 1,216 were living in courtyards. The municipality was considering removing all the cupboards, tables, and sofas from the houses occupied by Jews in the ghetto, to make room for at least half of the others. I am wondering whether my mother's friend Itzik was among those Jews who had a roof over their head? Did my mother have any idea where he was, and why he no longer came to play together with her that summer?

. . . On August 23, the largest mass murder operation in the Panevėžys district took place in nearby Pajuostė Forest, carried out by Joachim Hamann's Rollkommando. According to the Jäger Report, on that day, 1,312 Jewish men, 4,602 Jewish women, and 1,609 children "were handled." The children were buried separately. Itzik is probably among them, with his head smashed.

Antanas Stapulionis managed to remain in his position until the end of August 1941, when he was demoted to become a tax inspector. It is impossible to find out if he played any role in the liquidation of Jewish property which was carried out by the municipal administration. The Germans confiscated the most valuable furniture and other items, whereas the less-valuable items were given to the local drama theater, to the girls' gymnasium, orphanages, or hospitals, or sold to local residents. The items which could not be sold were distributed for free to locals, among them 2,636 men's pants, 7,644 sheets, 12,751 shirts, 8,235 pillowcases, 10,248 towels, 2,536 children's coats, 4,827 other items of children's clothing, and thousands of other items, from the mattresses to plates and cups. In all, about 80,000 items were distributed free of charge to Panevėžys residents in the fall of 1941.

According to the data of the Panevėžys municipality, after 4,423 Jews were murdered in late August 1941, there were 25,540 people living in the city. So, on the average, every resident received three to four items of the murdered Jews. I am wondering whether my grandmother received anything? Did my mother, who was fourteen, ever wear any of these clothes?

SEPTEMBER 2015

The building of the Panevėžys Yeshiva is now a confectionary and bakery. Two women selling cakes behind the counter don't know what was

Panevėžys yeshiva building, now a bakery. (Rūta Vanagaitė)

there before. The Panevėžys Synagogue belongs to the municipality, and the RE/MAX Agency now offers rental spaces for offices and stores there.

We find a building which has been returned to the Panevėžys Jewish community. The hall is full of people milling about. What is happening here? The Israeli ambassador and Panevėžys politicians are sitting at a table loaded with food. Speeches are being made. When they see the Nazi-hunter entering the room, all of them are shocked. The chairman of the local Jewish community jumps up to embrace him. The ambassador lowers his eyes to the plate before him and doesn't say a word. Perhaps the Israeli government doesn't like Zuroff, whom they fear is ruining relations with the Lithuanian government? The lunch ends and the politicians get into their nice black cars and drive away, carrying flowers to honor the victims of the Holocaust.

The ambassador's bodyguards carefully scrutinize the area of the mass murder site. The ambassador gives a speech. He wonders (or perhaps doesn't wonder at all) why the Lithuanian government and the administration of Panevėžys leave the upkeep of the mass graves to student volunteers.

The mayor of Panevėžys utters a few catchphrases about the Holocaust, how sad it was and so on. He lays a wreath. The motorcade departs. We are left with one teacher from Panevėžys whose pupils are maintaining the mass murder site. We stay at the site with the teacher. Of course, she asks us not to publicize her name, but she does share the following thoughts with us:

> One of the murderers of the Jews is buried in Panevėžys. His grave remains to this day without a cross. His relatives put one up, but someone keeps knocking it down. Everyone knew he shot Jews . . . One witness, a woman living in Panevėžys, watched through a window of the school on September 23, when children were being driven into Pajuostė Forest. When the truck stopped, some children didn't get off, while others jumped out and ran toward the pits. The executioners were blind drunk. All Lithuanians. And then they shot the children and spread quicklime over them so there wouldn't be a stench. They didn't put much of it down. All the [children's bodies] are in the trench by the side.
>
> [My students] and I clean up the mass grave every year, and a few years ago, as they were raking the leaves, the children found a gold tooth.

Efraim: It's a big monument, but there's nothing written in Lithuanian, and even the Russian inscription has mistakes. At least the grass is cut here, and it looks like the students did that. But if there's no inscription in Lithuanian, anyone who visits won't understand what happened here during the Shoah.

Rūta: Not unless they, too, discover a gold tooth . . . But since it's the students doing the maintenance, the city administration does not have any problems. Once a year they can drive up with flowers, as they did today, honoring the ambassador of Israel. And if someone asks the deputy mayor or mayor why the city isn't doing anything to honor the seven thousand dead buried here, the answer would be only one thing: silence. "They are not our people," meaning, "Let the Jews keep up Jewish graves." Or students, if they want to. It's not our problem. Our city has plenty of other problems.

With the help of our teacher guide, we find the Panevėžys Regional History Museum. Is there any information about the history of the Jews of Panevėžys? No, replies the museum employee on duty.

Efraim: Panevėžys was one of the most important Jewish centers in Lithuania before the war. Did you know that?

Museum worker: Everything's possible. But I think you should speak to our Jewish community about that.

Efraim: Sure, I visited them. But I think if you're working on the history of the city, and a large part of the city population were Jews who contributed to the city's development and culture, and who made Panevėžys known throughout the world . . . Did you know that? And do you know why Panevėžys is known throughout the world? Because there was a yeshiva here. At Savanorių street, number eleven. And to this day there is a yeshiva with the same name in Israel, the Ponevezh Yeshiva. Is that important? What are you telling me—that the history of the Jewish community is not Panevėžys's history? They weren't "our people," but someone else's people?

Museum worker: I think you should submit a complaint to the government or city administration. They established the museum, and they decide.

Efraim: But I want to ask *you* whether this community has given something to the city . . .

Museum worker: And I want to ask you, How many people in the world know about Panevėžys for the reason that you mentioned?

Efraim: Four million.

Museum worker: Do you really think so?

Efraim: I know this! Ponevezh was unique.

Museum worker: Okay, I will think about this. I'm glad I heard this so I can tell museum visitors now.

Rūta: Now I want to read you something special. There is a very interesting study—the social portrait of the killers. This is a study of forty-seven convicted Holocaust perpetrators done by historian Rimantas Zagreckas. The professions of these people: twenty-two of them were farmers; five teachers; three watchmen; two tailors; two farmhands; one insurer; one postal worker; one accountant, one smith; and one peat miner. Education: Out of forty-seven people, twenty-four were illiterate, or had only completed the third grade of primary school.

Efraim: The more I travel through the small towns and villages of Lithuania, the more I become aware of the gap that existed between the Jews and the farmers or peasants who were their neighbors. In most places in Lithuania, the Jews lived in the center of the town.

Rūta: Yes, and they were more educated, more wealthy, and very isolated.

Efraim: Their tradition was to maintain certain high standards, and maybe people looked at them with jealousy.

Rūta: Everyone had some kind of motivation when it all started. The government had its motivation, the clergy had a different motivation, the young boys who joined the self-defense forces had their motivation, as did the dregs of society.

Efraim: And there is no solution to that, except Hitler's "Final Solution."

Rūta: Yes.

Efraim: The Jews paid for their success—paid with their lives. Many Jews were generous and friendly to their Lithuanian neighbors. They were the merchants, and people from the villages used to come and buy things from the Jews. There were many stories about the generosity of Jewish shopkeepers who allowed their Lithuanian customers to buy on credit and waited until they could afford to pay for the goods they had purchased.

Rūta: No, no, no. Wait a second. Those Lithuanian farmers, or anyone else, were permanently in debt to a local Jew. But it was Lithuania, the farmers' homeland, so why were Jews better off? It is our country, but for some reason it was not we, the farmers, who lent money to the Jews, but them to us. So what went wrong? They must have robbed us at some point; that's why they were richer than us. Of course, those people were somehow grateful to the Jews who gave them merchandise and did not ask for money until later, when they were able to pay. But the feeling was not all that positive. This is maybe a starting point for alienation, hatred, and, eventually, revenge.

Efraim: What about the hundreds of years of Christian theology saying that Jews were damned? That Jews murdered Jesus? What about that?

Rūta. Of course you did this. We all know this. And that you put the blood of the Christian children into your matzah.

Efraim: If you start talking about this Christian blood nonsense, we may as well stop right now. This is not the basis for us to go on this journey.

Rūta: Okay, I will stop. But I know what the church is saying. I was listening to a priest on a Catholic radio station who said that God always punishes the people who betray him. He said, Look at the history of the Jews. It sounded like he was saying that the Jews got what they deserved.

Efraim: I do not know whether to laugh or to cry. That is the most fundamental anti-Semitism which has existed in the Catholic Church for centuries, and led to mass murder after mass murder. When the Jews rejected Jesus—who was supposedly the son of God, according to Christian doctrine—the Catholic Church became God's chosen people. In 1965 the Catholic Church officially changed its doctrine and said that the Jews cannot be blamed for the death of Jesus.

Rūta: Let's go back to the year 1941. Back then there was strong and influential LAF propaganda saying that the Jews had robbed us. They came to our country and took the best land and the best positions. On top of all this, you Jews embraced the Soviets, who deported our countrymen in June 1941, shortly before the war. You worked in the Soviet security services! Nice bunch of different reasons, isn't it? So let's get rid of the Jews!

Efraim: The Lithuanian people were not sophisticated enough to think of something else—that if the Jews wanted to survive as a nation, they had to be different, had to be apart. There wasn't total separation, just the elements of alienation.

Rūta: So finally it happened. The Jews were apart from us. Very much apart. And forever.

19

Belarus

The story of the murder of Jews in Belarus by the Lithuanian 12th Battalion is extremely disturbing. When the battalion's 474 soldiers left Kaunas, the capital of Lithuania, for Belarus, they did not know that in several months they would murder at least 15,424 Jews in fifteen different locations.

The commander of this battalion, major Antanas Impulevičius, an officer in the interwar Lithuanian Army, was arrested by the Soviets after they occupied Lithuania in 1940 and held for nine and a half months. So-called "physical coercion techniques" were likely applied during his interrogation.

Some historical sources say that some people of Jewish ethnicity were in charge of the Impulevičius case. After the war began, Impulevičius was freed from prison and became a commander of the TDA battalion. Then he asked for five weeks' vacation for himself, to "recover his health and his nerves." In August of 1941 Impulevičius became the commander of the 2nd TDA / Lithuanian Auxiliary Police Battalion. On October 6, this unit was sent to Belarus with much pageantry.

Petras Kubiliūnas, Lithuanian general counselor for the Nazi administration, sent his greetings to the ceremony. The Kaunas military commandant Stasys Kviecinskas was also present at the ceremony. He told the soldiers: "Departing soldiers, perform the tasks entrusted to you with resolute will, conscientiously and honorably. Always and everywhere demonstrate you are worthy of the noble name of a Lithuanian soldier, because you represent the entire Lithuanian nation."

Antanas Impulevičius, commander of the XIIth battalion. (Lithuanian Central State Archives)

The flag of the XIIth battalion. (Lithuanian Central State Archives)

WHAT HAPPENED HERE IN 1941?

The interviews below with soldiers from the Impulevičius Battalion are from the Jeff and Toby Herr Collection at the United States Holocaust Memorial Museum in Washington, DC. Film director Saulius Beržinis spoke with both of the murderers.

Battalion member Leonas Stonkus was born in Darbėnai, Lithuania, in 1921. During the Soviet occupation he and four friends tried to cross the border to Germany to look for work. They were caught by the Russians and experienced the first day of the war inside the Kaunas jail. The jailer later unlocked the cells and freed all the prisoners.

Leonas Stonkus recalls:

We went down and there, in the cafeteria, it was full of people, perhaps one and a half thousand. We were told to join the Lithuanian volunteers right away. I was thinking: My life is very sad, I should at least serve in the military . . . They told us where to go. Two of us joined the Lithuanian military volunteers. . . . We received Lithuanian Army uniforms and an armband, as a Lithuanian military volunteer. We trained for about five months. Later we were issued rifles. We guarded the train station and the airport in Šančiai. Later we suddenly received the order to go to Minsk. And that was it.

Did you take part in shootings?

They didn't press the young people harshly; they just assigned them more difficult jobs. And you didn't get money. Those who were at the shootings all the time, they were all older . . . No one knew we would have to travel to the shootings. They took us, lined the Jews up, and then you get the order: "Rifles up!" "Aim!" "Fire!" and you shoot. Those who shot got a bonus on top of their salaries for the work. They paid the most for shooting Jews.

How much did they pay?

They didn't say how much they got. At first a little, later more, and more still . . . Those who did the shooting were volunteers. The entire battalion were volunteers.

Was it possible to refuse to shoot?

It was possible. If the entire battalion had refused, hadn't shot, then our officers would have been really angry. We'd look at those officers, how awful they looked . . . I don't get it, did they receive gold? When they stood in the middle of the soldiers, ordering "Fire!" and they all shot. Everyone shot. If it's "Fire!," then he has to fire, too.

How far away were the shooters from the victims?

About ten meters.

How many people did you shoot?

Did I shoot? One. And it wasn't fatal anyway. I could not do that thing, that's all. I got sick, I trembled, I was finished.

How did the shooting proceed?

There were five shots in the magazine. You empty the five and the others come. The soldiers stood up after the Jews were brought in. Everything happened very quickly: They lined up quickly and right away ... Who buried them, I don't know— Byelorussians, or maybe there were some civilians who were paid ...

Did you see their faces?

Of the Jews? Ordinary people.

Where did you shoot?

It was straight to the chest. We didn't shoot at the head. You have to be accurate if you aim for the head. Many of the soldiers were excited and upset, doing that kind of work ...

Did they look at you?

Who, the Jews? No. They looked over there. They didn't see who was shooting.

How did you shoot?

I shot to the left side. He did not fall; he kept bending over, bending over, bending over. A petty officer was standing close by and he opened fire and then [the victim] fell down right away.

What happened after that?

Well, nothing. If you can't shoot, you withdraw, and the same day you don't enter into the formation. You don't join. Others come.

What did you do when you withdrew?

Well, I withdrew; I pointed my rifle up, I leaned on the barrel, and I stood there. A petty officer came by and said, What's this? You're not going to join the formation anymore? I said no, I could not do it anymore. I became so sick afterwards, really sick; I couldn't do it at all. [I said,] Do what you want with me, shoot me if you want. Then he said, Put your weapon down here next to all the weapons and get behind the soldiers.

So you returned home without a weapon?

Without a weapon. And straight to a jail cell. And later they interrogated me as to why I did that, why I was causing panic. I said I wasn't causing panic; I am not telling anyone that he shouldn't do this or that. I just can't do it anymore; do with me what you want—I didn't do this in my youth, and I won't do it now.

How many others were there like you who refused?

Many, it seems. It's hard to give a number; there were about twenty persons, all young. They hadn't served in the army. People from Kaunas, Plungė, Telšiai—a lot of people from Šiauliai.

Was everyone who refused punished equally?

Those who hadn't served in the army were punished equally. But whoever had been in the military and refused, that was considered more serious. They knew they wouldn't be able to make a soldier out of you. After I refused, I only did guard duty, watching the area.

Did they give you alcohol?

No. Well, maybe they gave it to the petty officers, but not to us. They were afraid. After all, we could turn around and attempt to kill the officers . . .

Did the Jews try to flee?

No. I don't know; maybe at such a moment, a person becomes paralyzed. All the people were as if they had already died. They saw why they were being brought there. To surrender their lives. Everyone seemed frozen. Nobody moved.

What about the children?

The children had no idea they would be killed. The children walked, the mothers behind them.

Was everyone undressed?

No, the children weren't undressed. Neither the women nor the children. Just the men.

Whom did they shoot first?

The men first.

Why?

So there wouldn't be any panic, you see. When they shot the men, the women would then lie down on the ground themselves, and it was over. But the children were jumping around; they had no idea at all what was going to happen there. The children did not understand their parents were no longer alive. The older ones, [whether] a girl or a boy, understood, but the younger ones kept on playing, and that's all.

They weren't frightened by the gunshots?

They weren't frightened. They weren't worried; [they] didn't understand that right here, right now, it's rest in peace for us, too. There was nothing horrible. The mothers brought the children. There was this order: Don't leave the children. Give them to your neighbor, let the neighbor bring them. They brought them to the pit together. It wasn't just soldiers shooting; there was [also] a machine gun set up.

What was the night following the shooting like?

The people who did that, well, look, at night they're singing . . . They used to bring in homemade alcohol, sold privately, and they got drunk and sang.

Did you used to go to confession?

There was a church in the center of Minsk, Byelorussian but Catholic. We used to go to church. The entire platoon went, with their weapons. Confession was together with about four or five people. Repent your sins. And then the priest crossed himself, told you to pray, and you prayed. We had a very good priest, Ignatavicius. You didn't need to speak into the priest's ear.

Why was it done that way?

I think because there was no reason to speak into that ear. If I had done something horrible, I wouldn't be forgiven. Kneel on your knees, kiss the sweet ground, and ask for God's forgiveness.

Have you told anyone you shot a man in Rudensk?

I did; when I went to confession, when I was on holiday in Darbėnai. I said I had shot one person and he died quickly, or didn't die—I can't say that [for sure]—but I didn't undertake those sorts of jobs anymore after that. And I still regret it to this day.

What did the priest tell you?

He said that that sort of sin in that sort of youth is horrible, and it seems you were forced. You didn't eagerly begin to shoot voluntarily. That's all.

Did you tell your children?

Yeah, I did. I said I joined the military. I didn't go especially so I could shoot Jews. It was volunteers for Lithuania, the battalion, that's all. It was to protect Lithuania.

I talked about it after the war. Everyone knew. I said I was in that sort of military unit and I happened to have been at those painful tragedies, where people of Jewish ethnicity were shot. It was my fate to be there, and that I happened to shoot one. They asked me, Daddy, why did you join that unit? Because I didn't have a home, [I said]. I didn't have anywhere to live; I had to join them, not to do those sorts of jobs. But if the government did that, then the government is the most guilty for this.

When you guarded Jews, did you think that perhaps they might again send you to the edge of the pit to shoot?

No; no one was going to send me. If you refused, then they [would] punish you by either the death penalty or incarceration, but they [wouldn't] dare send you to shoot again. Because the commanders weren't really sure where you would aim your shots. What if you suddenly turned around and emptied your magazine into the commander?

So you think that it was volunteers who did all the shooting?

Yes, of course it was volunteers. As if they'd force you! No one was forced.[1]

This interview was filmed on April 21, 1998.

Leonas Stonkus was convicted for his collaboration with the Nazis and served his sentence from 1945 to 1946.

In 1981 he was arrested again together with other soldiers from the Impulevičius Battalion. From the verdict of the court in the Leonas Stonkus case at the Lithuanian Special Archives (ap. 58, case file 47760/3):

In court Leonas Stonkus stated he "was in Rudensk when the Jews were shot. He shot five times. The first two shots were fired into the midst of people, while he fired the last three over the heads of the people. These three possibly could have hit and wounded people [p. 75]. The witness B. Guoga testified that Leonas Stonkus had shot at the people. He stood at the gravel quarry with his barrel aimed at the people. He shot about five to ten minutes and muzzle flashes and smoke were visible.[2]

The court meted out a rather mild punishment for Leonas Stonkus: twelve years' imprisonment. They took into account that Stonkus had served the Soviet Union as a Soviet partisan—a defender of the people— after the Great War of the Motherland.

Born in 1914, Juozas Aleksynas served in the army of independent Lithuania before joining the Impulevičius Battalion. Under the Soviets, he

---

1 Credit to: Jeff and Toby Herr Collection at the United States Holocaust Memorial Museum in Washington, DC.
2 LSA, K-1, ap. 58, b. 477603, p. 77.

was head secretary of a trade union in his village. He was twenty-eight when he participated in the mass murder operations in Belarus.

Juozas Aleksynas:

Kubiliūnas called [me] back from the reserves to serve in 1941. I was supposed to present myself at the kommandantur. He said it was for maintaining internal [military unit] order, for a half-year, to help the Germans. We guarded prisoners of war at work in the peat bogs.

When did they send you out of Lithuania?

I can't say when; I only know it was fall, toward the end of September or early October. We were driven to Minsk. They didn't say where we were going; they just put us in the cars. That was the first and last time I saw battalion commander Major Impulevičius, bidding us farewell.

How long did you stay there?

The snow let up in May, and that's when I fled.

Why did you flee?

I didn't want to fight for the Germans anymore. The Germans were no longer a true friend. We were just their tools, even though they weren't giving us orders—they just rode with us. We didn't understand their language, so our own officers gave us orders. Gecevičius was a unit commander, Plungė was a platoon commander. Of all the officers, I saw that only Gecevičius spoke German well, so he was in charge of communicating with the Germans. The orders he received, he passed on to us. We lived in Minsk—not in barracks, but separately, in small groups in rooms.

So they drove you all over Belarus?

They did.

To which cities did they post you to shoot Jews?

To all of them. Many cars drove, and the entire battalion was moved to larger cities. We rode in covered German vehicles. Nobody told us where we were being driven. The local police went through apartments and collected Jews, then herded them onto the square. Later they were sorted according to a list. The Germans kept for themselves whomever was useful, perhaps a doctor or something, perhaps an engineer, and herded the rest to the pit. The pits were already dug beyond the city limits, on slopes.

How many of these shootings did you witness?

I can no longer count. About ten, perhaps. We had to herd them from the square to the pits ourselves, and then shoot them at the end. We took small groups from the mass of people and murdered them.

Did they have things with them?

No, they were just dressed. They didn't let them take things from home. They were marched in a column, four people wide. The column became long in the larger towns. At that time some of the soldiers were already standing on the edge of the pit, and some [soldiers] were bringing them [Jews] to the pit. They were herded into the pit, laid on the ground, and then we shot them.

You shot people lying on the ground?

Lying on the ground. One group leaves [is shot], then another climbs on top, then yet another.

You didn't fill in the pit with dirt?

No. Later, toward the end, we just sprinkled some lime [on top]. Who finally buried them, I do not know. We finished shooting, and we left. We were only issued Russian rifles and Russian ammunition. The ammunition included both exploding bullets and burning bullets. Sometimes the clothes [of the victims] would catch on fire, while others were being brought in and the clothes were already on fire. Such a heavy smell comes from a burning body. It's horrible. I can't explain it to you; you have to see it.

People were being herded in and they were supposed to lie down on top of burning corpses?

Yes. They lay down, and that was the end of it. They went without any resistance at all. None of them stood at the edge of the pit and said, "I'm not going." [. . .] They got undressed, got in, and lay down.

At what spot did you need to aim?

Mainly at the chest. Or the back of the head. But there were exploding bullets, so the back of the head of the person shattered quite quickly.

How many people did you shoot during one operation?

Only the Devil knows. However many they brought, that's how many you shot. We didn't drive off until we [had] finished. They didn't bring anyone back from that group. Nobody announced that a thousand, or two, or a hundred, or however many were brought in. They went like some sort of little lambs, without any resistance.

But what about the children?

The small children were carried, the others were led. We murdered them all.

So if a mother or father was carrying a child in their arms, did they lie down together in the pit?

They did, and the child was next to the father, whose arm was placed over the child.

Did you then have to choose between shooting the father or the child?

First you shot the father. The children didn't feel any of it. Imagine for yourself: how a father would feel when his child was shot next to him? You weren't firing from an automatic weapon, [you were shooting] one bullet at the father, and another at the child.

When they used to send you to a shooting, what was your mood then?

Don't ask. You become a sort of machine. You are doing something but you don't know what it is. It is terrifying. The Germans shot rarely; mostly they used to shoot photographs.

When you were shooting, did you ever ask yourself, Why are these Jews being shot?

I don't blame anyone anymore—only God, if He exists, for allowing the murder of innocent people. And that's how I thought about it then as well.[3]

Stasys was the cook who fed the Impulevičius Battalion soldiers in the field. Stasys recalls:

At first they didn't used to say they were going to shoot. They were going to carry out "operations." They were mostly volunteers. It's not work that just anyone can do . . . It often happened that when they left the operations and came back, they didn't take any soup, so there was a lot left . . .

Why didn't they take soup?

There were times that they filled their pockets there. They would play cards, drink and party for several days.

What was the situation with the volunteers? Did they use the same people every time, or was it one group one time, another group another time?

---

3 Ibid.

There were those who were greedy, and they saw others coming back with expensive items and money, so the next time they asked to be included in the operation. There weren't a lot of people who went at first. Those who were more cowardly didn't ask to go and weren't taken along. But those who liked to gamble more, they used to request it.

Tell me how those who did go to the operations got along with those who didn't?

Those who went were happy they got loot. Those who didn't go didn't want the loot anyway. Both groups were happy . . .

This interview was filmed in 1998.

Impulevičius's soldiers usually spent their Sundays in Minsk, where they went to church. One soldier recalled:

There was a sermon at ten a.m. at the Minsk cathedral. Father Ignatavičius, who was the chaplain of the Lithuanian battalions in the east, read the sermon. During the sermon Lithuanian hymns rang out through the Minsk cathedral. The sermon ended with the national anthem. . . .

Continuing the program, the battalion choir sang several Lithuanian songs. Battalion soldiers recited several of our own poems and those of some of our poets. Later

XIIth battalion chaplain Zenonas Ignatavičius. (Lithuanian Central State Archives)

*there was a performance of "Tėvynės Aidai" [Echoes of the Fatherland] in which
lieutenant Juodys performed. The program concluded with the couplets called "Min-
sko Dzinguliukais" [Little Bells of Minsk], which featured events from the everyday
life of the Lithuanian battalion.*[4]

The "Little Bells of Minsk" singers did not have an easy life there. The
majority of the soldiers who joined the battalion in the summer of 1941
signed on for six months, but served twice as long. No one planned on
releasing them to go home to their farms and their wives and children.
The Germans didn't respond to the soldiers' requests to be relieved of
their duties, since they had already served more than a year longer than
the time they had initially signed on for.

One of the commanders of a Lithuanian self-defense battalion wrote to
the commander of a district behind the German lines in November 1942:

*When we arrived at the front in December of 1941, we were ragged, without shirts,
and some lacked shoes, but when a military task had to be carried out quickly, we
prepared ourselves, although those left on constant guard remained naked (without
shirts). Twenty-five soldiers were completely barefoot, but we came to serve. In January, 1942, we were without any winter clothing at all. But the Lithuanian performed
his duty at the front, even in extreme cold. These are the facts which testify to our
ideals.*[5]

OCTOBER 2015

We both agreed that it would be important for us to visit at least some of
the locations in which the Impulevičius Battalion carried out the murders,
so we set out on another journey, this time to Belarus.

We went to Dukara first, the first mass murder site where Lithuanian
men were sent. On October 6, 1941, the men of the battalion were sent off
in a solemn ceremony. Two days later, on October 8, these men went to
the small village of Dukara, some forty kilometers from the Belarusian
capital. When they arrived, soldiers surrounded the village and marched
the Jews to the market square for a "meeting." There they lined up the
Jews in one column and forced them to go to Recnaja (River) Street. From
there, the Jews were marched across the bridge to the large meadow near
the village. (On October 29, 2015, we saw the same stones on the road
leading to the river, the same ones from 1941.)

---

4 "Karys" (The Soldier), March 14, 1942, No. 12. From: *Masinės žudynės Lietuvoje* (Mass
Murder in Lithuania), pp. 319–20.

5 From: Rimantas Zizas, *Lietuvos kariai savisaugos batalionuose* (Lithuanian Soldiers in the
Self-Defense Battalions). From: *Lietuvoas archyvai* (Lithuanian Archives), t. 11, 1998, p. 62.

The soldiers were quite experienced killers; members of the first platoon had already murdered thousands of Lithuanian Jews in Kaunas in the Seventh Fort. They probably used exploding bullets for the first time at Dukara. According to battalion member Juozas Aleksynas, "When we used exploding bullets, the backs of the heads were blasted open very quickly." This killing operation was the very first one for platoon commander Captain Zenonas Kemzūra, but it would not be his last.

During the shooting, the bodies and the clothing of the first victims were burning, and additional people were then brought to lie on top of those already shot, layer upon layer, until the pit was full. According to Aleksynas, the battalion remained "until the job was finished and all the Jews were murdered."

After the exploding bullets blasted open the heads of 394 people, the Lithuanians together with the Germans went into the nearby forest to look for anyone who might have escaped. They found seven additional Jews. The Lithuanians murdered four of them.

In October 2015, we stand in the meadow near the small monument. The victims are most probably buried in thick forest next to the monument. This was the place where residents of Dukara were brought to bury their neighbors.

We ask two old women in Dukara about the murders, but all they could tell us was that, according to their parents, the earth at the mass murder site moved for several days. They have no idea about the killers. In their words, they were "Germans; who else?"

We are leaving Dukara and heading to Rudensk, where, according to the testimony of the soldier Leonas Stonkus, he shot a single bullet at the victims for the first and only time.

Rudensk is a small village near the railway tracks, not far from Minsk. Two days after the shooting in Dukara, a different platoon, this time the second, was sent to Rudensk. This was their first mass murder ever. In Lithuania the platoon had been assigned to guard the airport and other locations. This was the first time that their commander, Juozas Krikštaponis—the nephew of the president of independent Lithuania, Antanas Smetona—would give the command "Fire!" to his soldiers.

All of them arrived in Rudensk by commercial train. Some of the Lithuanian soldiers carried out the orders of their superiors, to surround the town and guard it so that no Jews would escape. Others, together with German gendarmes, went into the homes of the Jews to arrest men, women, and children, bringing them to the space in front of the post office. The victims were forced to march to the mass murder site near the railway tracks, near the local sand or gravel quarry, where the pits had already been dug.

Members of the second platoon, led by their officers, shot the victims. Around fifteen men from the second platoon refused to shoot, and their commander, Krikštaponis, ordered them to step aside. Apparently, Leonas Stonkus was among these men. According to his testimony, he shot only once, and wounded a middle-aged Jew. "I shot to the left side," Stonkus recalled. "He clearly did not fall; he kept bending over, bending over, bending over. A petty officer was standing close by and he opened fire and then he fell down right away."

After this shot, Leonas Stonkus moved aside. Krikštaponis allowed him to do so. After the Soviet invasion, this officer, Juozas Krikštaponis, became a Lithuanian partisan. Several years ago, he was declared a "hero" of Lithuania, and a monument in his honor was built in Ukmergė, where a square was also named for him. We saw this monument.

On October 29, 2015, we stand on the square in front of the post office where hundreds of the Jews of Rudensk had been gathered prior to their murder. We seek assistance from a local resident to find the site of the mass murder. At one of the shops we see a man who apparently had had a few drinks too many, but nonetheless, he gladly volunteers to take us to the place of the murder. "I have nothing to do anyway," the man said. He takes us to the quarry near the village, an ideal site for the murder.

Mass murder site in Rudensk.
(Rūta Vanagaitė)

On the edge of a deep pit, there is a fence to mark the border of the local farmers' land where they grow potatoes. This is the very spot where the killers stood, when they shot the seventy Jews of Rudensk.

There is a monument on the spot, at the base of which we found an old wreath of artificial flowers with the inscription "To the heroes of the Great Patriotic War—from the workers of the collective farm." Our guide does not know who the killers were. Nobody in the village knows, he says. We offer our guide 13,000 Belarusian rubles, less than a euro, which he initially refuses, saying that he hasn't done this for money. "I went with you because nobody ever visits this mass murder site."

One place that is particularly important to us is the town of Slutzk, where we want to commemorate the seventy-fourth anniversary of the tragedy that took place there on October 28, 1941. Over eight thousand people were murdered there. Impulevičius brought all three platoons of his battalion to do the job. Shocked by the cruelty of the killers, German *Gebietskommissar* Heinrich Carl wrote to his superior in a secret letter: "I beg of you, by all means, please never send this battalion to our area again." Like everywhere in Belarus, there are no signs to direct us to the mass murder site.

It is getting dark when we find an elderly woman near a market in Slutzk. She had just finished selling her apples from her country home, and tells us that the mass murder site is twelve kilometers away, in the village of Selisce. This old woman, named Evgenya, speaks with some difficulty, after having suffered a stroke. She lives alone on her pension of 100 euros a month. In Soviet times, Evgenya worked as a librarian in Selisce village, so every year on Victory Day, May 9, she was supposed to organize the pioneers to honor "the victims of the fascists."

Finally we find the site. Apparently nothing has changed here in the past fifty years. There are the same artificial flowers and the inscription, "To honor the soldiers—liberators." While Belarusian pioneer youth apparently still come here, they have no idea what really happened here in 1941—who the killers were, and who their victims were. According to Heinrich Carl's letter, some of the victims in Slutzk were buried alive, and several hours after the shooting they were able to crawl out of the pit.

The Lithuanian battalion members shot no fewer than 2,250 people at the site.

On October 30, two days after the shooting in Slutzk, the soldiers of the Impulevičius Battalion were brought to Kletzk, where they were supposed to murder five thousand people.

Olga, a worker at the local history museum, shows us the mass murder site. She is so sorry to say that there is nothing in her museum on the history of the Jewish community of the town, or on the Holocaust. The murder pit is in the middle of town, next to a beautifully preserved Orthodox cemetery on a hill.

The mass murder site is in the valley. We see an enormous pit and a small monument to the "peace-loving people killed by the German fascists." Olga has never heard that among the German fascists were many young Lithuanian men brought to her country to murder the Jews.

Next, we are heading toward Minsk, to see a mass murder site in a suburb of the city. It is called Maly Trostinec, where 220,000 Jews were incarcerated and murdered. The president of the Republic of Belarus, Aleksander Lukashenko, recently dedicated an impressive monument to the victims. Yes, it's impressive. Big and ugly. No sign of who was murdered here, when, how, or how many. The victims are referred to as "people."

We see a few boys who are probably around twelve years old or so, passing by. We ask them what they know about this place. The boys are very eager to tell us the story that they were taught at school.

"This is where our partisans and underground fighters were murdered," they tell us.

"Were those partisans Jews?" we ask.

"No, no, they were our people—Belarusians. Some of the victims were kids. The fascists kept them here and fed these kids beetroots."

"Why beetroots?"

"Because they wanted to take their blood. They needed the kids' blood for their experiments. Our history teacher told us all this."

Then one of the kids asks us where we are from. Upon hearing our reply, he says, with admiration, "It must be damn cool there in Lithuania."

Before leaving Belarus, we search for information in the regional and state archives. The KGB archives are inaccessible, unlike in Lithuania. There is just some general information in all of the other archives, so it is obvious why Belarusians do not know that more than fifteen thousand of the Jews of their country were murdered—not by German fascists, but by ordinary Lithuanian men who did not know that they were being sent to Belarus to kill, but who killed anyway.

The most shocking discovery in the testimonies of these killers was that the majority of these men did not even know the names of the Belarusian towns to which they had been brought, where Jews had been living for ages. Rūta's people were brought to these towns in order to take the Jewish families out of their homes and then murder them a few minutes later. The command was given to them in Lithuanian: *Ugnis!*

The very last word on earth that more than fifteen thousand Belarusian Jews heard was in Rūta's mother tongue.

IV

THE HELL
OF VILNIUS/VILNA

20

Portraits of the Witnesses

At the end of the nineteenth century, 63,996 Jews were living in Vilnius (41.4 percent of the local population).

Before the Shoah—around 57,000.

WHAT HAPPENED HERE IN 1941?

The Special Unit, which was better known by its Lithuanian name, *Ypatingas būrys*, was created directly under the command of the Gestapo in July of 1941. Most of the commanders and members were Lithuanians, but there were also a few Russians and Poles. Initially, when the unit's headquarters was on Šventaragio Street in Vilnius, where the Lithuanian Interior Ministry is currently housed, those youth seeking to join would come and submit an application. They didn't need to sign any sort of oath. After the unit moved to Vilniaus Street No. 12, oaths were required.

At the beginning, about one hundred men served in the unit, but in the second half of 1941, and later in the war, there were somewhere between thirty and forty. According to statements made by members under interrogation, the men in the unit received books of food-ration coupons with which they could enter any restaurant or cafe in Vilnius and present the coupons as payment. The men received salaries as well as food rations, including raisins and, once a week, vodka. Starting in November 1941, the commander of the squad was Balys Norvaiša.

The main area of operations for the Special Unit was Ponar. Many of these members had families or girlfriends. Veronika, a girlfriend of

Member of the Special Unit Vladas Kliukas. (Lithuanian Special Archives)

Special Unit member Vladas Kliukas (born in 1923), testified that she began her acquaintance with the murderer when she was eighteen and he was nineteen. Kliukas and Vladas Butkūnas lived together at Basanavičiaus Street No. 15 in Vilnius.

Veronika recalled:

Vladas Kliukas invited me to the apartment in which he lived together with Vladas Butkūnas. When we began our friendship I learned that he was serving in the Special Unit. During a session of drinking they boasted that they had shot citizens of Jewish ethnicity at Ponar, and had a lot of Jewish valuables. I noticed Butkūnas, Kliukas, and Čeponis had taken a lot of money and weren't responsible about how they spent it. They said they drank a lot of vodka and would then shoot citizens of Jewish ethnicity. They usually got drunk at Stasys Čeponis's apartment and then got into fistfights with each other, and shot a pistol.

I was dating Vladas Kliukas until about the fall of 1943, but later, when I became pregnant from Kliukas, he didn't visit me anymore and the relationship ended. Besides which, as I noticed, he had many girlfriends at the same time he was with me.[1]

Did Vladas support his girlfriend financially? It seems so: "He gave money, and once he brought me a blouse and a skirt," Veronika stated. Vladas and Veronika's baby was born but died before the age of two months.

Before the war, Ponar was a placid suburb of Vilnius surrounded by pine trees, where city residents came to enjoy the summer. A railroad line and the Vilnius-Grodno highway passed almost right next to Ponar. Just nine kilometers away from the city center, people could come by road, rail, or on foot. In 1941 the Soviets began setting up liquid fuel tanks there, digging seven large pits connected by ditches for laying pipelines in the ground. The five-square-kilometer territory was surrounded by barbed-wire fences. When the Germans selected Ponar as a mass murder site, the territory became known as "the base."

The Ponar base was situated right next to the railroad and residential homes. Railroad watchman Jankowski, who sat on guard in a booth next to the crossing, recalls:

[There were] two large pits twenty-five meters in diameter and five meters deep, and several pits of smaller diameter, and the channels between the pits were filled with the bodies of those shot. A German officer whom the murderers called "chief" gave the commands. He was a blond man of medium stature with glasses. When they brought the usual group of victims, the German and someone else arrived in a passenger car.[2]

Mečys Butkus, one of the members of the Special Unit, said under interrogation:

I was supposed to compile a list of the Jews who were brought to Ponar to be shot. There was a table placed at the entrance to the pit and I sat there making lists of those who were brought from that pit and led to another pit to be shot. I wrote down the surname, [first] name, and date of birth. That's why I remember there were two thousand people entered on the lists.

The main chronicler of the Ponar mass murders was Kazimierz Sakowicz, a Polish journalist who published the weekly newspaper *Przegląd Gospodarski* in Vilnius before the war. He lost his press and apartment in Vilnius during the Soviet occupation and moved to a small house in Ponar. The house was very close to the killing grounds. From the first days

---

1 LSA, K-1, ap. 46, b. 4914, p. 126.
2 LSA, K-1, ap. 58, b. 47746/3, t. 2, p. 20.

of the mass murders, Sakowicz observed events from a window under the eaves and secretly kept a diary. He placed the pages of the diary in empty glass bottles and buried them in his yard.

Kazimierz Sakowicz:

July 1943

Myszka—small, gray, with floppy ears and a long tail. The bitch barks terribly in the evening, even until late, but can be seen in the morning as she returns from the base. Och! The children of Jankowski and Rudzinski know Myszka because they herded cattle at the base; often they frightened her away from the pit. She digs up earth in the pit, then tears up the remains of the clothing of the victims and eats them. She tears up breasts, stomachs, legs—whatever she digs out: faces, cheeks. She is a small monster. But Siniuca is proud of possessing such a little monster. And Siniuca is himself of Jewish descent. Perhaps the bitch buries his very close relatives.

July and August 1943

That Myszka digs up corpses does not surprise anyone because they buried them badly (it's a waste of time to bury them deep). In general everything is only just covered, even if they were killed last year, so there is a horrible stench in the base. Everywhere one can see pieces of discarded clothing—men's, children's, women's, various bits of the wardrobe, underwear, women's slippers, men's caps, gloves, shirts, socks, some books, handkerchiefs, a coat and everything, or almost everything, unraveled by a hand searching for "treasures" hidden in the clothing.

Lithuanian members of the Special Unit in Vilnius. (Lithuanian Special Archives)

The route of Myszka's wandering and returns is always the same. She goes through the hole in Sieniuc's fence, toward the top [of the hill], then she wanders onto the railway track. She can be seen when she runs across the track, then she disappears from sight and after a while reappears at the base, on the sandy yellow road that cuts through and disappears among the trees. Occasionally she brings something when she returns. Once—it was in August 1943—she carried an intestine, but, terrified, dropped it down before Siniuca's yard. Children placed it on Siniuca's fence.[3]

Kazimierz Sakowicz's diary ends on November 6, 1943. His relatives say he kept the diary until his death on July 5, 1944, when he was shot riding a bicycle home from Vilnius to Ponar.

The glass bottles with Sakowicz's entries lay in the garden many years until they were discovered in 1952 when someone was digging up the ground there. Neighbors who believed gold might be buried there continued to dig, but only uncovered bottles with pieces of paper in them, and turned them over to a museum.

Sakowicz's *Ponary Diary* was published in Polish in 1999, in Hebrew in 2000, in German in 2003, and in English in 2005. It was published in Lithuanian as *Panerių dienoraštis* in 2012. The print run was five hundred copies.

---

3 Kazymierz Sakowicz, *Ponary Diary, 1941–1943: A Bystander's Account to Mass Murder*, edited by Itzhak Arad, New Haven: Yale University Press, 2005.

21

Portrait of a Student

Instead of messing around and doing nothing, the students at the Vilnius First School of Crafts spent the summer of 1941 working for the *Ypatingas būrys*, or Special Unit. Some of these students were sixteen years old. One of the craft school's students, future metalsmith Vladas Paulaitis, tells the story:

> I was in Vilnius in the summer of 1941 and lived at the craft school dormitory on Filaretų Street. Wanting to find some work during the summer vacation, I went to some sort of business organization and they assigned me work as a cashier at a food shop on Užupio Street. I worked there about two or three weeks but I made mistakes and I was fired.
>
> Around the middle of July 1941 I met an acquaintance of mine. He told me there was this work place where you could make good money. He explained to me that people were needed to collect expensive items from citizens of Jewish ethnicity, things such as rings, watches, and other gold items. He explained that during the collection you had to fill out some sort of documents, but that it was possible to take some things for yourself without recording them on the documents. Encouraged by that acquaintance, I decided to go work there. He gave me the address where I had to go to apply.
>
> It was on Vilnius Street, but I don't remember the building number. There on the second floor of a brick building was the so-called Special Unit. At first I didn't know it was called this, but I found out after they issued me an identification document showing I was a member of the Special Unit. I found out that Vladas Stavaras, who was also a student at the Vilnius First School of Crafts, and was studying metalsmithing with me in our group, was already part of the unit. A bit later, I noticed there were other students from the school in the unit.

The craft school students who belonged to the unit ate at the craft school dormitory on Filaretų Street. We students received no salaries for serving in the unit. I remained in the unit for about a month, then I left and continued my studies at the craft school.

Right from the beginning, when we joined the unit, they did not give us any guns. Our job was to evict citizens of Jewish ethnicity from their apartments to the street where soldiers from some sort of Lithuanian battalion took charge of guarding them and marched them in groups to Lukiškės Prison. . . . Then later they issued us Russian rifles. We had to march citizens of Jewish ethnicity from Lukiškės to Ponar, where they were later shot.

We, the members of the Special Unit who were armed with guns, went to the prison, but did not go inside, but rather waited at the gate. There were also a large number of soldiers from some sort of Lithuanian battalion who arrived at the prison, wearing the uniforms of the former bourgeois Lithuanian army. They were not armed with Russian rifles, but were armed with some kind which I do not now recall.

In the prison yard the citizens of Jewish ethnicity, men, women, and children, were lined up in columns, and when they began to exit the gate we, members of the Special Unit and the battalion soldiers, surrounded them on all sides and marched them to Ponar. We carried guns in our hands. At the head and tail of the column there were uniformed soldiers. I did not notice any soldiers dressed in German uniforms. Each time several hundred people were marched out, but I don't know the exact number. I don't recall which streets we marched them down. I do remember that in Ponar we had to cross the railroad, and right after the crossing there was a forest which is where the mass shooting site was.

There were several large pits dug there which the Soviet army units had dug for whatever reason before the war. As I recall they were pits with a diameter reaching twenty or more meters. We marched the condemned to one of the pits and they were held there before the shooting. Then we took groups from that pit to another pit and shot them there. The condemned were supposed to leave their things in the pit where they were held before being shot, things which they usually had taken tied up in bundles. In front of the pit where they were to be shot, they had to undress to their underwear, and only then were they taken into the pit and shot. . . . They didn't take us craft school students to do the shooting; instead, we were ordered to guard the condemned. Other unit members went to the shooting site and shot the condemned there.[1]

Special Unit commander J. Tumas:

I want to say that all Special Unit members took part in the shootings, because this unit was formed for exactly that purpose. If one day a member of the Special Unit stood guard over the condemned, then on another day that same member would shoot them. Some sort of Special Unit members, who did no shooting at all, did not exist.[2]

---

1 LSA, K-1, ap. 58, b. 20046/3, t. 2. pp. 64–65.
2 LSA, K-1, ap. 58, b. 47746/3, t. 2, p. 9.

22

Portrait of a Postman

One of the longest-serving members in the Special Unit was Vilnius Central Post Office letter carrier Vincas Sausaitis. Unable to flee to the West in 1944, Sausaitis changed his name and lived using forged documents. He was arrested in 1948 and sentenced to twenty-five years' imprisonment in a labor camp for transporting and guarding Jews during the Ponar mass murders. After he received amnesty in 1955, he returned to Lithuania, started a new family, and had children. During the interrogations of other members of the Special Unit in Poland, new facts came to light, and Vincas Sausaitis was arrested again on July 26, 1977, on suspicion of not only transporting Jews to Ponar, but of actually shooting them. Asked why he didn't admit to shooting Jews during the 1948 interrogation, Sausaitis gave a simple and clear answer: "I didn't say because no one asked me."

Vincas Sausaitis recalled:

The first shooting went like this: When they brought the condemned, they first put wedding rings, watches, and gold and paper money in Weiss's briefcase. Then they all undressed to their underwear and took off their shoes, throwing everything in a pile. Then Weiss ordered them to climb down a ladder into the pit, stand themselves in a single line on top of the corpses already there, and turn away. After that, after the condemned obeyed his orders, Weiss positioned us—that is, the Special Unit members and about ten more German soldiers—along the edge of the pit. We were all armed with army rifles.

I stood in the line of shooters, second from the first person. Weiss warned us not to shoot without being ordered. We all loaded our rifles and aimed at the heads of the condemned standing in the pit, and waited for Weiss's order to shoot. I aimed

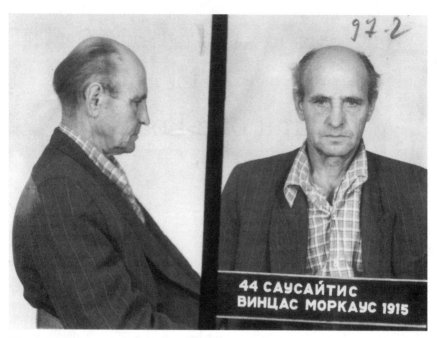

Vincas Sausaitis in prison in 1977. (Lithuanian Special Archives)

at the temple of the second condemned person standing in line in the pit. Together with me, aiming to shoot the condemned, stood Čeponis, Butkūnas, Granickas, and others. Weiss gave the order to fire, waving his hand at the same time. Together with the others I shot, and saw how the person at whose temple I had been aiming with my rifle fell into the pit.

Some of the condemned were only wounded. Weiss finished them off with his pistol. Then Weiss gave the order to bury the corpses. I buried them together with the Special Unit members and German soldiers. Then the Germans threw the clothes and shoes of the people who had been shot into a truck and we returned to Vilnius.

Besides this time, I personally shot condemned people several more times at Ponar. About three times, if I'm not mistaken. I cannot say now how many I shot during my period of service in the Special Unit, since no one counted the number of victims.

The method of shooting the condemned was the following. Those brought there were undressed to their underwear and valuable objects were collected from them: wedding rings, watches, money. Sometimes the shooters stood on the edge of the pit, but when they were shooting in the larger pits, then they were there in the pit with the victims. They lined the condemned up in a single column with their backs turned toward the shooters. Sometimes they themselves climbed down into the pit by ladder (when there was shooting in the smaller pits), but they were led by one of the Special Unit members into the larger pits. Before entering the pit they were ordered to hold each other's hands. As a rule ten of the condemned were shot at once. This same *number of shooters was allocated from members of the Special Unit. Weiss, Norvaiša, or Major Tumas usually gave the order to shoot. After the shootings we didn't always bury the bodies. As a rule they were left unburied until the next day's shootings. Those condemned the next day buried them, after which they were then shot.*

Members of the Special Unit shot people in other locations besides Ponar. I heard about their field trips from them themselves, but I don't remember the names of those locations. I only shot condemned people at Ponar. I didn't shoot them at other locations.

I don't remember the year, when I and other members of the Special Unit, whose names I cannot now recall, went to Eišiškės and Trakai. I don't remember what we did in Eišiškės, but it seems to me we didn't shoot people there. In Trakai, if I remember correctly, members of the Special Unit together with local police shot condemned people. I didn't shoot that time, but stood guard at the shooting location. I do not remember the number of those shot at Trakai, their ages, or other circumstances of the shooting.

Question: *What do you know about the use of alcoholic beverages during the shootings in Ponar?*

Answer: *During the shooting of people at Ponar the shooters, members of the Special Unit, frequently drank vodka. They drank it before shooting people. As I remember it, Special Unit chief Weiss supplied it at the shooting location. I understood that the Germans gave Special Unit members vodka to drink before the shootings so that they would shoot the condemned without becoming disgusted, so they'd be braver during the shooting. The box of vodka was placed several meters away from the shooting pit, on the edge where the shooters, members of the Special Unit, stood. They used to go to the box, drink vodka, then shoot the condemned.*

I want to say they didn't always bring vodka to the Ponar shooting site. They supplied it when there were many condemned to be shot. When I shot condemned people at Ponar, there was no vodka at the shooting site.[1]

A report on the arrested individual: "Attitude toward work: negative; works jobs for personal gain."

Entry in medical report: "Emotionally unstable, very quick to tears."

The last words of Vincas Sausaitis at his trial on February 16, 1978:

I am sorry I committed such heinous crimes against the Soviet order and all humanity. The executioners ruined my life and stained my conscience. . . . I think I am needed by my family, my children need me. I went there where I could earn a bit of bread. Please have mercy on my children.

Excerpts from Vincas Sausaitis's last letter to the Supreme Court:

For me, as an average uneducated village boy who had ended up in the city for the first time, and with such a group of bandits—mainly officers, commanders, petty officers, and other trained murderers—so I didn't understand the situation at all, what was happening there, I thought perhaps that's how things should be during

---

1 LSA, K-1, ap. 58, b. 47746/3, t. 2, pp. 177–88.

The victims. (Lithuanian Central State Archives)

wartime. . . . But I didn't serve in the military, so I had no understanding at all of the military's work. . . . I followed orders; if there was no way left for me to avoid that bloody work, I always requested of Tumas the same thing, but more often Norvaiša and Lukošius, because they relieved me of duty because I couldn't face the suffering and the blood. I frequently became sick from it . . . There were those who liked to drink, especially Lukošius, so sometimes I used to bring him a bottle of something, so when I made the request I was relieved of duty and put on guard duty, and often I didn't even show up for work.[2]

On April 28, 1978, Vincas Sausaitis was executed by a firing squad in Minsk. He was the last member of the Special Unit to be punished in this manner.

---

2 Ibid., pp. 352–53.

23

Dreams of a Killer

Vincas Sausaitis recorded his dreams in prison from March to April as he awaited his execution. This was in 1978. His descriptions of the dreams are still there, in a small envelope in his case file:

March 11

It seems Father taught me a poem of some kind in the morning, and I put it to song: "The feet have frozen, the hands and head are stilled . . ."

March 17

I dreamt I was in my yard and I remembered the cows hadn't been put out to pasture. I opened the barn doors and let them out. It was all dirty, as if it was not ours. And the fence was all broken up, and I listened: A young bull was bellowing. So I let him out, too, some sort of small black one. And I wanted to shoot some person; I was walking through some sort of ruins and aiming to shoot. Later, he went out into the road and there I shot at the person several times but completely missed him. And I took a large louse from my head and crushed it.

March 21

1. *I dreamt I went out into some corridor to urinate. And the corridor was so unclean, full of all these piles, but I stood in between and didn't get my shoes dirty.*
2. *It seems Jonas cut my hair. I said, Don't cut [it] too short. He said he would just give me a trim, but he didn't cut at all, just cut away from the ears and shaved my throat with a machine. At first it hurt, and I said, Don't press that hard, and then it didn't hurt. I looked good.*
3. *It seems Petraitis's Angelė ran up to me naked—she was so beautiful—and then [she] ran away again. Algirdas's Marcelė lay on our bed as though one of the condemned, so thin and pale, and I lay down on her. I don't remember if I got up, but it seems as if I got up.*

181

March 22

I dreamt: I was, it seems, at home, and an interrogator was interrogating a person, saying, Don't bother me, and I left the room and screamed, saying I had to get dressed, and as I went I slammed the door several times, but it wouldn't close. I went through the snow, and it was so clean . . .

March 23

I dreamt, it seems, I was eating large flour pancakes with my daughter, big white pancakes, and I ate only half of them, the thinner half . . . There was water, very dirty; I didn't drink it, I just stood and watched. And I lay down in some house like my own, and on my left hand there were two cuts. It seems my father was going to beat me for something, but this man said he shouldn't, because both incisions were of the exact same length and were already almost done healing, and didn't hurt. Then I went up to my father, my father was so big, and didn't seem like my father—and I began to apologize so he wouldn't beat me, and it seems he forgave me, and I cried.

Before [my] trial I dreamt Friday that some sort of ball was being prepared in our kitchen, but we neither drank nor ate. Two folded tablecloths were placed on the clean table. Jonas gave me a white shirt, but I said, It will be warm, so Julė brought me a checkered one, but not completely new, and I put it on. As I sat at the table I washed my hands, but they were not completely clean, some sort of spots remained, and I sat down, unhappy.

Before my trial I gave my father a white rooster without a head, but it was still alive, and Father vanished with the rooster. Pulling a board from the fence, I squirmed into a small hole; it was quite nice, and [I] waded through clean water.

April 13

I dreamt I was going through a riverbed and I climbed up this steep sandy bank. Pulling myself up on tree branches I came to a beautiful forest. I stood by a beautiful thin pine tree, without branches. A rabbit ran through the field; I shot at it, but missed. The rabbit jumped into a bush. I pressed it down with a stick and pulled it out by the tail. It turned out it was a small, black cat. It ate two dead mice. I didn't take it home.

April 14

I dreamt that I had come home. I spoke with Julė, but couldn't see her. I said I needed to shave because I would have to say farewell to everyone. I took the razor blades in hand; they were all old, I took one in my palm, but I didn't shave. I told my son to put the blades in place. He did, sitting on the sofa, looking so handsome. I went to him and kissed him over and over again. He began to cry.

Sausaitis's last poem:

> *In memory of the orphans who will be left without a father*

> *The hands and feet got stiff, the head got stiff*
> *But where are my little children*
> *Who protected me . . .*
> *The spring will come*
> *The little flowers will bloom*
> *But my stiff body*

Will lie in the grave.
The world will scream
About my horrible death
But in my breast
My heart will no longer beat.

Don't wait because it won't come
Daddy's not coming back
Because the yellow sand of the grave
Will cover my eyes
Forgive me for this
That I was bad
Just don't forget
That I raised you.

Note attached to the poem:

Honorable director,
Please don't destroy this poem, and give it to my children.
Please grant this request of mine.[1]

The poem was obviously not sent to the killer's children. Do they even know about it?

---

1 LSA, K-1, ap. 58, b. 47746/3, t. 4, envelope 98-57.

24

Portraits of the Victims

In August of 1944, after the Soviet Army entered Vilnius, an exhumation of the human remains of those murdered from 1941 to 1944 in the six pits at Ponar was carried out. The remains were numbered and described in detail in the exhumation report.

What was left of the victims, the Jews of Vilna, the Jerusalem of the North?

The findings of the report are as follows:

No. 9. *Male corpse with fractured and broken skull. Some bones missing. Civilian clothing: gray suit, shoes. Passport found in pocket, name illegible. Born in 1920.*

No. 24. *Corpse of a 20-year-old female. Clothes: cotton blouse, machine-woven underwear, rough leather skirt, silk stockings, women's shoes. Two gunshot entry wounds, right side of forehead, right side of back of neck, both 0.7 cm. One 8 x 6 cm exit wound at right temple under the skin where a 0.8 cm bullet was discovered. Other bullet discovered in mouth cavity.*

No. 26. *Corpse of a female, [age] 20 or younger. Clothes: machine-woven blouse, crêpe de chine dress, leather belt, shirt, underwear, stockings, women's shoes, cotton gauze scarf on head. Dark brown hair, up to 20 cm. Entry wound on right temple, 0.8 cm in size, exit wound at base of left orbital socket where a 0.8 cm bullet was found. Mammaries well developed.*

No. 36. *Corpse of a 50-year-old woman. Clothes: sweater, silken underwear, two skirts, one shoe where 1,000 marks were discovered in the padding. One tooth in mouth.*

Exhumation in Ponar, 1944. (Lithuanian Central State Archives)

No. 68. *Corpse of a girl under [age] 4. Clothes: short white dress, shirt, stockings, women's shoes. Skull and face bones unharmed.*

No. 78. *Male corpse; impossible to determine age. Clothes: shirt, underwear, socks, shoes, head missing.*

No. 80. *Corpse of a man of about 70 years old. Clothes: undershirt, underpants, shoes. Skull broken: hole there about 18 x 15 cm.*

No. 117. *Corpse of a girl, 4 or 5 years old. Clothes: shirt, underpants. Bullet entered from right side of forehead, a second through the right temple, both exit holes at rear base of skull.*

No. 123. *Corpse of a 12- or 13-year-old boy. Clothes: black cotton trousers, in the pocket of which were a notepad, pencil, and pencil sharpener. Base of skull fractured and broken.*

No. 192. *Corpse of an elderly woman with long gray hair. Clothes: coat, dress, two shirts, leotard, stockings, boots. Lower right jaw missing.*

And so on, to number 522. The report is eighty-three case-file pages long. The conclusion on the final page:

After exhuming 486 corpses from pits 1, 2 and 3, further investigation was halted because the cause of death was repeated over and over and is clear.[1]

---

1 LSA, K-1, ap. 58, b. 47746/3, t. 4, pp. 177–250.

Ponar victims. (Lithuanian Central State Archives)

Date: August 23, 1944.

Signatures: Senior medical expert from the Third Belarusian Front and six pathologist-anatomists.

25

Portrait of a Corpse-Burner

In the fall of 1943 the Gestapo began covering up the evidence of the mass murders at Ponar. A new pit eight meters deep was dug, covered with a roof, and bunks and a kitchen were set up inside. At the end of 1943, guards commanded by Vilnius Ghetto Gestapo officer Eugen Faulhaber brought about eighty Jews and Soviet POWs there. They were forced to live in the pit and perform "special work of state significance" — namely, to exhume and burn the corpses already there. The Jewish and Soviet prisoners dug the corpses up and stacked them in four- to five-meter-high pyramids for burning. The smell of burning human flesh lingered, polluting the environs of Ponar for a long time afterward.[1]

Avraham Blazer fled the Ponar killing grounds on October 13, 1941, and was returned there in November 1943. Blazer testifies:

When we arrived at Ponar all of us were chained together. Our job was to dig up all the corpses buried from the beginning of the mass executions and to burn them in specially prepared bonfires. The work was set up like this: Fifteen people cut firewood for the bonfires. Ten people dug up corpses and hooked them using special hooks 1.5 meters long and 25 centimeters across, with sharpened ends. They had to bury the end of the hook in the body of the exhumed corpse and use the hook to pull the body from the pit. Sometimes we found mummified corpses instead of rotten ones, and in those cases we could determine the hair color.

We pulled the really decayed bodies out in pieces—the head separately, arms and legs separately, and so on. Ten people worked with stretchers and two people carried a single stretcher on which a single [corpse] or two corpses were placed. Two people

---
1 Arūnas Bubnys, *Mirties konvejeris Paneriuose: budeliai ir aukos*. From: Kazimieras Sakow-iczius, *Panerių dienoraštis, 1941–1943* (Ponar Diary, 1941–1943), Vilnius: LGGRTC, 2012, pp. 17–18.

The structure for the burning of the corpses at Ponar. (Lithuanian Special Archives)

constantly tended the bonfires upon which the corpses were placed. We placed the corpses in rows and poured gasoline over each row. One person with a 2-meter-long fire poker constantly tended the fires, making sure the flames burned in the right places, and removing the ashes.

We removed the bodies of eighteen thousand men, women, and children from the first pit, and the majority of their heads were mangled from exploding bullets. The first pit was where the victims of the liquidation of the second Vilnius Ghetto were buried. There were many Poles whom we recognized from the crucifixes on their chests. There were also priests, which we saw from their clothing. Most of the Poles had their hands tied behind their backs with cords, belts, often barbed wire. Some of the corpses were naked, some were half-naked, others wore only socks.

From the fourth pit we exhumed eight thousand corpses, all young people, often with eyes blindfolded or heads covered.

In the fifth pit, whose dimensions were 21 to 30 meters across and 6 meters deep, there were about twenty-five thousand corpses. Here we found the residents of the shelter and the patients who were brought here with the medical personnel; we recognized this from the patients' gowns. The children from the orphanage were also shot in this same pit.

We exhumed a total of about sixty-eight thousand corpses from the eight pits.[2]

---

2 Testimony of Avraham Blazer to the Extraordinary Commission, August 15, 1944. From: *Masinės žudynės Lietuvoje, 1941–1944: Dokumentų rinkinys. I dalis* (Mass Murder in Lithuania, 1941–1944: Documents), Vilnius: Mintis, 1965, p. 167.

On the night of April 15, 1944, thirteen of the corpse-burners escaped by digging a tunnel about thirty meters long out of the pit. Eleven of the escapees joined the Soviet partisans in the Rūdninkai Forest. A group of Vilnius Jews was brought to Ponar to replace those who had fled, and they continued the work of burning corpses right up until almost the end of the German occupation. When they had completed the task, all of them were shot.

26

+

The Fates of the Killers

According to witness Juozas Mekišius, questioned in Poland, in total about five hundred people served in the Special Unit over four years. Several Special Unit members hid in Poland living under assumed names, until they were arrested in the 1970s. Vladas Butkus, who lived in Poland under the name Vladislavas Butkūnas, jumped out of a window during his first interrogation and injured himself, and was later convicted and received the death penalty. In total, twenty members of the Special Unit were executed in Poland, Byelorussia, and Lithuania.

Some Special Unit members were punished not for the mass murders which they denied or omitted from their testimonies, but for guarding and transporting the victims to the killing sites. The charges against some of them were renewed after new facts came to light; they were later convicted, and received much harsher punishments.

Some members of the Special Unit who were sentenced to twenty-five years in labor camps served less than that, and after 1990, they were rehabilitated by the Lithuanian Prosecutor's Office. They received a certificate with the following text signed by Prosecutor General Artūras Paulauskas: This is to certify that [name] "was illegally and unfairly repressed and is not guilty of crimes against the Republic of Lithuania, and his rights are restored. The repressed person is allocated compensation to be paid by the local municipality, and his property is returned." One member of the Special Unit worked as an orchestra conductor and artistic director at cultural centers after the war.

A significant portion of the members of the unit fled together with the German Army to the West, and later emigrated to the United States, Canada, Australia, or the U. K. They died of old age, most likely surrounded by their loving children and grandchildren. The man whose face is on the cover of this book, Balys Norvaiša, is rumored to have emigrated to the United States, although according to one of his relatives, he was killed near Dresden in a bombing raid before the war ended.

The most fascinating fate befell those members of the unit who, according to top-secret KGB documents, "belonged to the agency network" or "were turned into agents," or were simply called "Agent Jonas." What did the KGB offer them? A lighter sentence? The cook at the Special Unit cafeteria also found work as a KGB agent—"Agent Irina." One of the members of the Unit, Vladas Korsakas, was rehabilitated in 1990 and got his property back, along with some financial compensation.

One member of the Special Unit by the last name of Ivinskis ended his life by suicide. During the shooting operations at Ponar, he shot himself in the stomach and died immediately thereafter at a hospital. Is that what really happened? Other testimonies say he was just cleaning his rifle.

SPECIAL UNIT ACTIVITY STATISTICS

1941–1944, Vilnius, Paneriai—Up to 70,000 Victims

One fortnight in 1941:

  September 22, Naujoji Vilnia: 1,159 victims
  September 24, Varėna: 1,767 victims
  September 25, Jašiūnai: 575 victims
  September 27, Eišiškės: 3,446 victims
  September 30, Trakai: 1,446 victims
  October 6, Semeliškės: 962 victims
  October 7–8, Švenčionėliai: 3,476 victims

27

✛

The Last Day

Our journey is ending. We are visiting a place right outside Vilnius in the area of Naujoji Vilnia. There is a hill called Plikas, or Bald Hill, next to which, on September 22, 1941, the Special Unit, with the "poet" participating, shot 1,159 Jews. Before they were shot, the Jews were held at the Veliučionys manor, now a children's institution, which hasn't been repaired since probably Czarist times. It has been in existence since 1900, and is now called the Children's Socialization Center, housing children whom regular orphanages and children's homes can't handle. During Czarist times boys aged ten to sixteen from Vilnius, Kaunas, Grodno, and the Minsk *guberniya* were brought here, according to the center's web page. After World War I, the place was turned into an agricultural training center for Jewish boys. This manor was one of the possible places for the Vilna ghetto suggested by the Vilnius city administration in the summer of 1941. Instead of Veliučionys, twenty thousand Jews were concentrated in the Old City of Vilnius.

According to the colony's website, a Jewish children's camp was established here during World War II, from which the children were taken, to be shot. "Where they were taken, even old-timers of the village don't know," the website says.

They weren't taken far. More precisely, they were all taken away on a single day by the Special Unit, which was used to dealing with even larger numbers of Jews. While village old-timers may not know the

195

details, it's likely their parents heard the gunshots when the Jewish boys and a thousand others were murdered, just a kilometer or two away.

You won't be able to find that shooting site, either.

We wander in vain down paths ending in heavy foliage. Finally, we see an elderly man at a farm next to the railroad tracks, and tell him about our mission. The man is a dedicated mushroom picker, and that's how several years ago, he discovered both the site and the small monument. He hadn't been back to the site for perhaps five years. It seems there weren't a lot of mushrooms to be found in the area of the murder.

We ask him to get into our car and show us the Jewish mass murder site, called a Jewish cemetery, for some reason. There is no road. Neither is there a path. We push through nettles taller than a person, but the way is blocked by a ditch. We have to go back and try to reach it from the other side. There are nettles there, too, and a large pile of garbage. According to the directive of the European Union, such dumps are supposed to be cleaned up. This one was closed, but our mushroom picker says the local residents don't care, and continue to throw their garbage there out of habit.

"This is a symbolic monument to the murdered Jews," Efraim says as we gaze at the stinking hill of trash.

The mushroom picker is persistent, just as we are. After about an hour, we finally find what we are looking for—a Soviet monument erected in 1951 surrounded by brush on a slope: 1,159 murdered, including 495 women and 196 children. The Special Unit murderer Vincas Sausaitis was here too. Thirty-seven years later, in 1978, he as an elderly man wrote bitterly as he awaited his execution in prison: "And where are my small children who protected me?" and "Don't wait because it won't come / Daddy's not coming back / Because the yellow sand of the grave / Will cover my eyes."

The mushroom picker accepts a tip of five euros for his trouble. He complains that the children's home is too close by. Everyone is tired of it, because the elderly women in charge fail to supervise the children, who are always running away and stealing from the local store. In fact, a group of them recently murdered one of their friends, a thirteen-year-old boy, by burying him alive in the sand.

We are fifteen kilometers from Vilnius. We are silent as we return, checking to be sure we haven't collected any blood-sucking ticks. We need to buy some sort of ointment for the nettle stings on our arms and legs. We are heading back to the civilized world, to where we haven't been before, but must go.

We spend our last afternoon going to the home of the late Efraim Zar, Zuroff's namesake, at Šopeno Street no. 3, apartment 19, near the railroad station.

On July 13, 1941, Rabbi Efraim Zar left his apartment on Šopeno Street and turned onto Pylimo Street. That day the white armbanders were out looking for rabbis to kidnap, recognizing them by their beards. They seized Efraim as well, and took him away. The story is that they took him to Lukiškės Prison, but we have checked the list of prisoners taken there in 1941, which is in the state archives, and we didn't find his name. It's probable that Efraim Zar was taken directly from Pylimo Street to Ponar and shot there, along with the first groups of Vilnius Jews murdered. According to Sakowicz's diary, the shootings began at Ponar on July 11. Several days, or weeks, later, his family, his wife Beyla, and their two sons, Hirsch and Eliyahu, were most probably murdered in Ponar, likely at a different pit.

We find a couple in the courtyard of Šopeno Street no. 19. The building is being renovated, and a young man and woman are working there. They both smell of alcohol. The woman carries a baby girl a few months old in her arms. They will get us into the entrance. They call someone to open the door.

Finally a man pokes his head out of a window in an apartment next to the stairwell. He looks at Zuroff with an angry face and says: "What does he want?"

We say he has come from Israel and wants to see where his great-uncle, who was murdered at Ponar, once lived.

"He's lying," the man says. "That's not what he wants. I know from television. This man is Zuroff."

After considering the matter for some time, he nonetheless does let us into the stairwell, where apartment no. 19 is located, on the third floor. We ring the doorbell. Nobody answers. The man in the window eyes us warily and mumbles angrily: "Let's just not hear any tales; he had no grandfather or brother here. What is he looking for here?"

After we leave the stairwell, we want to thank the young couple with the baby girl.

"Could we perhaps buy something for your daughter?"

"I don't know what she eats," the mother says. "We just took her from the children's home. We don't even know what to give her. They took her away from us when our house burned down, and now they've given her back, just for the weekend. Could you buy some diapers?"

The last destination on our journey.

In Ponar, some ten kilometers away from Vilnius, in the woods, where Efraim Zar's family were shot in the head by the Special Unit and fell into pits filled with Jewish corpses.

The Ponar Museum is really just a little hut, a single large room. The names of perhaps a dozen Jews are listed on the walls of the room—for some reason, only a dozen or so out of the seventy thousand murdered here. There are several dozen photos, some portraying Jews, others Poles, still others Soviet POWs and Lithuanians who also died here. There is a looped film being shown on a screen about the Japanese diplomat Sugihara, for some reason. It costs three euros to enter the hut.

The roads on which the victims were marched and driven are not marked. We ask people at the store; perhaps they know something. No, no one knows anything. No one speaks Lithuanian. They say, Go ask Mama Rial; go there and ask. Where does Mama Rial live—which house? No, it's not Mama Rial, it's the Memorial. Ah, *Memorial*.

Finally we do get some answers from a memorial guide. The road the victims traveled on is not the same road on which people arrive at Ponar today. They came from the side, from the direction of the railroad. Where was the booth of the railroad worker named Jankowski? Where is Sakowicz's house, out from under whose eaves he witnessed the mass murders happening right in front of his eyes? Where is the yard of Siniuca, from whose yard the horrible dog Myszka left in the evenings, running to the pits and returning in the morning with human intestines?

There are only four houses here. We go from one to another. Some are in ruins, uninhabited; others have been renovated. There are no people there. Dogs bark. Right next to the former military base there is a barn returning to the elements. We watch as a large black dog slowly emerges from within. It does not bark. It slowly walks toward us, pulling a chain on the ground behind it. The dog stops. It looks at us very strangely, almost through us, as if he cannot see us. It has clear blue eyes, without pupils. The dog is blind. The Hellhound of Ponar is blind.

Our Journey to Hell is over.

V

CONCLUSION

28

Human Faces
of the Murderers

W ho were those men, our Lithuanians, who shot men, women, children, and the elderly?

Historian Rimantas Zagreckas's unique study is called *The Social Portrait of the Holocaust Perpetrator*. The author used modern interdisciplinary methods in researching material from the criminal case-file collection at the Lithuanian Special Archives, where there are "several thousand cases connected to the Holocaust." He examined the personal information and autobiographies of 205 people from five Lithuanian regions provided in the interrogation records and in witness testimonies.

Rimantas Zagreckas concludes:

All of the people who were convicted of crimes connected to the mass murder of Jews were members of units which had taken part in the June 1941 uprising, or units which still hadn't been disbanded, or police officers.

The social status of those convicted more or less fits the sociological cross section of the residents of Lithuania (the majority were farmers, the minority craftsmen and artisans, hired hands, servants and intellectuals).

The largest portion of convicted Holocaust perpetrators had little education, and at most had finished the fourth grade at a primary school, or had no schooling at all.

The convicted Holocaust perpetrators were apolitical in independent Lithuania.[1]

---

1 Rimantas Zagreckas, *Holokausto dalyvio socialinis portretas* (The Social Portrait of the Holocaust Perpetrator). From: *Genocidas ir rezistencija* (Genocide and Resistance), 2012, No. 1 (31), pp. 63–64.

Who participated in the mass murder of Jews?
Historian Alfredas Rukšėnas:

One group of these people participated in the June 1941 uprising and served at various levels of the Lithuanian government departments restored after the uprising. Others were members of armed Lithuanian security units—the Lithuanian Auxiliary Police, TDA, units of white armbanders—and were usually subordinate to the chiefs of the Lithuanian police departments. A third group served in self-defense battalions. There were twenty-six self-defense battalions formed in Lithuania, with a total force of twelve thousand to thirteen thousand soldiers. Those who served in these units did so out of a sense of duty, to obey orders and carry them out. The soldiers' duties also included carrying out orders to commit the genocide of the Jews and other groups of people. This task was unexpected by the soldiers; they didn't know that their duties would include committing war crimes.[2]

The web page www.bernardinai.lt/tv published a very important interview with Alfredas Rukšėnas in 2012 about the motivations of TDA soldiers who murdered Jews. Here are a few of the highlights from that interview.
Alfredas Rukšėnas:

I would differentiate three kinds of behavior by Kaunas self-defense battalion soldiers based on their sense of duty: average, active, and nonconformist. The average type of behavior is more mechanical than anything else, without any special features. This was the behavior of the majority. They carried out orders only because it was demanded of them, and not for any other reason. Another, smaller group of soldiers were quite active and volunteered to shoot. Some of the active types behaved very brutally toward the victims. I think they were motivated to carry out their duties so energetically out of a sense of pleasure, i.e., they had sadistic impulses. The nonconformists were soldiers who refused to follow orders during operations.

Asked whether it was possible to refuse to shoot, and whether many people did so, the historian replied:

There was no case in which soldiers en masse refused to shoot the victims, i.e., entire units and platoons. I did manage to find information about one soldier who refused to shoot Jews in July of 1941 in the Mickevičius ravine in Kaunas during an operation staged by the Germans. He was shot for this. There is also information about one soldier who refused to shoot victims at the beginning of July 1941, at the mass murders being carried out at the Seventh Fort in Kaunas. A Lithuanian officer yelled at him for this and sent him to do guard duty. One Kaunas TDA officer and perpetrator at

---

2 Alfredas Rukšėnas, *Kauno savisaugos batalionų karių dalyvavimo žydų ir kitų asmenų grupių—žudynėse vokiečių okupacijos laikotarpiu: 1941–1944 motyvai* (Motives of the Soldiers of Kaunas Self-Defense Battalions to Participate in Mass Murder of the Jews and Other Groups of People (1941–1944). From: *Genocidas ir rezistencija* (Genocide and Resistance), 2012, p. 42.

the Seventh Fort in Kaunas recalled that the Germans threatened to shoot anyone who refused to shoot victims.

Although there was the threat of such a punishment by the Germans, many officers and soldiers participated very enthusiastically in the mass murders for different reasons. As I said earlier, they were motivated by both orders and hate. I will give an example from Belarus. On October 10, 1941, the second platoon of the 2nd Auxiliary Police Battalion carried out a mass murder operation against the inmates of the Jewish ghetto of the city of Rudensk. About fifteen soldiers refused to shoot victims. On October 14, 1941, soldiers from the third platoon of the same battalion shot the Jews living in the town of Smilovichi. They carried out the shooting reluctantly, and some soldiers refused to do it. So soldiers from the first platoon replaced the third platoon.

It needs to be stressed that the soldiers who refused to shoot at Rudensk and Smilovichi nonetheless did raise their rifles against victims who had done nothing to them during other murder operations. It was possible to refuse once or twice, but not all the time. There is no indication that those who refused were punished. Most likely they weren't.

Vladas Kliukas with his girlfriend. (Lithuanian Special Archives)

Who were the Lithuanians who murdered Jews?

I think that the Lithuanians who served in the battalions and murdered innocent peo-
ple were no better or worse than their contemporaries. Not worse than people now. If
not for the Soviet and German occupations, the soldiers who served in these battal-
ions would have done the same thing they had done during the period of Lithuanian
independence. The battalion officers would have served in the Lithuanian armed
forces, which were at the same time their workplaces. They would have climbed the
ranks successfully in their careers; they would have taught youth drafted for military
duty and national defense work. Retired officers would have served in the Lithuanian
police and other jobs. Other soldiers would have worked as farmhands, construction
workers, and factory workers. Some of them would have been considered good and
exemplary workers; others would be regarded as failures. Still other soldiers would
have been reserve petty officers in the Lithuanian armed forces. Soldiers who lived
near the German border possibly might have become successful smugglers. Many of
the soldiers would have been active participants in the Lithuanian Union of Rifle-
men. A few soldiers with a greater sense of religiosity might have entered the semi-
nary [to become priests] or might have become monks.[3]

---

3 Alfredas Rukšenas, *"Jie pakluso isakymui, o ne sazinei"* (They Obeyed the Orders, Not
Their Conscience), www.bernardinai.lt/tv, January 17, 2012.

29

+

Lithuania Got Richer

During the Nazi occupation of Lithuania, about two hundred thousand Jews were murdered. Two hundred thousand Jews is about fifty thousand families. Left behind were their homes, land, livestock, furniture, jewelry, and money. Left behind were their factories, shops, pharmacies, hospitals, taverns, restaurants, schools, synagogues, and libraries, with all of the valuable property and inventory they contained.

What happened to all of that? Who got rich? Was it just the Germans, who ordered all the valuables turned over to the Reich? Or just those who did the shooting, and later pulled out gold teeth and divided up the clothing? Or was it perhaps also Lithuanian enterprises and even average Lithuanians, who were able to buy this or that better thing at the auctions held by the town administrations? Who knows?

In the summer of 1941, Lithuanian national police chief Vytautas Reivytis proposed that during the liquidation of Jewish property, it might be possible to settle forever the problem of supplying the police department and their personnel with premises and housing.

We know that some of the property of those murdered never reached the storehouses. It was stolen by local residents before the auctions could take place. Police officers also took belongings when they performed searches of Jewish homes ("The looting of property takes place in broad daylight and is compromising the reputation of the police," officers complained to the chiefs of police of Vilnius).

After the auctions were over, some property remained, so the Rokiškis Jewish Property Liquidation Commission turned over the unsold property to a warehouse keeper.

Among the things left over were dishes, pots, buckets, 2,399 dresses and blouses of all sorts, 1,661 towels, 894 tablecloths, and 837 women's shirts. But there were only a few radio receivers, telephones, watches, and gramophones left over. Some organizations received Jewish property free of charge; among them were shelters for the young and elderly, primary schools, forestry agencies, and local municipal bodies. Clinics and hospitals got the medical equipment.

Life got better.

> *The majority of Jewish farms were taken over by real people, the absolute majority of whom were Lithuanians. [. . .] The registration, supervision and allocation (sales) of all remaining Jewish property was supposed to be executed by the local administration, rural district heads, city council members, police and others. The commandant of Rokiškis complained that "because of the huge wave of buyers it was impossible to maintain appropriate order at the point of sales."*[1]

What did the Catholic Church have to say to the looters, buyers, and receivers of Jewish property?

> *The position of the Catholic Church of Lithuania regarding stolen Jewish property is partially revealed by the reports read at a 1942 conference of bishops. The predominating attitude in the reports is that if the property was stolen by a poor parishioner, and only for his most urgent individual needs, then that property could remain at his disposal. But if a person had taken more than he was able to use, then that person had to return it, and optimally to the Church, although he was allowed to give it to the poor as alms or to charitable organizations. An exception was made for the immoderate looters of Jewish property who were former partisans and who became partisans for noble reasons. Restitution was not required of them because they had risked their very lives at the beginning of the war. The Jewish property acquired was said to be recompense for the risk taken.*[2]

Saulius Beržinis filmed an interview with a simple Lithuanian woman named Regina Prudnikova, in April of 1988.

> **Regina Prudnikova (RP):** *Many Lithuanians who were poor worked as servants in Jewish homes. The Jews were merciful people. I also worked as a servant, but later left because I was plump and healthy, and they said Jews can't live without the blood of Christians; when they have their holidays, they need to taste at least a drop of blood. When the Germans invaded, the Jews didn't have the right to anything. The Lithuanians looted the shops and carried everything off . . . They took a bit of everything, and I took [stuff] home, too.*

---

1 Valentinas Brandišauskas, *Žydų nuosavybės bei turto konfiskavimas ir naikinimas Lietuvojs Antrojo pasaulinio karo metais* (Confiscation and Destruction of Jewish Property in Lithuania during World War II). From: *Holokaustas Lietuvoje 1941–1944 m.* (The Holocaust in Lithuania 1941–1944), Vilnius: LGGRTC, 2001, p. 475.

2 Ibid., p. 501.

Saulius Beržinis (SB): What did you take home?

RP: *I took material from a Jewish shop, and shoes, but the shoes didn't fit. And later they herded the Jews out of their homes and onto the square, with guns. And surrounded them. They put them in rows. Everyone herded them because they asked everyone to go; they said they would give them property, homes, an apartment. Later many people here lived off Jewish property.*

Later there were auctions at Lipke's restaurant, which was filled with clothes which had been brought in by horse. They threw blankets, pillows, [and] bedding out the windows and people grabbed at them. Some got something; Jesus, what went on there . . .

SB: Who was doing the throwing?

RP: *Those who had done the shooting; they did the throwing. The better things, furniture, they kept for themselves.*

SB: Did you see that furniture in homes?

RP: *You know that they had nothing—they were hoboes. Then later when I came over I saw fur coats. My cousin's wife was wearing one. The corridor was full of shoes. I took a pair of red soft lambskin women's shoes, but my cousin's wife came after me and she took them away. She said they belonged to her. I said they weren't hers—they belonged to Jews.*

There were . . . those who were richer; [they] were undressed—naked. They took their teeth out . . . And I bought one tooth.

SB: You bought a tooth? It was possible to buy a tooth?

RP: *Yes, yes, [a gold tooth]. I got it cheap. When the Russians invaded, I bought it from this one woman.*

SB: Where is that tooth now?

RP: *Right here (points to a gold tooth in her mouth). They melted it down and made a tooth for me. That woman's husband shot Jews, and sold me the whole crown.*

SB: So you bought the crown along with the whole tooth?

RP: *Yes, with the tooth.*

SB: So that means you profited from the Jews, too?

RP: *How did I profit? I paid for that tooth!*[3]

---

3 Credit to: Jeff and Toby Herr Collection at the United States Holocaust Memorial Museum, Washington, DC.

30

The Farewell

Efraim: Let's end our journey. I think that we both have a heavy heart. Not exactly the same heavy heart—different nuances, different emphases—but what we clearly share is a sense of anger and frustration at what happened.

Rūta: No anger from my part. I have a very strong sense of shame. And of disgust. Because of what happened then, and because of how we forgot all this. For the criminal indifference of many people in Lithuania.

Efraim: That's the difference between us. I feel the anger. Because no explanation in the world is sufficient to explain—and certainly not to justify—what happened. And that leaves us with the crime itself.

Rūta: Our journey with an enemy ends. After this we have one common enemy: indifference.

Efraim: Two enemies. Indifference and ignorance. The book is mostly to fight the other enemy. I understood a lot of things during this journey. I internalized one thing: how small a country Lithuania is. On a certain level you were simply incapable of doing what I had hoped you would do from the beginning of independence. That's why I said that it took France fifty years to accept responsibility for Vichy. And France is a very strong country. Lithuania is small and it is also weak. It is traumatized. It does not have a magnificent tradition of human rights or justice. These traditions take many years to build up.

Rūta: You came in 1991 after we became independent, and hoped that our country would become strong and democratic overnight?

Efraim: Yes; it was unrealistic. It was unrealistic to expect a true confrontation. But having said that, I could not ignore the situation. I had to bring this issue to public discussion. But it is also Lithuania's fault. If they would have put a few of these war criminals on trial, that would have been such a positive thing for the country. With one or two public trials you could have advanced your country by twenty to thirty years.

Rūta: Now it is too late for regrets. None of the war criminals are still alive. And maybe it helps people to forget the Holocaust. The murderers are dead, and those whom were murdered would be dead by now anyway. So why dig up the past?

Efraim: I am thinking about my mission in Lithuania. The time that we spent in the National Library of Lithuania was very frustrating for me, and only reinforced the fact that someone who is not from here stands almost no chance of being able to convince Lithuanians to confront their past. One thing that surprised me is the extent of the detailed research by Lithuanian historians about the murderers. Even historians I did not know about. I did not have access to this information because I do not read Lithuanian. I felt like an invalid, in a sense. I should have tried to get this information translated so I could deal with it.

Rūta: I do not agree. What you were fighting against was the official position of the Lithuanian authorities and the public perceptions of the Holocaust, which were not influenced by the academic research of our wonderful historians.

Efraim: So you are saying that it is all there, but it's never been read. These articles are published in journals that are printed in only a few hundred copies, and are sent to libraries where they lie unread. Certainly not by politicians who only say what serves their public, what the voters want to hear. That's why this book is so important. You are bringing the issue of the Holocaust down to the level of the individual. Presenting these individuals to the general public, who they were, what they did, what kind of motivation they had. You are using their stories as a prism through which you expose larger issues to Lithuanian society. You want the average person to understand what you are talking about. It will be a very emotional book.

Rūta: It was a very emotional journey for me—both the research in the archives which I did on my own, and the journey with you, the enemy. Before this journey I was not able, and I am still not able, to think about the figures of how many Jews were killed in our country. Nine thousand in Švenčioneliai, seventy thousand in Ponar—two hundred thousand in Lithuania . . . I remember one Holocaust educator who said, quoting someone else: "There were not six million Jews killed during the Holocaust. There were six million murders, and in each case, one particular human being was murdered."

All I can imagine is just one person being killed. He is a man. I see his figure, with his back turned toward the killers, facing the pit his corpse is going to fall into. Fall and stay forever in a pile of other dead bodies. I see his manly skull and then the killer's bullet entering it. The incoming hole will be 0.8 centimeters, the outgoing hole, -8 centimeters. The bullet literally blows up the skull from the inside.

Then I think of the man killed by Impulevičius Battalion soldier Leonas Stonkus. When he shot this middle-aged Jew, as he said, the Jew was bending, bending, bending, and then some other soldier shot him dead. I feel sick as I think of it. Leonas Stonkus also felt sick after he shot. It makes him one of *my people*—people I understand. You don't understand my understanding, but it's okay.

Efraim: No, I don't, and never will.

Rūta: Before we part, maybe we should listen one more time to the "anthem" of this journey, the Yom HaShoah psalm?

Efraim: Sure, why not.

As we are getting closer to the turnoff to the airport, Efraim suddenly starts crying very hard, harder than ever before.

Rūta: Are you okay? I thought that we were past the crying stage?

Efraim: [*still crying*]

Rūta: You don't want to talk?

Efraim: Not really. Or maybe yes. I just felt engulfed by a horrible feeling of betrayal—that by leaving Lithuania, I was betraying the victims. I thought to myself, how could I leave them there in the pits, hidden away, not only physically, but also from public memory and consciousness?

Rūta: You did a lot for them. Remember that. And remember that I am staying.

Efraim: You're right. I did not betray them, but now someone like you has to carry the torch of memory. The only way that Lithuania will ever face its past is if someone like you, a true-blue Lithuanian, will be the bearer of the message. And you know what? In that case, something very interesting will happen. My people will become your people, but your people will never become mine.

Rūta: I understand you, my friend.

EFRAIM'S LETTER TO RŪTA
FROM JERUSALEM, AFTER THE JOURNEY

One of the things that endeared the song to us was that we were completely clueless about the words. It was supposedly Hebrew, but even I could only decipher two words: Yerushalayim *(Jerusalem) and* Hashem *(G-d). The music spoke for itself and touched us both.*

So when you sent me the words, I was literally in shock, especially by the second line:

Yerushalayim, harim saviv la; ve-Hashem saviv le-amo. (Jerusalem is surrounded [guarded] by mountains and Hashem surrounds [guards] his people.)

The words couldn't be further from the truth in Lithuania, especially in the places we visited.

How many times while saying Kaddish, El Maleh Rachamim, and in some cases adding a chapter of Psalms, did I ask myself, Where was the G-d of Israel?

How could such atrocities against the Jews of Lithuania (not to mention the rest of the crimes of the Shoah) have taken place?

The victims were so helpless; they needed Hashem's protection, not his absence.

Shabbat shalom,

Efraim

Afterword

Lithuania Is Angry, Lithuania Is Sad

Rūta Vanagaitė

This book was written in the fall of 2015 and published in Lithuania in January 2016. We planned the book launch for January 26, the eve of International Holocaust Remembrance Day. On January 27 Lithuanian officials would, as they do annually, go to the mass murder site in Ponar and lay the same sort of wreath they always do at the base of monuments to the murdered Jews of Lithuania. A Jewish violinist would play some Jewish music. The Israeli ambassador would say a few words, as would the leader of the Jewish community. Some vice minister or deputy chancellor would represent Lithuania officially. No one would visit any of the other 226 mass murder sites that are registered in Lithuania. Most people have no idea where they are.

This time we hoped that Holocaust Remembrance Day would be different. We wanted to launch the book in an important and half-forgotten site connected to the history of the Holocaust in Lithuania. So where should a book about the real, hitherto suppressed history of the Holocaust be launched, in a way that would shake up my country?

First possibility: Lukiškių Prison. No book had ever been launched in a Lithuanian prison. Yes, this is the same prison from which members of the Special Unit brought people to be murdered in Ponar in 1941–1943, where Efraim Zuroff's grandfather's brother, also named Efraim, was most likely held in the summer of 1941 before he was shot at Ponar. This is also where my grandfather, Jonas Vanagas, arrested by the Soviets in Kavarskas, was held in 1945 before being deported to Kazakhstan. I know the director of the prison, after all. Call after call, so many letters. No. It won't happen. After long deliberations, the prison director refuses to allow us to launch the book in the prison, due to the increased security such an event would require. The journalists cannot be allowed to enter the prison, let alone thirty kids who would sing a memorial psalm.

Second possibility: the headquarters of the Special Unit, where the Lithuanian Interior Ministry is currently located, in the very heart of Vilnius. I know the minister, who helped me once. I also know his adviser, my former classmate. I call and ask the adviser, who asks the minister. The minister asks the adviser: "Have you read this book? Will its launch harm us?" The minister has enough problems already. He is thinking politically, i.e., will the Lithuanian government understand why the minister hosted the launch of "a book which slanders Lithuania"? I apologize to my classmate. I understand the book most probably would "harm" him.

Another possibility remains: a pizzeria, in the center of the city, which served as the base of the Special Unit. On the second floor, above the pizzeria, are the police department offices, now empty, where the murderers slept. We need the permission of the chiefs of police to get in, and request their approval through someone who knows the responsible officer well. We don't tell the police chief the truth—that the book is about the role of Lithuanians in the mass murder of Jews. All we say is that we need the premises for just one hour, for a project. Not a word about the Holocaust. We don't want to harm anyone, but even more, we don't want to lose our last important symbolic venue for the book launch.

Everything goes well. We get permission to use the facilities. The book—*Our People: Journey with an Enemy*—is launched in the pizzeria on a cold day in January, with both "enemies," the coauthors, present, as well as the two most popular priests in Lithuania, who also speak about Lithuanian complicity. Reporters from all of the television stations and Internet news outlets are there in the small pizzeria, elbow to elbow. It's hard to breathe.

A sixteen-year-old boy reads the testimony of another sixteen-year-old, a Ponar murderer, on how he killed his victims. Thirty children sing a psalm in Hebrew in memory of those who were killed. (The principal of the school had asked us beforehand whether the kids' participation might "harm" the school.) Efraim Zuroff says Kaddish. Efraim Zuroff cries. Several others who are present do so as well. One of my friends cries so badly that she has to leave the event. Later she said that while she was listening to the presentations, she suddenly realized her own mortality, and the fragility of human life in general.

The entire print run of two thousand copies is snatched up in two days. By January 28, it is no longer available in bookstores. Another four thousand copies are printed quickly, then another run, of five thousand.

A book with a print run of five thousand is considered a bestseller in Lithuania. During the first several months after its release, nineteen thousand copies of *Our People* are printed. The book has unexpectedly taken Lithuania by storm.

The Internet is all abuzz, with thousands of comments about *Our People*. Lithuania is divided into two camps. One side says: "Finally, we will know the truth." The other side says: "The Jews deported us, so they got what they deserved." This other side says the book serves Putin's propaganda purposes, and that maybe it's inspired and/or financed by the Kremlin. Most people don't read the book, but everyone has an opinion about it. People are fighting over the title. "Our people were the killers? No, they were not our people; they were *her* people!"

The discussion spills over into readers' lives—at work, around the dinner table, even becoming the topic of conversation at funerals. Husbands get angry with their wives; parents and children argue. At an Armenian restaurant near my home, prosecutors dine and discuss the book. The consensus: "Vanagaitė obviously works for Putin." The owner, an Armenian, goes over to them and physically grabs them by their collars: "Do you actually know Vanagaitė? You want me to call her?" Mechanics at auto-repair shops read *Our People* with motor oil on their hands. I go to the hospital for a minor operation and a line forms in the post-op ward: The young nurses want me to autograph the book.

An endless series of telephone calls begins. People are opening up to me; they want to tell me what they've seen. No one has ever interviewed them before, but now there is somebody to whom they can tell their stories. My son and daughter take the calls to protect me in case someone is very aggressive. I just hope nobody will puncture my tires or attack me or my kids physically.

"You know, Mom, we are very proud of you," my kids say to me.

This is music to my ears. I've never heard such words from them.

"What do your friends say about the book?" I ask my son, who is twenty.

"They say, Look, your mom got a lot of money from Putin, so you should pay for our beer."

Kids understand. They don't have the dark prejudices of middle-aged Lithuanians.

The Russian media literally attack both Efraim and me, asking for interviews. We both agree to keep silent because we don't want the book used as a Russian propaganda tool. Western press and TV crews arrive. Foreign journalists are escorted by local cameramen, translators, and coordinators, middle-aged Lithuanian men who have never before visited a Jewish mass murder site.

One educated man who worked for Lithuanian national television, and was a member of the prime minister's office staff, stands at a mass grave in Naujaneriai, in Vilnius. The bones of 1,769 people lie here.

"Look, Rūta," he says to me. "I don't get it somehow. So they're lying here now, just as they were murdered? Piled up haphazardly?" I see that he is shaken. He has never before thought about *how* they were buried. About how many *layers* of corpses—bones, hands, heads—about how many of them were shot, while the toddlers were smashed against trees. He has never even tried to imagine, but now he has seen with his own eyes, as it were, and is in a state of shock.

The annual Lithuanian book fair is held in February. Efraim is back in Israel, so I am there alone. There is so much hate, anti-Semitism, and threats directed against me on the Internet that the publisher hires a security guard, who stands next to me for four days, the entire duration of the book fair. Elderly patriots who had wanted to hit me in the head with my own book are now afraid to do so. They're intimidated by my bodyguard.

"Are you walking around like this, without a weapon?" a cab driver asks me when I leave the premises of the book fair, too tired to drive myself.

A TV host invited to my presentation at the book fair makes a drastic proposal: He suggests that we give everyone in the hall a stone, and after my talk everyone who is absolutely sure that no one in their family participated in the Holocaust could throw the stone at me. The publishers were frightened by the idea and said it would only take one ultra-patriot for me to end up wounded. My children also talked me out of it.

So, fifty kilos of small stones were distributed to the approximately five hundred people who came—not to be thrown at me, but to be placed on the graves of the victims as a symbol of respect and repentance at some point in the future, when they might drive past a mass murder site.

There is a long line in front of the *Our People* booth at the book fair. Young people are buying the book for their grandparents who have kept silent and never related what they saw in their towns in 1941, or have only spoken about it briefly, in whispers. Now, having heard about the book, they finally understand that their experience was not unique—that the same thing happened everywhere throughout Lithuania, as part of the systematic murder of hundreds of thousands of victims. Now, book buyers say, they want to tell the truth to their children and grandchildren. Finally they have the courage to do so.

A woman from the Varėna district, an acquaintance of Ponar murderer Vincas Sausaitis, about whom we wrote extensively in the book, comes up to me.

"Sausaitis was a nice person," she says. "Very considerate and helpful. Everyone liked him. No one knew he had served in the Special Unit and shot people for several years. But when his daughter was born, he couldn't hold his baby in his arms. As soon as he picked her up, he began to tremble all over, to shake, and he had to put her back in the crib. Later when they came to arrest him and put him on trial, we understood why. I guess he had murdered too many children."

Another woman comes over and says quietly: "I am the relative of one of your heroes."

"Which one?" I ask.

"I'm from Darbėnai," she says.

"I see. Are you a relative of Leonas Stonkus—the man who shot only one Jew?"

"No," she says. "Not just one."

"How do you know?"

"You see, when there were family parties, Leonas used to get drunk, and he would grab an imaginary machine gun and shoot at everyone present. Later, when they came to arrest him, when he saw the police, he said: 'I have been waiting for you for thirty years.' Leonas was a very handsome man. And his son was also very handsome, and horribly unhappy. Later Leonas's son committed suicide. His father was still alive, serving his sentence."

Story after story makes clear something I didn't expect when writing the book: The fate of the majority of the killers was horrible. But not just their fate; the fate of their children was often tragic as well.

My good friend from Samogitia comes up to the booth and says that the faces of the children of the local murderers were different somehow; they were marked in a horrible way. They were heavy drinkers, just like their fathers who had shot Jews. There was something wrong with them: They were born deaf, or they became very ill and died young. They were killed in an accident, or they committed suicide.

Here's a typical story sent in by an elderly woman from Mažeikiai. The woman, formerly a judge, is paralyzed, but she still has the use of her right hand. Her handwritten testimony consists of thirty-five pages. It begins with the story of her cousin, a tailor named Ignas Galminas, whom she describes as a murderer of Jews. The woman saw with her own eyes how he took Jews in a truck to the murder site in 1941. He was tried—twice even.

> [Ignas] came back after the second trial and lived in his house in Mažeikiai. He died at the age of eighty, from cancer.
>
> His son, Ramutis Galminas, was studying at the Vilnius Construction Technical Institute in about 1962, and he did his apprenticeship that summer at some construction company in Panevėžys. During his apprenticeship he vanished without a trace. A year later, his decayed corpse was discovered in a canal in Panevėžys. His

father only recognized the body from the clothes he himself had sewn for his son. His remains were brought home and he was buried in the Mažeikiai cemetery, where his parents were later buried.

How he died has remained a mystery to this day. He was an upstanding, reserved, hardworking young man, not some sort of fool or lowlife. So no one knows why he would have been targeted. There was talk that it was vengeance from Heaven for the dark deeds of his father.

What were the reactions of my friends and relatives—those who told me I should not write this book—that I should not betray my family and my country? Of course, they will not read it. They refuse to have the book in their homes. They will not forgive me.

But these are not the only opinions.

Two cousins congratulated me on my courage and told me some terrible stories about the mass murder of Jews that they had heard from their neighbors. Another cousin wants nothing to do not only with me, but also with those cousins who said that I'd done the right thing. Her sister, who is my own age, nonetheless read the book.

"You know, I read it as some sort of task," she said, "as if I were preparing for an exam. Yes, the book is moving, but can it change my attitude toward Jews? Is it possible for Jews to become our people, for a person who from early childhood was told by her mother that Jews put children in barrels, nailed them shut, and rolled them down hills, so that the child's blood would be more concentrated, and the matzah would be more delicious?"

One of the most interesting events which took place was a discussion between some of Lithuania's leading psychotherapists, all university professors. They openly admitted that while they personally had been aware of the basic facts of the Holocaust, until reading the book, they had never fully internalized the scope of the tragedy. Although there was, and is, a formal consensus that Jews were a part of Lithuania, this is not what ordinary people felt. For Lithuanians, the Jews were always "them."

Two hundred thousand murdered, and we do not feel the loss. You cannot mourn if you do not know what you have lost.

A historian who participated in the panel also surprised me by openly criticizing the efforts of the Lithuanian political elite to whitewash the role of the Lithuanian Provisional Government in the Holocaust. He also called the government-sponsored double genocide theory "merely a rhetorical weapon." Participants in the discussion said that the Lithuanian people know practically nothing about the Jews, and until now, it wasn't important to them. With the publication of *Our People*, written in a popular, conversational style, the Holocaust in Lithuania suddenly became a major issue. We, as a nation, can't ignore the truth any longer. We are experiencing a very deep sense of shame, and even if many of us want to reject it, we as a nation will have to find ways to deal with it.

And finally, there is the reaction of the political elite of Lithuania. Lithuanian Holocaust professionals from the Genocide and Resistance Research Centre and the State Commission on Nazi and Soviet Crimes continue to fight against the book—not the book so much as the fact that Efraim Zuroff was involved in the project. After all, for years they have sought to belittle him in Lithuania by all means available, to defend themselves against his constant attacks. Jewish representatives of the Lithuanian political elite refuse to take part in television shows discussing *Our People*, and attempt to talk others into ignoring those shows, and the book itself. The Lithuanian political elite do everything possible to ignore the book, but sometimes they stumble. Former Lithuanian leader Vytautas Landsbergis, son of a minister of the Provisional Government of 1941, wrote an article about the book and its unreliability, most importantly stressing the fact that he wouldn't bother to read *Our People* because everything is already so clear without it.

The Lithuanian political elite are convinced that the book is not a book; instead, it's merely a "project," coordinated "from elsewhere." (Their proof: Another book about local Holocaust perpetrators appeared at the same time in Poland.)

Politicians on television call *Our People* dangerous and harmful, especially to young people. On television, a spokesperson for the State Security Department says that the book discredits the entire Lithuanian partisan movement and should probably be deemed a threat to national security. Incensed "patriots" repeat the mantra *Išsigimėliai nėra mūsiškiai* ("Degenerates are not our people").

Even more infuriating to the self-styled patriots of Lithuania is the fact that the book was written in an emotional and conversational way, not academically, and it's practically flying off bookstore shelves while their books continue to gather dust. The patriots tried to start a campaign on the Internet with the slogan: "Lithuanians unite! Let's not buy or read Vanagaitė's book, no matter how interested we are!" The appeal was not very successful, as *Our People* remained on the Lithuanian bestseller list for four months.

The ice has finally begun to melt irreversibly in Lithuania.

A few months after the book was published, the Lithuanian parliament assembled to discuss the topic of the Holocaust. During the session, Lithuanian historians told members of parliament that the Jews of Lithuania were not shot by a handful of lowlifes. Thousands of average Lithuanians shot Jews—perhaps four thousand, perhaps as many as six thousand murderers in total. They said that we shouldn't only consider those who personally shot the Jews to be Holocaust perpetrators, but also those who drew up the lists and guarded and transported the victims, along with those who dug the pits and stole the victims' property.

After the book was published, the Lithuanian Jewish community sent a request to the Office of the Prosecutor General to investigate a list of 2,055 alleged perpetrators and to take action against them. The Office of the Prosecutor General investigated and found that all of the 2,055 people on the list had died, and therefore could not be prosecuted. The circle closes.

The Genocide and Resistance Research Centre of Lithuania says that the government should publicize the names of these people, but the government refuses. The circle closes even tighter. The Genocide Centre said they couldn't investigate the veracity of the list because there were no living witnesses.

No living witnesses? But we, the authors of *Our People*, found living witnesses at many of the mass murder sites we visited. The witnesses who told us about the mass murders were perhaps eight or ten years old in 1941, so now they're in their eighties. Many of them are still alive, in good shape, and very easy to find. You just go to any mass murder site and knock on the door of a house nearby.

Our People has affected many Lithuanians, leaving many readers, especially women, in tears. Each of the nineteen thousand copies of the book sold in Lithuania is read not just by one person, but by three, four, or five different readers. There is a waiting list to borrow the book at all of the libraries in Lithuania, meaning people have to wait several months to read the book. It doesn't matter that *Our People*, like all of my other books, has been removed from the bookstores in Lithuania, and that no bookstore dares to sell it anymore. The learning process has already begun—an important part of healing for Lithuanian society.

Index

221

Orlovas, Vladimir, 68
Ovchinnikov, Yakov, 90
Ovsey, Dr., 76

Pabradė, 85
Padumblė, 84
Paleckis, Algirdas, 32–33
Palestine, 123, 134
Panevėžys (Ponevezh), 26, 27, 44, 141, 143–148, 217; Pajnostė Forest, 144, 145, 147; Savanorių Street, 148
Paris, v
Paulaitis, Vladas, 175
Pažiezdris, 73, 76
Petraitis, Angelė, 181
Pilanis, Mykolas, 75, 78
Platakis, 115
Plateliai (Plotel), 125–130; Plateliai, Lake, 126
Plungė (Plungyan), 69, 70, 121–124, 128, 155
Plungė, Jonas, 158
Pocevičius, 116
Poland, 4, 12, 47, 94, 122, 129, 177, 193, 219
Polygon, 85
Ponar (Paneriai), x, 4, 19, 20, 21, 28–29, 30, 169–198, 210, 213, 214, 216
Prague, 7, 11
Prudnikova, Regina, 206–207
Pumpučiai, 91, 92
Putin, Vladimir, 32–33, 50

Radviliškis, 111
Rainiai Forest, 115–119
Raižys, Aleksas, 66
Raižys, Jonas, 65
Raseiniai, 134–135
Raslan, Pyotr (Raslanas, Petras), 116–117
Reivytis, Vytautas, 44–45, 55, 205
Riga, 19, 20, 46
Riveris, 65
Rocienė, Antanina, 116
Rocius, Domas, 116
Rokiškis, 46, 205, 206
Romania, 12

Rudensk, 156, 157, 163–165, 203
Rūdninkiai Forest, 191
Rudzinski, 172
Rukšėnas, Alfredas, 66, 202–204
Rumbula, 20
Russia, 117. *See also* Soviet Union

Sabaliauskas, Pranas, 116
Sakalauskienė, Elena, 83
Šakiai, 45
Sakowicz, Kazimierz, 171–172, 197, 198
Samogitja, 122–123, 125, 128, 217
Šančiai, 153
Sar (Zar), Bertha (Beyla), née Gifter, 109
Sar, Samuel L. (Shmuel Leib Zar), 17, 109
Sausaitis, Vincas, 177–180, 181–183, 196, 216
Savickas, 135–136
Scotland, 45, 55
Šeduva (Shadeva), 109–112
Šėgžda, Antanas, 131–132
Selisce, 165
Semeliškės, 194
Senulis, 111
Šerėnas, Jurgis, 74
Šernas, Tomas, x
Šešuoliai, 105
Shvartsman, Daniel, 116
Šiauliai (Shavl), v, 4, 141, 155
Siberia, 40, 79, 112, 139
Šimkė, Balys, 90, 97
Siniuca, 172, 198
Skabickas, Klemensas, 66
Škirpa, Kazys, xi, 37, 41, 43, 44
Slutzk, 47, 165
Smetona, Antanas, 103, 163
Smilovichi, 203
Sobibor, 4
Soviet Union (USSR), 1, 2, 18, 19, 20
Stalin, Joseph, 25, 26, 50
Stapulionis, Antanas, 26, 44, 144–145
Stapulionis, Gene (Genovaitė), 144
Staugaitis, Bishop, 117
Stavaras, Vladas, 175